# AMERICA LOOKS TO AUSTRALIA

# AMERICA LOOKS TO AUSTRALIA

## THE HIDDEN ROLE OF RICHARD CASEY IN THE CREATION OF THE AUSTRALIA–AMERICA ALLIANCE, 1940–1942

JAMES PRIOR

Australian Scholarly

© James Anthony Prior, 2017

First published 2017 by
Australian Scholarly Publishing Pty Ltd
7 Lt Lothian St Nth, North Melbourne, Vic 3051
TEL: 03 9329 6963   FAX: 03 9329 5452
EMAIL: aspic@ozemail.com.au   WEB: scholarly.info

ISBN 978-1-925588-32-3

ALL RIGHTS RESERVED

*Cover design:* Wayne Saunders

*Cover:* Richard Casey, Washington, 1942. NLA, CDC-10602277;
Sir Winston Churchill, 1942. Library of Congress, LC-USW33-019093-C;
John Curtin, 1942. NLA, CDC-10602298;
Franklin D. Roosevelt signing the declaration of war against Japan,
8 December 1941. National Archives and Records Administration, 520053

*To the memory of John Prior, my Father, who lived not quite long enough to greet me into this world and to the memory of Anne Prior who was both Mother and Father for much of my life.*

# Contents

*Preface* ix
*Acknowledgments* xiii
*Introduction* xv

1. What We Know of Casey  1

2. Casey, Australian Diplomacy and the American Challenge  30

3. Casey in the United States: Roosevelt's 'the washing of the hands'  49

4. Spring 1940: From the Phoney War to the Fall of France  64

5. Summer 1940: Casey's Battle for Britain  94

6. Autumn and Winter 1940–41: America Moves into the Pacific  122

7. From the Menzies Visit to Pearl Harbor  142

8. Curtin and Casey  157

9. Pearl Harbor and Its Aftermath  173

Conclusion  188

*Appendix: 'The Task Ahead' by John Curtin*  193
*Bibliography*  197
*Index*  210

*Preface*

# Casey/Curtin. Have we got it all wrong?

Has the adulation of John Curtin gone too far? Bob Hawke is on record as saying he was one of the greatest Australians. Similar sentiments can be found in countless books and articles. This belief seems to be based on two major achievements. The first was his standing up to Winston Churchill when the British Prime Minister attempted to stop the return of Australian troops from the Middle East, in 1942. The second was the creation of the alliance with the United States, forged at a time when a Japanese invasion seemed not only possible but probable. This alliance is generally seen as the reason Australia was not invaded, hence the catch phrase, 'Curtin saved Australia'.* Because this reasoning involves his supposed influencing of American foreign and defence policies, it is permissible to include the name of the American President, Franklin Roosevelt, as part of that equation.

No one can deny that Curtin, in 1942, bravely confronted Churchill when he insisted that the sixth and seventh divisions of the Australian army be brought back to Australia. Churchill wanted to send them to Burma which would have been a strategic mistake and lessened Australia's defence capabilities. Curtin's robust response to the cables that passed between him and his adversaries, including Earle Page, Australia's High Commissioner in Britain, in which the writers attempted to get Curtin to agree to send at least one division, the 7$^{th}$, to Burma, make inspiring reading.

---
* Norman E. Lee, *John Curtin. Saviour of Australia* (Melbourne: Longman Cheshire, 1983).

Curtin fought that encounter virtually alone. Even today, seventy-five years later, reading those cables defines Curtin's courage and determination.

Curtin's role in establishing the close alliance with the United States however, is not so clear. Should the acclaim be directed to an Australian diplomat who was Curtin's political rival, Richard Gardner Casey? Consider: Before being sworn in as Prime Minister, in October 1941, two months before the war in the Pacific began, Curtin had been Leader of the Opposition since 1937. There are limitations on how far an Opposition Leader may go in speaking with foreign governments. Yet, he could have sought agreement from the Menzies or Fadden governments to visit the United States, where undoubtedly he would have been granted an interview with the President. Even if that wasn't possible he would have been granted access to senior American diplomatic and defence officials, to whom he could have emphasised the relevance of Australia in American defence planning in the South Pacific.

But in those ominous years before 7 December 1941, Curtin felt that he was needed in Australia, as much for political reasons as anything else. Both the Menzies and Fadden governments survived only with the support of two independent members, a situation that could and did open the possibility of the conservative government collapsing, and Curtin becoming Prime Minister at short notice. Additionally, he disliked flying and the prospect of a long journey to Washington, crossing the Pacific in wartime, constituted a major hazard. He thus forfeited the opportunity to directly bring pressure on the American President to recognise the key role that Australia could play in the event of hostilities breaking out in the Pacific. It would be three more years before Curtin met Roosevelt, by which time, the United States was clearly getting the upper hand over the Japanese. Moreover, by this time, the Americans had recognised Australia's strategic importance.

Yet, from early 1940, nearly two years before the Pacific War broke out, Australia's interests were being well looked after by the Australian Minister to the United States, Richard Casey. He took up his appointment as Minister, two steps below Ambassador, in 1940 and initially set about convincing the Roosevelt Administration of the need for greater American assistance to Britain, at that time facing the threat of a German invasion. When that danger passed in late 1940, Casey began convincing the Americans that when and if Japanese hostilities began in the Pacific and Asian regions, the only feasible jumping-off point for an American response was Australia. Casey was a strategic thinker who, more than Curtin, or any other Australian, facilitated the transformation of Australia into a vital American ally.

Moreover, Casey proved himself to be a successful networker. No one in the United States, occupying any sort of influential position, whether it be in the Roosevelt Cabinet, defence, the armed forces, diplomatic, banking and finance, newspapers and radio escaped his attention. He had access to the Oval Office where he had discussions with Roosevelt on sixteen occasions.

Despite the effectiveness of Casey's endeavours, there has been an absence of acknowledgment of the success of this campaign. Rather, in much of the literature of the Pacific War, Casey has been a non-player, his efforts to involve the United States in the planning of the strategy ignored or belittled. His efforts were generally unknown to the Australian people then or later, after the war.

Casey was a wealthy man and his costs of travel and entertaining his guests (invariably lunch or dinner at the Australian Legation) exceeded the official allowances, requiring him to pay from his own resources. His dinner parties were renowned for the company a guest was likely to encounter, ranging from the Vice-President, the Chief of the General Staff, the publisher of the *New York Times*, the Chairman of the National Broadcasting Company to the Secretary of State, a Senator or two, at least one being a chairman of a Senate Committee. Casey and his wife were keen aviators and flew their own aircraft, a Fairchild, on visits to interest groups, such as farmers' organisations and chambers of commerce, where Casey delivered what he called 'the Gospel', a plea for greater American interest in Australia and the Pacific region. This, of course, was before Pearl Harbor.

No one believes any longer that Curtin's well-known declaration of 27 December 1941, that 'Australia Looks to America', played any part in the American decision to establish its major base in Australia, a decision that was based entirely on strategic considerations. Casey himself was aghast at the declaration because it suggested a split with Britain that was seen in Washington as almost treason against a major ally. The Curtin declaration's publication in American newspapers, just a few weeks after Pearl Harbor, so angered Roosevelt that he summoned Casey to the Oval Office and told him that if Curtin thought that the declaration would attract favour in the United States, he was quite wrong. Casey knew that Churchill and Roosevelt had divided the world into war theatres and Australia had been placed in the American theatre. Did Curtin not know this? Curtin's declaration embarrassed Casey as much as it angered Roosevelt. The arrival of American troops and supplies, ultimately growing to enormous numbers had already started before Curtin's declaration. (The Pensacola convoy, the first of many, arrived in Brisbane on 22 December.)

This reappraisal of Casey's endeavours in the United States will examine the role he played in thrusting the importance of Australia in any defence planning, upon a nation that barely knew of Australia's existence.

# Acknowledgments

I have had an interest in Richard Casey and John Curtin over many decades. They were both of the same generation, yet their backgrounds could hardly have been more contrasting. Similarly, their careers differed hugely. Casey's C.V. if he had one, could have been almost book length, while Curtin's major achievement before becoming Prime Minister was editor of a political newspaper. However, Curtin achieved the position, Prime Minister that eluded Casey for the whole of his public life.

***

I must offer my heartfelt thanks to my wife Jan and the support and patience that I have had from my children. For the many years I spent in researching this book, Jan has been at my side engaged in our searching the archives in New York, Washington, London, Cambridge University, the National Archives, Kew, Canberra (both the National Archives of Australia and the National Library of Australia) and Sydney, including both the State Library and the Mitchell Library. It would be remiss of me if I did not refer to the wise and comprehensive advice I received from Professor Carl Bridge, Kings College, London and Professor David Lowe, Chair in Contemporary History, Deakin University. I am also grateful to Dr Stephen Brown, who took a keen and helpful interest in the creation of the book and the development of my arguments. Without their counsel, this book would have been a lesser work. Dr Ken Knight, former Assistant Vice Chancellor of the University of Sydney and foundation Principal of Kuring-gai College of Advanced Education played a not insignificant role in keeping me on the straight and narrow path of academic procedures.

In researching this book, I visited institutions ranging from the National Library of Australia to the MacArthur Memorial Library in Norfolk, Virginia and including the Public Records Office (now known as the National Archives), in Kew, Britain, the Roosevelt Library, Hyde Park, Poughkeepsie, New York, the National Archives, Washington, the State Library, Sydney, the National Australian Archives, and Churchill College, Cambridge University.

In all of these institutions I received the utmost assistance, that was both efficient and friendly. I regret that I cannot now recall the names of every one of those good folks and because of my failure to do so, I think it best that I name none of them.

# Introduction

Richard Gardiner Casey was, by any standard, a distinguished Australian. Trained as an engineer, he became, in turn, a decorated soldier, diplomat, parliamentarian, member of both the British War Cabinet and the Australian Cabinet and Australian War Cabinet, company director, party chief, peer, Privy Councillor and twice, vice-regal envoy. His efforts were usually attended by success and encomium. For the most part, his abilities were recognised by his peers. The Department of Foreign Affairs in Canberra is today housed in a building named in Casey's honour. Australia's Antarctic base also carries Casey's name. Yet, in the eyes of many of his fellow countrymen, he is not held in the high regard that his accomplishments would suggest is warranted. His devotion to his country, even his patriotism have been seen as qualified by self-interest. Moreover, within the confines of his political reference groups, his limitations robbed him of the political reward that he most coveted – the prime ministership.

Thus, the perception of Casey in Australian history accords him a minor role. Because of his failure to achieve any kind of domestic political eminence, he has been relegated to that large band of political identities who had the misfortune to reach near the top, but never the top itself, of the political plum tree during the long period of what has become known as 'the Menzies years'.

This book is an attempt to conduct a closer examination of Casey in one specific period in his career, 1940 to 1942, when he represented Australia in Washington. This period has been chosen because his responsibilities as Australian Minister in Washington could be regarded as the most important responsibilities he ever undertook. In the years immediately leading up to the outbreak of the war in the Pacific, the government and the people of Australia realised, with increasing dismay, that the nation would be virtually defenceless in the event of attack by the forces of Japan, an attack long feared and expected. With Britain fighting for its very survival and unable to offer any kind of military or naval aid and much of the Australian defence forces engaged in the Middle East and the European theatres, Australia increasingly perceived the United States as the only power capable of bestowing assistance.

It is not an original observation to argue that the years 1940 to 1942 included the most significant events of the twentieth century. The historian, Ian Kershaw, claimed that 1941 was the most momentous year in modern history.* According to Kershaw: 'That year, the most awful in history ... took its shape largely from a number of fateful choices made by the leaders of the world's major powers.' This was certainly true of Australia's situation. As Harry Gelber described Casey's mission to the United States: 'never before and never since has any Australian Ambassador been called upon to serve in so vital a post at such a critical turning point not only in Australian but world history'.†

Whilever the United States remained the focus of Australia's endeavours to enlist massive military aid in the feared conflict with Japan, Casey's role as Australia's chief representative in the United States carried grave responsibilities. It was he who would argue the justification for American participation in the defence of Australia, not only with the Roosevelt Administration but with the American people, who were deeply committed to an isolationist stance, as the rest of the world erupted into war.

When Casey first arrived in the United States, he received the worst possible news from the American President. At their first meeting, when Casey presented his credentials, Roosevelt confirmed to Casey that his Cabinet had decided that assistance in the event of war breaking out in the Pacific could not be offered to Australia, which was so distant from where the United States' believed its principal strategic interests lay. Casey was quickly made aware that one reason for the Roosevelt Administration's view was that public opinion would not allow any offers of help to Australia.

* Ian Kershaw, *Fateful Choices. Ten Decisions That Changed The World. 1940–1941* (London: Penguin, 2007), p. xv.
† Harry Gelber, 'Turning Points. Richard Casey and the Development of An Australian Foreign Service', *Quadrant*, April 2009, Vol. 53, pp. 74–9.

For the entirety of his term in the United States, Casey strove to turn around public opinion, Administration thinking and American naval and military strategy.

It would not be too blunt to claim that the American refusal to come to the military aid of Britain in May–June 1940, when that nation was seemingly threatened with invasion, boded ill for Australia. The survival of Britain was far more important to the United States than Australia, yet Washington was not prepared to give that aid in any substantial and meaningful measure. Australia, obviously, was not seen as being worthy of more sympathetic consideration. Casey's mission therefore was to convince the United States that Australia should be looked upon not as a distant outpost of the British Empire, but as a key element of its strategic thinking.

This book seeks to add to our understanding of the degree to which Casey's adroit lobbying took the concept of an Australia-America alliance to the point where United States strategic thinking would perceive Australia as an integral part of that thinking. Casey's efforts were directed to the coming together of Australia and the United States and the creation of an alliance between the two nations. Casey's efforts in 1940–42 were undertaken in the context of Australia's very survival being guaranteed only with American help. Casey's achievement was that, more than any other Australian, he facilitated the movement of Australia from the periphery to near the centre of the United States' strategy in the Pacific War.

Yet this is not the most common or popular view of Casey's achievements in the United States. Although there is a general recognition of Casey's active and successful efforts in making Australia better known to influential figures in the Administration and the American media, there is little recognition linking Casey with the United States' strategic decision to use Australia as the base for the repulse to the Japanese attack. In most academic studies, Casey is accorded only a minor role, given that the Americans only entered the war after the events at Pearl Harbor seemingly gave them no other choice than to turn Australia into their Pacific base. Popular representations and much of the historiography of this period clearly perceives the Prime Minister John Curtin as the catalyst in the Australian defence strategy moving from its traditional reliance on Britain to a new alliance with the United States. As the historian James Curran explained Curtin's enduring popularity:

> In a land that has seen no civil war or engaged in no act of military rebellion against the 'mother country' to act as the baptismal font for a self-sustaining national mythology, the Curtin story offers a tale rich in the vital ingredients of nationalist drama and human experience.*

Or to quote the journalist Alan Ramsey: 'If anyone was ever the political father of Australia's security ties with Washington, however much they were formalized by the Menzies coalition government's negotiation of ANZUS in 1951, it was without question, Labor's John Curtin'.†

The conventional wisdom holds that Curtin's initiative in gaining American support at this very crucial time led to the development of close and enduring ties with the United States, ties that since 1941 have remained the foundation of Australian defence policy, endorsed by both major political parties. As one recent study has put it, 'the alliance with the United States remains the universally-supported centrepiece of Australia's foreign policies'.‡ The role of Curtin in this hugely significant development in Australian defence and foreign policy has become part history and part folklore, made immeasurably easier to understand by the adoption of the simple tag, 'Australia Looks to America'. This was a key phrase in the statement, issued by Curtin as a New Year's Day message to a Melbourne newspaper on 27 December 1941. As Lionel Fredman has put it: 'Curtin's statement of 27 December 1941, has become a landmark in our history'.§ Or as former Prime Minister Bob Hawke put it in a book entitled *John Curtin: Saviour of Australia*, Curtin

---

\* James Curran, *Curtin's Empire* (Melbourne: Cambridge University Press, 2011), p. 5.
† Alan Ramsey, *Sydney Morning Herald*, 10 October 2001.
‡ Mark Beeson, 'Australia, the United States and the Unassailable Alliance', in John Dumbrell and Alex Schafer (eds.), *America's 'Special Relationships*  (London: Routledge, 2006), p. 76.
§ L.E. Fredman, *The United States Enters the Pacific* (Sydney: Angus and Robertson, 1969), p. 55.

was 'the greatest of Australians'.* This link between Curtin's appeal, the wartime alliance with the United States, the transformation of Australia into an American bridgehead for the Pacific War and the formalising of the alliance in the ANZUS treaty of 1951 appears well established. Curtin's declaration, 'Australia Looks to America' has come to convey a precise meaning of where Australia stands in relation to the rest of the world. Because Casey's work was what might be described as 'behind-the-scenes' diplomacy, his writings left no such identifiable marker to compare with 'Australia Looks to America'. Writing in 1982, Carl Bridge noted that Casey's mission to the United States was widely understood to have produced little that was positive:

> Existing accounts are harsh in their assessments of the effectiveness of Australia's first Washington legation in the two years from its establishment in March 1940 until the fall of Singapore in February 1942.†

Over the years, Bridge and others have fought to correct this impression of Casey as a failure, but, even today, doubts remain. Certainly, there is no widespread recognition of Casey as the foundation stone of Australia's alliance with the United States. Bridge, in 2008, noted the continuing neglect when he wrote that:

> Few today realise that when Curtin issued his famous 'Australia looks to America' statement in December 1941 he was actually following the trail blazed and prepared brilliantly by Casey over the previous two years. It was then that the seeds of the future Australia-United States alliance were planted.‡

As Bridge is acknowledging here, the standard accounts of the dramatic events of 1940–42 rarely if ever, directly credit Casey with

---

\* R.J. Hawke, 'Foreword' in Norman E. Lee, *John Curtin. Saviour of Australia* (Melbourne: Longman Cheshire, 1983).
† Bridge, 'R.G. Casey, Australia's First Washington Legation and the Origins of the Pacific War, 1940–1942', *Australian Journal of Politics and History*, 1982, Vol. 28, No. 2. pp. 181–9.
‡ Carl Bridge 'The Other Blade of the Scissors', in Baxter, Christopher and Andrew Stewart, *Diplomats At War, British and Commonwealth Diplomacy in Wartime* (Leiden: Martinus Nijhoff, 2008), p. 148.

an important role in the American decision to turn Australia into its base in the South West Pacific. Yet there are good reasons for thinking that this was Casey's legacy.

It was the Japanese attack on Pearl Harbor on 7 December 1941 that caused the United States to come to the aid of Australia. In the weeks that followed Pearl Harbor, General George Marshall and his staff came up with a new plan for war against Japan which situated Australia as its principal Pacific base for waging that war. The standard accounts of how Australia became an American base make the point that the decision was 'coldly strategic'.[*] With the Philippines under attack and likely to fall, Australia, which had barely entered the consciousness of the United States eighteen months earlier, now became a strategic priority.[†] Perhaps General Douglas Macarthur summed it up best when he told Curtin in June 1942 that the interest of the United States in Australia was purely 'from the strategical aspect of the utility of Australia as a base from which to attack and defeat the Japanese'.[‡] Implicit in that was the cold, hard fact that emotional ties between the United States and Australia had no bearing whatsoever.

Yet, what is striking about the American decision is how quickly and easily it was made, and how effectively it was implemented. An awareness of Australia and what it had to offer the United States had obviously grown, thanks to the efforts of Casey and others. Casey learned of this felicitous turn of events from Harry Hopkins, and recorded the news in his diary:

> December 22, 1941. Winston Churchill and the Chiefs of Staff arrived in Washington. Harry Hopkins telephoned and cheered me up a good deal by saying that he thought I would be pleased at what was in train so far as Australia was concerned. I told him that I was feeling a little 'blue' at which he said that I had no reason to do so, as the representations that I had made were bearing very promising fruit.[§]

---

[*] See, e.g., Anthony Burke, *Fear of Security. Australia's Invasion Anxiety* (Cambridge: Cambridge University Press, 2008), p. 74.
[†] Alan Watt, *The Evolution of Australian Foreign Policy 1938–1965* (Cambridge, Cambridge University Press, 1968), p. 68.
[‡] Quoted in Peter Stanley, *Invading Australia. Japan and the Battle for Australia, 1942* (Camberwell: Penguin, 2008), p. 168.
[§] Casey Diaries, 22 December 1941. The Casey Diaries are held at the

Harry Hopkins, a former Secretary of Commerce, was Roosevelt's personal and unofficial representative to the British government. His closeness to the President is exemplified by the fact that he lived in the White House. The implications of the Hopkins' message are worth noting. They convey the thoughts of a close Presidential adviser, probably the closest Presidential adviser. Hopkins' comments clearly recognise the work and effort that Casey had put into the campaign to make Australia front and centre of the new American political and military strategy.

At one level, the decision to turn Australia into its Pacific base was an obvious choice in the context of December 1941. As a result of the attack on Pearl Harbor, the Americans had few options and so decided to 'look to Australia'. A more accurate and valid way of understanding the situation is to view the United States as being gradually drawn towards looking at Australia as a base. As Bridge has described this evolution, the Roosevelt Administration was badly shaken by the fall of France. In September 1940, Roosevelt and Churchill signed the 'Destroyers for Bases' deal, which provided no real military help to Britain but proved that the 'biased neutrality' of the United States favoured the Allies. In early 1941, the secret military ABC1 talks in Washington suggested that 'Australia would be a principal Pacific base and a significant supply provider for the global war effort'.* On 1 December 1941, the United States finally made an 'explicit guarantee to come to Britain's and Australia's aid should the Japanese attack Malaya'.† Finally on 17 December 1941, Roosevelt approved the Marshall/Eisenhower plan to turn Australia into its Pacific base. From that moment, the 'saving' of Australia was more or less assured.

Casey's achievement was to encourage this process of American recognition of what Australia had to offer to the United States. Roosevelt himself, after Pearl Harbor, credited Casey with being in tune with his own thinking. Casey quoted the President as saying

---

National Library of Australia, Canberra, at MS6150, Vol. 1, Box 24. In this book, I simply cite 'Casey Diaries' and the date of entry.
\* Carl Bridge, 'Poland to Pearl Harbour' in Carl Bridge (ed.), *Munich to Vietnam. Australia's Relations with the United States since the 1930s* (Melbourne: Melbourne University Press, 1991), pp. 45–7.
† Bridge, 'The Other Blade of the Scissors', pp. 140–3.

that: 'As I have always realised and as you have said in your speeches here, the South West Pacific is one unit'.\*

As to why Casey has not been acknowledged for what he achieved, several factors are at work. Bridge and others have pointed out that Casey is a convenient villain in a nationalist myth. According to this myth, it was only after conservative United Australia Party politicians, such as Casey, left the stage that the Labor team of Prime Minister Curtin and Minister for External Affairs Doctor H V Evatt' carved out a new independent path for Australia that genuinely reflected Australia's national interests.†  Casey, as a consequence, is more likely to be remembered as too attached to the British Empire to have been of much use to Australia.‡

It can also be added that in the context of Australian politics, Casey does not present as a dynamic, engaging personality capable of turning around world events. Casey never boasted publicly that he had played an important role in the creation of the Alliance. Over time, Americans came to realise the value of Australia to American strategic interests. The remarks by Harry Hopkins, speaking on behalf of the President and referred to earlier, have remained largely unknown.

Finally, Casey's achievement in the United States is often described in terms of his remarkable publicity and networking achievements. What is often forgotten was that Casey was a true diplomatic 'renaissance man'. With experience of the academic, military, business and political spheres, Casey was better placed than most career diplomats when faced with the task of convincing Americans to come in on the side of the Allies in World War Two. Casey was a superb salesperson of Australia in the United States and a tireless 'networker', but he was also capable of thinking strategically and mastering the technical detail of Australia's military needs. Australia was indeed fortunate to have Casey as its representative in Washington in 1940–42.

Casey should be remembered as a highly effective advocate

---

\* Casey Diaries, 17 December 1941.
† Bridge, *'Poland to Pearl Harbour'*, pp. 38–9.
‡ Christopher Waters, 'Casey: Four Decades in the Making of Australian Foreign Policy', p. 381.

of Australia's national interests because he, more than any other Australian politician or diplomat, facilitated the changed perception of Australia in the United States. Casey was successful because he understood an important fact of political life, that national interests and not brotherly concerns or the 'civilisational ties' of the British speaking world, would stimulate American interest in Australia. Where he saw his role, was to endeavour to change the perception of what the United States thought its national interests to be.

As Christopher Waters has put it, Casey was a realist in international relations terms.[*] According to Michael Wesley, Australian realism has three key elements. The first was 'experientialism' – meaning a consciousness of Australia's isolation and its security threats. Secondly, Australian realists are sceptical about the stability of the international system and are prone to see the world in terms of threats. Thirdly, Australian realism favours pragmatic or 'common sense' solutions to international problems. There is little faith in multinational efforts to solve problems or keep the peace. Instead, realists recommend that Australia look out for its own interests, usually through bilateral relationships.[†] These views were a clearly identifiable part of the conservative tradition of Australian politics and not simply a product of Menzies' political strategies in his fight with the Labor Party.[‡]

Casey is a prime example of this type of realism. Casey's experiences of diplomacy in the 1920s and 1930s led him to the conclusion that national interest was what mattered in international relations. He was deeply pessimistic about the enforceability of the Treaty of Versailles and sceptical about the League of Nations.[§] Casey was an enthusiastic 'appeaser', long before the word took on its defeatist and pejorative connotation of submission to naked power. Casey, understandably, favoured negotiation over war. Appeasement, for Casey, was the logical way to maintain the peace

---

[*] Ibid., p. 383.
[†] Michael Wesley, 'The Rich Tradition of Australian Realism', *Australian Journal of Politics and History*, Vol. 55, No. 3, 2009, pp. 324–34.
[‡] David Lowe, 'Brave New Liberal: Percy Spender', *Australian Journal of Politics and History*, Vol. 51, No. 3, 2005, pp. 389–99.
[§] Waters, 'Casey. Four Decades in the Making of Australian Foreign Policy' in *Australian Journal of Politics and History*, Vol. 51, No. 3, 2005, p. 383.

for an Australia that had nothing to gain and much to lose from a new world war.

It was this realism and pragmatism that underpinned Casey's approach when he arrived in the United States in February 1940. Casey quickly came to the view that interesting Americans in Australia's defence on the basis of a common civilisational bond was simply futile. He was proved right on this score. As Bridge has put it:

> When the United States came to Australia's defence in 1941 and 1942 they did so not just to protect 'kith and kin' or to reward an ally, but to protect a vital source of human resources, food supplies and other materials for the global war effort and to preserve a basis for the reconquest of their territories in Southeast Asia.*

Understanding this reality was one of Casey's strengths almost from the outset of his work in the United States. Casey was immediately struck by the fact that isolationism in the United States meant that there was virtually no solidarity at all among what is today described as the 'Anglosphere'. There was no way that the United States was going to aid Australia because of their shared civilisational values. Casey had to sell Australia as a vital American economic, political and military resource. This he did brilliantly.

Casey's barnstorming of the United States was done in two separate stages. For the first six months, the thrust of his efforts was directed to attempting to generate greater American support for Britain in her hour of need. By the end of 1940, when there was no longer the threat of a German invasion of Britain, Casey threw himself into the real purpose of his appointment, that is, greater recognition of the significant role Australia could play in the event of hostilities breaking out in the Pacific. This, after all, could well be a global war. Casey endeavoured to emphasise the strategic value of American involvement in the South West Pacific, specifically the huge landmass of Australia. Casey's prioritising of Britain in the first phase would lead to the unwarranted tag that Casey was, as one historian has put it, just 'another good boy scout for the Empire'.†

---

\* Bridge, '*Poland to Pearl Harbour*', pp. 50–1.
† Stephen Alomes, *A Nation at Last. The Changing Character of Australian*

Yet this type of criticism is unjustified. For Casey, Britain was the first line of defence for both Australia and the United States and its defeat would be a military catastrophe for both counties, indeed for the whole world. Once the threat of a German invasion of Britain had been deferred or, as quickly became evident, cancelled, in the northern autumn of 1940, Casey concentrated on getting Australia included into American strategic planning for the looming conflict in the Pacific. Casey mingled with key Administration figures, tirelessly worked the press and town halls, and, especially in the second half of 1941, shared his view with key American military leaders, gradually improving American appreciation of what it was that Australia had to offer.

At this point, it is fair to ask, what if Casey had been ineffectual? Would the Americans have come to the same conclusion about Australia, given the turn of events? No doubt the US would have eventually seen that Australia was a logical choice from which to fight. However, Casey's groundwork, not only in the political sense, but in providing details of harbours, airfields, geographical possibilities, his own WWI experience assisting his assessments, meant that the US decision to use Australia as a base could be made quickly with no need for detailed enquiries. The speed with which the decision could be implemented is demonstrated by the arrival of the Pensacola convoy in Australia on 22 December 1941.*

The task of discovering, examining and documenting Casey's actual impact on the development of American strategic thinking has been an exhausting one, extending over more years than the author cares to count. The research has involved documentation from a variety of secondary and primary sources in Australia, in Britain, and an even greater number of primary sources in the United States. It must be admitted that the secondary literature is daunting and much the same is true of primary sources, given that this was an era when powerful players kept diaries, sent letters, and wrote long confidential reports that are now available to the public.

---

*Nationalism 1880–1988* (Sydney: Angus and Robertson, 1988), p. 116.
* Maurice Matloff and Edwin Snell, *The War Department Strategic Planning for Coalition Warfare 1941–42* (Washington, DC: War Department, 1953), pp. 72–3; James Prior, 'The Friendly Invasion', *Weekend Australian*, 2–3 January 1982.

Casey is already the subject of a vast academic literature.* Casey's critics have been an academic, David Day, who knew him not, and a colleague, Paul Hasluck, who knew him well. Casey wisely intended to make sure that his side of the story would be told by keeping a diary, albeit a very incomplete and quite an inadequate one. Menzies' biographer A.W. Martin described Casey as 'Canberra's most notorious diarist'. Martin tells of Casey almost daily, distributing to friends and colleagues his versions of daily events. Menzies was apparently opposed to the concept of diary-keeping and told the Governor-General, Lord de Lisle, that he did not trust people who kept diaries.† Although Menzies instructed Casey to cease his diary-keeping, Casey clearly ignored his Prime Minister. Instead, he became more discriminating in choosing readers of his daily thoughts. His diaries for the period March 1940 to March 1942 have been minutely examined and published as *The Washington Diaries* edited by Carl Bridge.‡ The unabridged Casey diaries, used for the research for this book, are available at the National Library of Australia.§ Casey's diaries are testament to the multiplicity of repeat meetings with officers and officials holding senior positions in their respective fields, which clearly show that Casey occupied an unusual, if not a unique position of both importance and influence in the Washington firmament. Of course, with any diary, one needs to question the audience for which it was intended. As Casey's will left his

---

\* W.J. Hudson, *Casey* (Sydney: Oxford University Press, 1986), Carl Bridge, 'R.G. Casey's Contribution to Australian War Policy', *Journal of the Historical Society of South Australia*, Vol. 9. 1981, pp. 80–90, Bridge, 'R.G. Casey', pp. 181–9, Bridget Griffen-Foley, 'The Kangaroo is Coming into Its Own: R.G. Casey, Earl Newsom and Public Relations in the 1940s', *Australian Journal of American Studies*, Vol. 23, No. 2. December 2004, pp. 1–20, Gelber, 'Turning Points', pp. 74–9, David Ellery, 'Furphies a'plenty in Long ANZUS Alliance', *Canberra Times*, 18 November 2011, Michael Birgan, 'Lord Casey: Britain's Secret Agent', *The Bulletin* (Sydney) 20 November 1984, pp. 60–2.
† A.W. Martin, *The Whig View of Australian History* (Melbourne: Melbourne University Press, 2007), pp. 122–3.
‡ Carl Bridge (ed.), *A Delicate Mission. The Washington Diaries of R.G. Casey, 1940–1942* (Canberra: National Library of Australia, 2008).
§ The reference is NLA, MS 6150, Vol. 1, Box 24. All further references to Casey's NLA records are at this number.

diaries to the National Library of Australia, he clearly meant them to be publicly available after his death. He knew they would be an addition to archived official documents and so they add a personal aspect to formal documents and provide an insight into the commitment to official duties and participation in the 'social whirl' and the manner in which Casey combined the two to achieve his aims.

There were three Prime Ministers – Robert Menzies, Arthur Fadden and John Curtin, and four Ministers for External Affairs – Henry Gullett, John McEwen, Frederick Stewart and Herbert Evatt – while Casey was in the United States. Casey, of course, wrote cablegram reports and letters to them all. Much of this correspondence is available through the National Library and the National Archives.

Despite the high offices that Casey held in a singularly successful life, his ability to mix easily with the powerful and the influential and his propensity to gravitate towards the centres of action, there has been only one full-length biography, by W.J. Hudson, published in 1986.\* Hudson's work is an important source of biographical material about Casey, but, by no means, the only source. Apart from familiarity with the more commonplace documents and personal writings, Hudson had the advantage of having worked on the publication of a large volume of correspondence that flowed between Casey and Stanley Melbourne Bruce, Australia's eighth Prime Minister and Casey's principal supporter.†

Hudson recognised perhaps the major hazard confronting a biographer: 'If one invests some years of one's own life in the exploration and presentation of another's, one tends to justify the investment by exaggerating the qualities of the subject'. Hudson, to his credit, achieved exemplary balance in his account, noting Casey's strengths and weaknesses. According to Hudson, Casey sought to live 'a highly gregarious life and a very public life'. Yet, Hudson, after years of researching the 'millions of words' that, as a compulsive writer, Casey left behind, concluded he was extremely

---

\* W.J. Hudson, *Casey*, p. ix.
† W.J. Hudson and Jane North (eds.), *My Dear P.M. R.G. Casey's Letters to S.M. Bruce, 1924–1929* (Canberra: Australian Government Printing Service, 1981).

careful in what he wrote.* Carried through to his personal relationships, this characteristic would have ensured a good fit into the higher echelons of government in both London and Washington and an acceptance by the diplomatic communities in both capitals.

Yet Casey's discretion and modesty present a real difficulty in assessing Casey's achievements. In some ways, Hudson concedes the frustrations of writing Casey's biography in his own, Hudson's failure to reveal the complete man, because of Casey's refusal to ever reveal his innermost thoughts. Although he left behind a massive amount of personal and official records, some going back to childhood, there was nothing intimate or confessional in any of his papers, his personal relations with men and women were seldom explored in any detail, and the daily reality of politics was rarely described. Perhaps the lowly, almost invisible place that Casey occupies vis-à-vis the Alliance lies in Casey's own inability to talk about himself, or create any written record of his personal feelings, a characteristic that Hudson found deeply frustrating.†

Since Hudson, it has been Bridge who has brought to life Casey's efforts as a diplomat and Australian representative in Washington.‡ Bridge described Casey's achievement thus:

> As Australia's envoy, Casey had two objectives: to gain American support for the Allies' war effort against Germany; and to alert the Americans to the common danger from Japanese aggression in the Pacific. He set about achieving these in three ways. First, he mounted a public speaking and media campaign which succeeded in putting Australia on the mental map for millions of Americans. Secondly, he networked, particularly among the Washington administrative

---

\* Hudson, *Casey*, p. x.
† Ibid.
‡ Bridge, 'R.G. Casey', pp. 181–9, Carl Bridge, 'Menzies, Casey and the Politics of Australia's Participation in the European War, 1939–40', *Flinders Journal of History and Politics*, No. 11, 1985, pp. 79–90, Carl Bridge, 'Casey and the Americans. Australian War Propaganda in the United States, 1940–41', Working Paper No. 30, Australian Studies Centre, Carl Bridge 'Poland to Pearl Harbour' in Bridge, Carl (ed.), *Munich to Vietnam. Australia's Relations with Britain and the United States since the 1930s*, Melbourne: Melbourne University Press, 1991; Bridge, 'The Other Blade of the Scissors'.

elite. And thirdly, he made some timely, well-directed and effective diplomatic interventions.*

This book endorses this summary of Casey's goals and achievements, because Casey is not given the credit he deserves for Australia's transformation into a wartime base of the United States. His public reputation and recognition are not what they should be.

In terms of American sources, the author has examined State Department archival records. Historians have not needed to accept Casey's own account of his role in Washington; all of the important American decision makers of this period have left behind observations about Casey. I have used the Adolf Berle papers, especially Berle's diary, which Bridge has used but which are not often cited in the Australian literature, to understand Casey's thinking and influence.† According to the historian David Reynolds, Berle, Assistant Secretary of State, 'combined one of the sharpest minds in the State Department with an obsessive hatred of Britain'.‡ Winning over Berle was the type of challenge that Casey relished. I was also able to consult other documents not much cited in the Casey literature such as the blatantly anti-British 'Briefing Notes' produced by the State Department for use by President Roosevelt, when preparing for the visit to Washington of Prime Minister Menzies in May 1941. A number of official notes kept by Dean Acheson, another Assistant Secretary of State, were consulted. In neither the archives of the State Department, nor the personal writings of Berle and other leading figures in the Administration, is there any hint of Casey being regarded as less than a diligent, worthy representative of his country.

The author was able to interview only two people who knew Casey personally, his daughter Jane and the former Prime Minister, Malcolm Fraser. I was also fortunate enough to engage in correspondence with Hudson, Casey's biographer.

Out of this long search and study, it became impossible to avoid

---

* Bridge, 'The Other Blade of the Scissors', p. 127.
† Adolf Berle Diary, Berle Papers, Box 212, Roosevelt Memorial Library.
‡ David Reynolds, *Creation of the Anglo American Alliance. 1937–1941. A Study in a Comparative Co-operation* (London: Europe Publications, 1981), p. 256.

the conclusion that Casey exercised an influence way beyond that ascribed to him. All the networking, the speeches, the interviews, the meetings, the conferences, the dinners, the arguments that took him from the Oval Office to the backwoods of small town America, his close relationships with the opinion makers and decision makers, with the editors and publishers of the major American newspapers and periodicals, with the top echelons of both the army and the navy, with the diplomats and politicians and in particular, with the American President, bore fruit. He was preaching the 'gospel' (his phrase) of the need for a close relationship between Australia and the United States. The relationship that exists today can be traced back to Richard Casey in 1940–41, albeit through a tortuous journey with many vicissitudes.

Few aspects of Australian foreign policies or Australian defence policies have been subject to the same forensic examination as the American connection. It needs to be emphasised that this work is not concerned with the place of the Australia-United States alliance in contemporary Australia. That is not a pretty story. Rather, it is the beginning of the alliance and Casey's place in that beginning that prompts this study. Nor would I assert that the ANZUS alliance of 1951 flowed naturally from the wartime alliance that was in place after Pearl Harbor. The United States looked to Australia as its wartime basis, but this was not in itself, a guarantee of continuing American interest in Australia. After the war, the United States reviewed its commitments in the context of the Cold War. Percy Spender, Casey's predecessor as Minister for External Affairs, contributed to the decision made by the Americans in 1951 to extend their security network southwards from the Philippines to Australia and New Zealand.* Casey welcomed ANZUS, but the focus here is Casey's mission in 1940–42, which revolved around engaging the United States in the defence of the South West Pacific.

Chapter One is an examination of the literature about Casey. This chapter offers a brief account of Casey's career with a view to helping to understand why Casey has not received the accolades that at least some historians believe that he deserved. His career was

---

* David Lowe, *Australian Between Empires. The Life of Percy Spender* (London: Chatto and Pickering, 2010), pp. 135–6.

one of both remarkable achievement and nagging doubts about his capacity to influence events. Judgments about Casey often carry the suggestion that he was too 'British' to be an effective representative of Australia, too 'good' a man to be successful in politics, and that he was a politician of style rather than substance. It will be described how many of the alleged political weaknesses ascribed to Casey were also his strengths during his period in Washington.

Chapter Two looks at the context of Casey's Washington appointment by describing the state of Australian diplomacy before the sending of the first legation to Washington. In the 1930s, the senior members of the Lyons' and Menzies' governments were for the most part supporters of appeasement as the most likely way to achieve a lasting peace.* While Casey can be criticised as an advocate of appeasement, his decades of involvement in shaping Imperial foreign policy should be viewed instead as excellent preparation for his taking up the post in Washington. He saw the world of the great powers, accurately, as driven solely by considerations of power and self interest.

Chapter Three looks at what Casey was faced with when he arrived in the United States. It is often assumed that the Roosevelt administration was waiting its chance to involve itself in the war against Nazi Germany and only the November election of 1940 prevented earlier assistance to the Allies. Yet the evidence suggests that much the reverse was true. Casey found himself confronted with a vast array of challenges, including Anglophobia, ignorance about Britain and Australia, and an isolationist public. At his first meeting with Roosevelt, the American president confirmed that Australia was too far away to interest the American public and equally too far away to figure in American security concerns in the Pacific region.

Chapter Four looks at how Casey developed his strategy during spring 1940, the Phoney War period. This was an information-gathering period where Casey set down his basic operating principles. It was also a period when Casey established the contacts needed to influence events in Washington. It was at this point

---

* Christopher Waters, *Australia and Appeasement. Imperial Foreign Policy and the Origins of World War II* (London: I.B. Tauris and Company, 2012), p. 243.

that Casey showed one of his greatest skills – the careful use of information – to advantage.

Chapter Five looks at the summer of 1940 and why saving Britain became Casey's focus in that summer. It was during this period that Casey developed a much more accurate, global picture of the war. Despite his tireless efforts to involve the United States in the defence of Britain, his gospel placed Australia at the centre of his strategic message about American security concerns in the Pacific.

Chapter Six looks at the autumn and winter of 1940–41 when Casey was able to turn most of his attention to Pacific affairs. After the November election, there was an expectation that Roosevelt would offer more wholehearted support to both Britain and Australia. This didn't eventuate. Casey worked hard in particular to make the United States pay attention to the strategic keys to the south of the Philippines, that is, Singapore and Australia.

Chapter Seven looks at the Spring and Summer of 1941 especially the Menzies visit. By this time, the Americans were beginning to see Australia as important to its security needs in the Pacific. However, Casey had now to fight skilfully to convince American strategists that the South West Pacific was one unit and that concentrating upon the defence of the Philippines at the expense of Singapore and Australia was unwise, a broad hint that the Philippines were indefensible.

Chapter Eight explains how the contribution of Casey to the defence of Australia is best understood in the context of comparing Casey's efforts with Curtin's 'Look to America' appeal. While Curtin's appeal achieved virtually nothing except the hostility of the American President and others, Casey achieved much more tangible outcomes.

Chapter Nine looks at events after Pearl Harbor. They confirmed that Casey was a superior strategist, with a remarkable mastery of the technical and tactical detail that Australia needed if it were to wage war against Japan.

The Conclusion, sums up the evidence for crediting Casey with successively impressing upon the Americans why it was in their interests to turn Australia into their principal Pacific base.

*Chapter One*

# What We Know of Casey

Casey's stay in Washington represented only two years of an extraordinarily rich political and diplomatic career. A study of the literature about Casey reveals three main themes. The first theme might be described as Casey's personal attributes. He was often described as a 'good man' but an indifferent politician who lacked the necessary toughness to influence events. The second theme is Casey's allegedly incompatible loyalties to Australia and the British Empire. Thirdly, Casey's well-known ability to charm his audience has been interpreted as the triumph of style over substance. Casey is remembered as a 'networker' but not as a thinker, strategist or policy maker.

In Casey's biography. Hudson describes Casey as a child of his class and his time. He was born in Brisbane in 1890 into a prosperous family, one of 'the landed families of Queensland, the Australian robber barons of the nineteenth century', according to the historian, Manning Clark.* As described by his daughter, Jane MacGowan, there is no denying that despite his being a conservative politician, Casey formed friendships with people on the other side of the political spectrum.† His grandfather, Cornelius was a medical practitioner who, after arriving in Australia in 1833, married Loetitia Gardiner, daughter of an Army captain. Their first son, Richard Gardiner Casey senior, born in 1846, became a successful businessman and a member of the Queensland Parliament before losing most of his fortune through the gambling activities of his partner. By diligent work, he later recovered and

---

* C.M.H. Clark, *A History of Australia,* Vol. 6 (Carlton: Melbourne University Press), p. 235.
† Phone conversation with Jane Macgowan on 14 March 2012.

with wise investments in the new Mount Morgan Gold Mining Company and, later, Goldsbrough Mort and Company, rebuilt both a fortune and a reputation. He moved to Melbourne with his family in 1893, where his growing prosperity enabled his two children, Richard junior and his brother Dermot to step into what Hudson referred to as a 'comfortable bourgeois life'.[*]

Although Richard could number a father, maternal grandfather and maternal great-grandfather as past members of the Queensland Parliament and a great-uncle as a former Premier, Hudson claims that Richard and Dermot would have found social and school life intolerable had it been known that their mother's great-grandfather had been sentenced to death at the Old Bailey for theft or that one of her great-grandmothers was an unknown convict woman. According to Hudson: 'From the time that he became aware of the world about him, Richard Casey knew only material privilege. Emotionally, he was less privileged'.[†] Writing of him at the beginning of his career, Clark less kindly described him as 'a young man of promise, one of those men known to his friends as a man of infinite desire and limited capacity'.[‡] It is not clear how Clark formed this conclusion. It might well be that Casey's failure to meet his own goal of becoming Prime Minister justified Clark's judgment.

The *Australian Who's Who* entries for Casey over a period of some years are hopelessly confused with alternating references to a B.A. and an M.A. The University of Cambridge has explained that he gained B.A. in June 1913 and M.A. by proxy in November 1918, as is the custom at both Oxford and Cambridge Universities.[§] Casey was not an academic star at Cambridge, but he engaged with American students more successfully than with British students. His writings show that their gregariousness appealed to him more than the reserve he found in the British-born students. Possibly, Casey's favourable introduction to Americans at Cambridge may have played some part, years later, in his achieving such easy rapport

---

[*] Hudson, *Casey*, p. 7.
[†] Ibid., p. 9.
[‡] Clark, *History of Australia*, Vol. vi, p. 235.
[§] Correspondence between Cambridge University and the author, 1997, held by the author.

during his diplomatic appointment in Washington.

In World War One, Casey served as a Staff Officer at both Gallipoli and the Western Front. Although he spent the entire war years on staff duty, he never commanded men.* On the other hand, Casey was an engineer, a technical training considered useful by the military. He collected both a Military Cross and a Distinguished Service Order. His status as a staff officer did not provide him with any sort of immunity from danger. He was frequently under fire at Gallipoli and was with General William Bridges when the Australian commander was picked off by a sniper, a shot that proved fatal.

After demobilization in 1919, Casey served in the Army Reserve, working part-time as an Intelligence officer in Melbourne. Casey pursued various business interests after the war and visited the United States in an unsuccessful bid to convince Ford to use an Australian-designed motor engine. Casey's friendship with the newly elected Prime Minister, Stanley Bruce led to his appointment as Australian Liaison Officer with the British Cabinet Office in 1924. He was in effect, Bruce's political agent, separate from the High Commission. Although the High Commissioner kept Bruce and the Australian government well informed of decisions made in London, Bruce considered it necessary for this information to be supplemented by a close observer capable of discerning 'developing problems before they reached crisis and decision point'.†

Casey thus became Australia's first diplomat, garnering information and gossip not only from Whitehall and Westminster but from the various strata of London society. Casey's easy fit into that London society as well as his ready acceptance by the mandarins of Whitehall, enabled him to offer an interpretation of whatever intelligence he passed onto Bruce. Moreover, his distinguished military career led to his acceptance by Britain's service chiefs. In effect, he was Bruce's eyes and ears in London. the Imperial centre, reporting to Bruce on everything from British

---

* *Australian Dictionary of Biography*, Vol. 13 Bede Nairn (ed.) (Melbourne: Melbourne University Press), p. 382.
† I.M. Cumpson, *History of Australian Foreign Policy. 1901–1991* (Canberra: I.M. Cumpson, 1995), p. 9.

defence policy to club gossip.* When Casey was appointed to the London post in 1924, he was given an office in 2 Whitehall Gardens, the office of Sir Maurice Hankey, the Cabinet Secretary and probably the most influential and best-informed civil servant in Britain. Far from resenting the presence of a colonial outsider in his sanctum, Hankey eventually came to regard Casey as his 'confidential Australian assistant in imperial policy-making, rather than as a prying foreign diplomat'.†

Bruce himself described Casey in glowing terms, suggesting that his role embraced not only reporting on matters but influencing them: 'From the time [that] Casey went to London as my liaison officer until I ceased to be the High Commissioner in 1945, Australia was invariably better informed on international affairs, and had far more influence on the UK government and its policy, than all the rest of the Empire put together'.‡ While in London, Casey married Ethel Ryan, known as Maie, from a well-connected family in Victoria and later remembered as an author, artist, composer, aviator, an acquaintance with members of the Royal Family and bon vivant. The Caseys slotted easily into inter-war British high society.

With the defeat of Bruce in the 1929 Election, Casey had no further purpose in remaining in London. He returned to Australia and won election to the Federal Parliament as a United Australia Party (UAP) candidate. Casey was in Federal Parliament as the member for Corio from December 1931 to January 1940. In all the years he spent in Parliament, he escaped any time in Opposition. Prime Minister Joseph Lyons appointed Casey Assistant Treasurer in 1933 and Treasurer in 1935. Under Menzies, Casey served in the crucial role of Minister for Supply and Development in 1939. Although he was a worker, what would now be called a workaholic, Casey left no significant monuments as treasurer.§ The problem, according to Hudson, was that Casey was not a natural politician.

---

\* *Australian Dictionary of Biography*, Vol. 13, p. 382.
† P.G. Edwards, 'R.G. Menzies Appeals to the United States. May–June 1940', *Australian Outlook*, XXVII, 1974, pp. 64–70.
‡ Cecil Edwards, *Bruce of Melbourne. Man of Two Worlds* (London: Heineman, 1954), p. 87.
§ Hudson, *Casey*, p. 98.

The 1930s had been for Casey years of remarkable success. Without any grounding in local government or state government and without the basic political gifts of the gab and a thick skin, through some highly placed connections, he had entered Federal Parliament at his first attempt, becoming a junior minister after less than two years and a senior minister after less than four.

In career terms they were successful years. In terms of concrete accomplishment, the times, the company and Casey's own inability to wheel and deal made the decade for him, less memorable.[*]

It was this apparent inability to 'wheel and deal' effectively with his Cabinet colleagues that bedevilled Casey for the whole of his political career and beyond. Years later, Casey himself virtually confirmed this judgment by admitting the failure of his strenuous efforts as Treasurer to convince his Cabinet colleagues to boost defence expenditure in the years immediately before the outbreak of the Second World War.[†] Of Casey's tenure in the Lyons Ministry, the economic historian, Boris Schedvin wrote that 'Casey was energetic but uninspired in his several Treasury capacities'.[‡] Casey can take some credit, however, for the fact that, in the case of Australia, rearmament did finally get under way in the last years of the decade so that ten times more was spent on defence in 1938–39 than was the case at the height of the Depression in 1932–33. Indeed, Casey and other UAP politicians did a great deal to help Australia save itself in the Second World War by strongly developing its industry and military technology.[§]

The suspicion that Casey, who had spent the best part of a decade in London, had a dual allegiance to the Crown and to the Australian government was a constant refrain from his critics.[¶] In his examination of Anglo-Australian defence relations during the inter-war years, J.M. McCarthy accuses Casey of revealing

---

[*] Ibid., pp. 111–12.
[†] Quoted in David Day, *The Politics of War* (Sydney: Harper Collins, 2003), p. 7.
[‡] C.B. Schedvin, *Australia and the Great Depression* (Sydney: Sydney University Press, 1988), p. 316.
[§] Andrew T. Ross, *Armed and Ready: The Industrial Development and Defence of Australia, 1900–1945*, p. 68.
[¶] J.M. McCarthy, *Australia and Imperial Defence. 1918–1939* (St Lucia: University of Queensland Press, 1976), pp. 116, 182.

Cabinet discussions to the British High Commissioner, Sir Geoffrey Whiskard, in 1936, during the negotiations about the construction of aircraft for the R.A.A.F. While I have been unable to verify this allegation, it has the ring of accuracy about it. Similar allegations exist of a more substantive nature that Casey was advising the King's Private Secretary during the emerging crisis in 1936, about the King's determination to marry Mrs Simpson. The Prime Minister, Joseph Lyons carried the burden of reporting the Australian government's opposition to the marriage, and if the allegations were true, they reflect poorly on Casey's judgment.

Descriptions of Casey as 'British' or 'English' in appearance and style abound in the literature. Gavin Souter, quoting the US Consul-General J.P. Moffatt, creates a vivid word picture of Casey sounding and looking like 'an Englishman, perhaps a Guards' officer in well-cut mufti, rather aloof most of the time, but affable when he chose to be ... travelled widely in Europe and North America, spoke good French and some German, and had the knack of impressing people in high places'.[*] Fred Alexander noted that 'in dress, manner and personal appearance, he possessed 'many of the outward marks of an Englishman – 'the Anthony Eden of Australia'.[†] Evatt's close friend, Sam Atyeo, described Casey as 'the poor man's Anthony Eden'.[‡] Clark's word picture of Casey follows the familiar theme: 'English, Melbourne Grammar and Cambridge, while his manners were impeccable, his clothes straight from Bond Street and his voice from the Old Country'.[§]

A Parliamentary colleague, James Killen, wrote of Casey as 'English in appearance, in manner, in dress, with a clipped English style of speaking ...'.[¶] In a review of Parliamentary performers in

---

[*] Gavin Souter, *Acts of Parliament. A Narrative History of the Senate and House of Representatives, Commonwealth of Australia* (Carlton: Melbourne University Press, 1988), pp. 307–8.
[†] Fred Alexander, *Australia Since Federation* (Melbourne: Thomas Nelson, 1967), p. 280.
[‡] Ken Buckley, Barbara Dale, and Wayne Reynolds, *Doc Evatt. Patriot, Internationalist, Fighter and Scholar* (Melbourne: Longman Cheshire, 1994), p. 414.
[§] Clark, *History*, Vol. vi, p. 235.
[¶] James Killen, *Inside Australian Politics* (Sydney: Methuen Haynes, 1985), p. 33.

1950, Casey was said to have 'a rapid, eager stutter' found more often in Britain than Australia.*

There was both an irony and a practical difficulty here given that the man who had to explain Australia to the Americans at the outset of World War Two looked and sounded like a stereotypical English diplomat. Fred Daly, a Labor Member of Parliament with a reputation as a humorous participant in debates, tells how he ridiculed Casey by asking him a prank question during Question Time and Casey taking it seriously, suggesting either a poor sense of humour or unfamiliarity with the sardonic aspects of Australian humour.† Trevor Reese considered Casey's parliamentary speeches 'unimaginative and woefully tedious'.‡

Given these attributes, it may well have been that Casey slotted easily into a more formalised relationship with the colleagues that he had found in London than the more robust and casual relationships found in Australian male groups. It is also possible that the very qualities that were seen as detrimental to political success in Australia were regarded highly in London and Washington. Indeed, more than one observer concluded that Casey appeared more at home when overseas than he did in Australia, a personal characteristic occasionally applied to Menzies. T.B. Millar, a former Director of the Australian Institute of International Affairs, while judging that Casey was an excellent choice as Australia's first Minister to Washington, claims that he was 'perhaps more at home in foreign fields than in his own'.§ A similar belief is expressed by W.J. Hudson and Wendy Way: 'Casey was wealthy, more at ease in London society'.¶ It would be fair to say that his Labor opponents disliked Casey's upper-class origins, imperial politics, and British loyalties. Given Australia's relative isolation from Europe and North America at that time, it would be reasonable to conclude

---

\* Quoted in K.S. Inglis, *This is the ABC* (Carlton: Melbourne University Press, 1983), p. 145.
† Fred Daly, *From Curtin to Hawke* (Melbourne: Sun Books, 1985), pp. 89–90.
‡ Trevor R. Reese. *Australia, New Zealand and the United States. A Survey of International Relations* (London: Oxford University Press, 1969), p. 173.
§ Millar, *Australia in Peace and War: External Relations 1788–1977* (Canberra: Australian National University, 1978), p. 140.
¶ W. Hudson and Wendy Way (eds.), *Letters from a Secret Service Agent* (Canberra: Australian Government Printing Service, 1986), p. xiv.

that Casey's upbringing, including a Cambridge degree and a long sojourn in the British Foreign Office, had prepared him not so much for the rough and tumble of the Australian political milieu but rather for life in the upper reaches of British society.

Having a dual allegiance to Britain and Australia was commonplace in inter-war Australia. Casey, as Waters has put it, 'was a firm believer that the English-speaking peoples had a special role in world affairs' and in the saving of 'Western civilisation'.* Casey in the 1930s was an enthusiastic imperialist on both economic and defence grounds, and as a strong supporter of the 'one voice theory' of imperial foreign affairs. Yet Casey emphasised that Australia had very practical reasons for its close relationship with Great Britain. In 1938, Casey summed up his reasoning thus:

> between Australia and Great Britain there is a community of interest that probably does not exist with equal force between any other two countries in the world. On those very material grounds we are, in a unique degree, dependent on the continued existence of Great Britain, and that is why I say I am an Imperialist as well as an Australian.†

Thus, Casey emphasised the 'material' link to empire and believed that the security of Australia and Britain were closely linked. Given that the United States was in no mood to offer protection to Australia and given the parlous state of Australia's military preparedness, Britain's was the logical, indeed, the only source of protection on offer. Like most Australian leaders, Casey wanted to forge closer links to Britain with a view to influencing British thinking. This did not rule out a closer relationship between Australia and the United States. Bringing the United States and the British Empire closer together was a strong theme among Australian politicians, as well as the British Prime Ministers, Chamberlain and Churchill.‡

Lyons' sudden death in 1939 enabled Casey to stand for the leadership of the United Australia Party (and Prime Ministership) but he was easily beaten by Menzies. Hudson claims that the

---

\* Waters, 'Casey. Four Decades', p. 382.
† Cited in Waters, 'Casey. Four Decades', pp. 382–3.
‡ Ibid.

leadership was denied Casey because he was 'far too modest and too inept in organizing support for himself'.* As Bridge has pointed out, Casey ran an abysmal third after Menzies and the indefatigable former Prime Minister, Billy Hughes, having made the dual mistakes of first backing the candidature of Bruce and then courting the Country Party.† Thereafter, Casey's role was always focused upon the international arena, though Casey himself continued to harbour leadership ambitions in the decades that followed.

Both Lyons and Menzies made use of Casey's international connections and diplomatic skills. Casey was an important contributor to the Imperial Conference of 1937, which he attended with Lyons, Hughes, Archdale Parkhill and Bruce, High Commissioner in London since 1933. Casey in the 1930s, like Menzies, Gullett, Lyons, and the majority of Australia's political class, sat firmly in the appeasement camp. Or, as David Lowe has put it, 'to divide Australians into "appeasers" and "anti-appeasers" is an historic nonsense, collapsing a broad range of positions, most of them involving concessions or efforts to improve relations between the major nations, into opposing camps'.‡

Casey, as Bridge has put it, was one of the 'ultra' appeasers.§ The aim was to keep Australia out of a war with Japan and to ensure that Britain did not become entangled in a war in continental Europe with the result that it would be unable to assist in the security of Australia.

Australian political leadership on both sides of the left-right divide recognised Australia's vulnerability in the face of German aggression, Japanese militarism, and the threat posed by the arms race. After the beginning of the European conflict, it was not difficult for Menzies to be won over and to agree to a rapid expansion of Australia's diplomatic positions. Despite the almost prohibitive cost of a legation with its own staff and premises, Australia would now have a voice in Washington as insurance against the ever-increasing danger of Japan embarking on a rampage in the Pacific.

---

\* *Australian Dictionary of Biography*, Vol. 13, p. 383.
† Bridge, 'The Other Blade of the Scissors', pp. 129–30.
‡ Lowe, *Australian Between Empires*, p. 54.
§ Bridge, 'R.G. Casey', pp. 372–9.

In June 1939, the British Prime Minister, Neville Chamberlain had promised Menzies:

> in the event of war with Germany and Italy, should Japan join in against us, it would still be His Majesty's government's full intention to dispatch a fleet to Singapore ... it would be our intention to achieve three main objects, (1) the prevention of any major operation against Australia, New Zealand or India, (2) to keep open our sea communications, (3) to prevent the fall of Singapore.[*]

Menzies gave every indication that already he was convinced that Britain could not sustain war with Germany and simultaneously send vast resources to defend British interests in the Pacific and Asian regions. This showed no great perspicacity. Britain's long period of running down defence preparations during the 1920s and 30s,

> inevitably raised doubts about her ability to cope with major conflicts in two parts of the globe. Even Bruce was privately doubtful that Britain would, or even could live up to its commitments.[†]

Menzies sent Casey to London late in 1939 to evaluate assurances from Britain about the Far East. The 6$^{th}$ Division of the Australian Imperial Force was about to be sent to Britain to help in the war against Nazi Germany. Casey reported that he found the assurances of the British government about Singapore satisfactory but with worrying questions. He accepted the view that the main enemy for Britain and Australia in 1939 was Nazi Germany. In reality, unless Australia could generate American interest in the South West Pacific, the Australian government had little choice other than to hope that Britain would live up to its promises.[‡] Menzies and his cabinet made the decision to send the 6$^{th}$ Division

---

[*] Chamberlain to Menzies, 29 June 1939, cablegram, unnumbered, PRO, CAB 21/893 (Kew: Public Records Office).
[†] David Lee, 'Stanley Bruce at the Wartime Australian High Commission' in Christopher Baxter and Andrew Stewart (eds.), *Diplomats at War*, pp. 153–4 (Leiden: Martinus Nijhoff, 2008).
[‡] Lee, 'Stanley Bruce', pp. 153–4.

on the basis of Casey's recommendations.* Bridge explained Casey's logic in the following terms: 'regardless of all else, the Pacific defence situation depended upon the survival of Britain and her fleet. Thus by defending Britain, the Australian 6th Division would be indirectly defending Australia'.†

While Casey was in London, Menzies appointed him as Minister heading the Australian legation in Washington. Casey was not Menzies' first choice, but he was the obvious appointment. As Waters has put it, Casey was 'Australia's first diplomat of significance in the 1920s and a well-connected senior minister in the 1930s'.‡ Casey was certainly better versed than most in United States government affairs. In July 1937, Casey, as Australian Treasurer, visited Washington and spoke to Secretary of State Cordell Hull and other high-ranking American officials about the contentious Empire-United States trade relations. By that time, Britain was viewing favourably the signing of a reciprocal trade agreement with the United States, a development that owed as much to Britain's desire for closer ties to the United States as it did to easing up trade restrictions. However, this would involve Australia losing much of its advantages under the Imperial preference scheme and abandoning high protective tariffs. Casey's talks achieved little. He was able to give the Americans an assurance that the Australian government would be prepared to make concessions, but only on the condition that the United States government indicated beforehand the extent of its concessions. This was the stumbling point. From the American viewpoint, Casey's offer was an advance in negotiations but in effect, it achieved nothing. His talks with leading figures in the State Department, however, had left a very favourable impression. According to Moffat, the American Consul-General in Australia, the Washington officials believed 'Casey the smartest of the lot ... a future PM'.§

---

\* Ibid., pp. 155–6.
† Bridge, 'R.G. Casey's Contribution to Australian War Policy', pp. 80–90.
‡ Waters, *Australia and Appeasement*, p. 6.
§ Quoted in Raymond A. Esthus, *From Enmity to Alliance. US-Australian Relations, 1931–1941* (Seattle: University of Washington Press, 1964), pp. 39–40.

Yet the context of Casey's appointment to the United States revealed personal qualities in Menzies that would eventually contribute to his downfall in 1941 and cast a shadow over Casey's suitability for the job of leading the Australian legation in Washington. Despite knowing of Casey's reluctance to terminate his political career in Australia for the diplomatic posting to the United States, Menzies advised the Dominions Secretary in London, Anthony Eden, that Casey would be going to Washington. This was before Casey had definitely accepted the post.*

Casey, from London, told Menzies that he (Casey) could render more valuable service in Australia, but that he would go if that was what Menzies wanted.† At this time, Casey confided in Bruce that the reason he wanted to remain in Australian politics rather than take up the Washington appointment was to be available should Menzies cease being Prime Minister, a distinct possibility at that time.‡ Casey's response to Menzies' request may be seen as loyalty to his leader, especially in the increasingly fraught times or alternatively as reluctance to press his own interests. His language in the reply to Menzies carries some significance: 'With the knowledge I have acquired here [in London] I feel that I could be of some assistance to you in the serious times that lie ahead ... my judgment is that I could render more valuable service in Australia [than in the United States]'. He was thus arguing, perhaps to himself, that taking over from Menzies would be of far greater service to Australia than accepting the Washington post. Yet, he seemed incapable of asserting that argument.§

In a cablegram to Bruce in London asking him to visit Washington 'to negotiate with the American administration for establishment of reciprocal Legations and to inaugurate our own', Menzies let slip his doubts about Casey: 'I have had some reservations about Casey, but on the whole I think that a man of political experience is essential at Washington, and he appears to be

---
\* Hudson, *Casey*, p. 115.
† Casey to Menzies, 1 November 1939, CP290/6 Item 1, NAA.
‡ Note by S.M. Bruce of conversation with R.G. Casey, London, 8 November 1939, *Documents on Australian Foreign Policy* (hereafter *DAFP*), Vol. II, 335, p. 381.
§ Casey to Menzies, 1 November 1939, cablegram, CP 290/6, Item 1, NAA.

the most suitable of those available'.* No matter how it is read, this was hardly a ringing endorsement of Casey.

In taking up the post of Australian Minister to the United States, Casey was breaking new ground. Australia had never had an independent diplomatic presence in the United States. Given the fact that Casey was not Menzies' first choice, it could be seen as almost serendipity that Casey was appointed to be Australia's first senior diplomatic appointment. Certainly the appointment was fortuitous given Australia's lack of experience in foreign relations; Casey was, by Australian standards, a veteran of international diplomacy. As Cecil Edwards has put it, before the outbreak of the Pacific conflict, Australian foreign policy was 'being formulated largely by the triangular traffic of cables between Bruce in London, Casey in Washington and Menzies in Canberra'.† On the other hand, the United States certainly represented a major personal challenge for Casey. After the years spent in London, working with British mandarins at the centre of the Empire, would Casey be able to assert an Australian role in international diplomacy?

The verdicts were mixed. For Carey's supporters, his appointment to the Washington post enabled him to exercise the diplomatic and public relations skills that he had exercised so effectively in London. For the representative of a small nation, entirely without influence, Casey, after assuming the post on 6 March 1940, quickly gained frequent access to President Roosevelt, himself renowned as a politician of engaging charm. Casey cultivated Administration officials and the service chiefs. As the *Australian Dictionary of Biography* put it: 'Although he was now 50, boyish charm and courteous deference opened doors to him, and he was a keen convert to the American craft of public relations'.‡ Indeed, he engaged the services of a public relations consultant and showed remarkable energy in promoting his mission. While not a typical day, Casey's account of his movements for 3 December 1940 illustrates his energy in undertaking what he saw as his responsibilities, his diary noting simply: 'Saw the Secretary of State,

---

\* Menzies to Bruce, 27 October 1939, cablegram, CP 290/6, Item 1, NAA.
† Edwards, *Bruce of Melbourne*, p. 284.
‡ *Australian Dictionary of Biography*, Vol. 13, p. 383.

Dinner at Legation, Justice Frankfurter, Joseph Alsop (Columnist), Admiral Stark (Chief of Naval Operations), John Foster and Danish Minister. Left on midnight train to Hartford Connecticut'. On this occasion, Casey was to remain in Hartford for just one day, meeting persons of influence, especially newspaper and university people, inspecting munitions factories and addressing meetings before flying onto Boston and then New York in a similar routine.*

The American press certainly approved of Casey. The *New York Times*, commenting on his appointment to Washington, reported that 'Australia has given her best in sending us Richard G. Casey'.† Casey had a rare talent for charming important people, evident in both his London and Washington years:

His natural shyness and boyishness, now a little at odds with his age (when he arrived in the United States he was nearly fifty) made for a socially powerful combination. President Roosevelt liked him and took him up, and when Maie (Casey) arrived in Washington, the President's wife, Eleanor, had the Caseys to tea at the White House. He melted the austere heart of Cordell Hull, also a shy man. He wisely took the precaution of courting Harry Hopkins, Roosevelt's closest and most privileged adviser and paid close attention to the President's man at the State Department, Adolf Berle, Cabinet members, Supreme Court justices and servicemen.‡

Casey became 'a trusted, informal intermediary'.§ Millar argues that so far as anyone could do it, he put Australia on the map in America.¶ Alan Watt, who took over from Keith Officer, an Australian diplomat in the Washington legation, noted that, 'it is clear that Roosevelt had a high opinion of Casey', and recounted a number of incidents when Roosevelt and the Roosevelt Administration employed Casey on delicate diplomatic tasks that were apparently beyond the capabilities of their own people.**

An example of Casey's high standing became apparent when United States Supreme Court Justice Felix Frankfurter, avowedly

---

\* Casey Diaries, 3 December 1940.
† *New York Times*, 21 February 1940, p. 5.
‡ Hudson, *Casey*, pp. 118–19.
§ Millar, *Australia in Peace and War*, p. 141.
¶ Ibid., p. 140.
\*\* Watt, *The Evolution of Australian Foreign Policy*, pp. 34–5.

pro-Allied and a personal acquaintance of Casey, requested Casey to give to Churchill a personal message before he met Harry Hopkins, who was about to spend some time in London with the Prime Minister. The Justice was anxious that Churchill express to Hopkins his great admiration for the American president, to match Hopkins' admiration which bordered on worship. It says a great deal about the relationship that Frankfurter selected Casey as the one most suitable to carry the message.\*

Maie Casey is worth special mention. Although Maie Casey remained in the background of Richard Casey for most of her life, in the words of the writer, Kay Saunders, she was a bohemian, adventurous and unconventional at one level but deeply status conscious, snobbish and demanding on another. Saunders describes the marriage as close but puzzling. Saunders claimed that she moved in the highest international circles, 'a confidante of Gandhi, Churchill, Noel Coward, Dame Judith Anderson and Eleanor Roosevelt'.† The inclusion of the name of the President's wife in Maie Casey's circle may have gone some way towards Casey's apparent ease of entry into the Oval Office and his attempts to establish an influential presence in the White House. Eleanor Roosevelt's winning personality and the active role she played in the Roosevelt administration is well documented. Maie Casey was a talented artist who furnished her Washington abode with her private art collection brought from Australia and she enchanted Washington with an exhibition of Australian settler and Aboriginal art.

Edwards views Casey as having successfully worked towards a better understanding between Britain and the United States. One of Evatt's biographers, Kylie Tennant, takes a similar view: 'Casey's extraordinary charm had brought him such success in Washington that the British Embassy had been only too glad to follow his advice'.‡ A like judgment by Watt throws some light on Casey's actual activities in America: 'Casey was an excellent host, with

---

\* Casey to London, 6 January 1941, cablegram, 96, A3300, NAA.
† Kay Saunders, *Notorious Australian Women* (Australia: Harper Collins Publishers, 2011), pp. 136–47.
‡ Kylie Tennant, *Evatt. Politics and Justice* (Sydney: Angus and Robertson, 1970), p. 140.

a flair for starting a conversation and inducing men of different outlook and views to carry it on'. Further, Watt writes of Casey that:

> His university and official experience in England and his understanding of the English temperament and outlook made it possible for him to explain Englishmen to Americans and Americans to Englishmen, and often to bring together on social occasions representatives of the two countries whose direct contacts had been formal rather than close.[*]

Paul Hasluck, usually numbered among Casey's critics, had no reservations about Casey's Washington appointment: 'Early in 1940, the appointment of Casey as first Australian Minister to the US had robbed the government of an experienced, energetic and tactful minister who could push ahead with a job and still be pleasant about it'.[†] Bridge claims that Casey's contribution to Australian war policy was 'fundamental': Casey 'served with great distinction, especially in the dark and difficult days before Pearl Harbor'.[‡] Tennant refers to Casey being popular in Washington, 'in the handsome tradition of old-time diplomacy'.[§] Taking a slightly different slant, Hudson has claimed that Casey personified to Americans 'the Hollywood notion of a handsome Britisher enlivened by New World zest'.[¶] Hudson also noted that senior British services personnel 'liked the cut of his jib',[**] an old-fashioned saying, but one that conveys a particular admiration.

On the other hand, it should be noted that Casey worked hard at achieving his preferred self-image. Hudson goes so far as to claim that this meant that Casey used 'a mask' when his views differed from those of the person to whom he was speaking.[††] Hudson may be referencing an earlier book by Percy Spender, who knew Casey for over thirty years and wrote of him: 'In many ways, his demeanour appeared to mask the inner man, and the mask and the

---
\* Watt, *The Evolution of Australian Foreign Policy 1938–1965*, p. 33.
† Paul Hasluck, *The Government and the People. 1939–1941* (Canberra: Australian War Memorial, 1965), p. 243.
‡ Bridge, 'The Other Blade of the Scissors', p. 127.
§ Tennant, *Evatt*, p. 135.
¶ Hudson, *Casey*, p. 118.
\*\* Ibid., p. 139.
†† Ibid., p. 144.

man, it may happen, become in the end, indistinguishable one from the other; the mask indeed can become the man behind'.* Spender suspected that, despite his confident image, Casey, at heart, was a somewhat shy man and 'this may account for the mask which I think was always with him'.

An alternative explanation is that Casey had learned from his diplomatic experience that masks were a necessary part of the job. Indeed, Casey's Washington diary is full of bitter and sarcastic comments about influential Americans and the American people more generally, but no hint of these heartfelt views was allowed to contaminate Casey's gospel of goodwill to the United States from Australia. Casey certainly made no secret of his admiration for British stoicism in the face of the Nazi onslaught, telling his diary on 27 June 1940 that 'The British race is the finest race in the world'.†
The contrast was with the Americans and their complete failure to live up to their duty to 'come in' and join Britain's fight against the dictators. In one of his darker moments, Casey speculated on the reason for the American failure to help Britain in 1940:

> May it not possibly be that there is the same sort of feeling between USA and Britain as there is between Japan and China? – i.e. the one having drawn its civilization from the other – hating to acknowledge it – having a sense of inferiority from it?‡

Casey met Roosevelt one-on-one on no fewer than eleven occasions.§ On five other occasions, he accompanied Lothian and Halifax. Although he is on record noting the difficulties in arranging to see Roosevelt, his relations with the President became closer over time.¶ Before Pearl Harbor at least, these Presidential conversations tested Casey's patience, though he usually described their outcome as useful. Casey described an interview with Roosevelt as being something of a monologue: 'It is not easy to get an opportunity to express oneself and you have to hop in while

---

\* Percy Spender, *Politics and a Man* (Oxford: Blackwell, 1972), pp. 32–3.
† Casey Diaries, 27 June 1940.
‡ Ibid.
§ Bridge, 'The Other Blade of the Scissors', p. 135.
¶ Casey to Menzies, 15 June 1940, cablegram, 123, A3195. 1/4326, NAA.

he's pausing for breath'.* Hudson confided to this author that 'in my judgment, Casey had so recommended himself at every level in Washington, including the White House, that there was nothing inherently improbable in Roosevelt having confided in him'.†

Even so, the critics have tended to disparage even Casey's seemingly easy access of Roosevelt. David Day has noted that Casey mostly accompanied Lord Lothian, the British Ambassador, when he visited the White House. For Day, Casey did on occasions make Australia's voice heard but he was more likely to be perceived as a British cipher.‡ It is certainly true that the British Embassy in Washington, was soon drawing attention to Casey's skills in the area of disseminating its message.§ Just about every source noted that Casey worked closely with Lothian and later with Halifax, both of whom had the principal responsibility for arguing Britain's case in Washington. Casey was himself so good at arguing the British case that some American press writers assumed that Casey would replace Lothian when the latter unexpectedly died in December 1940.¶ All of this makes Casey an easy target for those who prefer to see Casey as a British 'agent' pushing the 'Empire' line.

The diplomat Malcolm Booker summed up the charge against Casey: 'Throughout his stay in Washington, Casey invariably deferred to the British Ambassador, as is indicated in his own writings'. While conceding that Casey and his wife occupied an influential position in Washington, Booker claims that he used that influential position not so much to promote a specifically Australian point of view as to act as a broker between the British and the Americans.** This is not correct. In 1940, Casey directed his energies to seeking American aid for a Britain facing possible invasion. When that threat had passed, he concentrated on securing American involvement in the Pacific region. However, Booker claims that, as a senior cabinet minister in the Menzies Cabinet,

---

\* Casey Diaries, 5 June 1940.
† W.J. Hudson, Casey's biographer in a letter of 20 July 1988, to the author. Original held by the author.
‡ Day, *The Great Betrayal*, p. 97.
§ See, e.g., Bridge, *A Delicate Mission*, pp. 6, 17.
¶ Bridge, 'The Other Blade of the Scissors', p. 142.
\** Malcolm Booker, *The Last Domino. Aspects of Australia's Foreign Relations* (Sydney: Collins, 1976), pp. 41–2.

Casey showed surprising humility in accepting the secondary rank of 'minister plenipotentiary'. This was a rank below ambassador, making it clear that Britain was the senior partner in the Imperial alliance.

Booker makes the point that the terms of his Washington appointment placed him in a position of inferiority to all the important diplomatic representatives in the capital. According to Booker: 'In particular, it symbolized to the rank-conscious Americans, Australia's readiness to accept a role subordinate to the British'. Booker asserts that this relationship was doubtless confirmed by the *Note* which the British Ambassador delivered to the State Department declaring that the Casey appointment was not to be regarded as denoting 'any departure from the diplomatic unity of the Empire'.[*] In the words of the historian, L.E. Fredman: 'The fiction of the diplomatic unity of the Empire was still maintained even in announcing this first appointment'.[†]

Stephen Alomes is even less kind, portraying Casey as an 'imperial boy scout' and 'another good boy scout for the Empire'.[‡] According to Alomes, Casey was 'more British than the British'.[§] A similar conclusion can be drawn from Roger Bell's account of Casey's years in Washington. Conceding that the Australian minister developed close associations with Roosevelt's personal adviser, Harry Hopkins and with Secretary of State Hull and close but unofficial contacts with Generals Marshall and Arnold and Admiral King, Bell claims that these were inappropriate and insufficient to meet the needs of intimate war-time collaboration.[¶] Bell does not explain how these contacts were neither appropriate nor sufficient. While acknowledging that Casey is entitled to some of the credit for a changed American attitude to Australia's defence needs in 1942, Reese claims that 'Casey had a high opinion of his own work in Washington'.[**]

---

[*] Ibid.
[†] Fredman, *The United States Enters the Pacific*, p. 55.
[‡] Alomes, *A Nation at Last*, p. 116.
[§] Ibid., p. 180.
[¶] Roger Bell, *Unequal Allies* (Carlton: Melbourne University Press, 1977), p. 59.
[**] Reese, *Survey of International Relations*, p. 13.

According to Alomes, Casey was 'more concerned with bringing the United States into the war [as Britain wanted] than with avoiding a Pacific war [as Australia wanted]'.*

Writing of the withholding from the Australian government of the policy adopted by Churchill and Roosevelt to 'Beat Hitler First' in 1941, Day describes the violent reaction by Evatt upon learning of the existence of this policy when visiting London in May 1942. Day speculates who was responsible for concealing the 'Beat Hitler First' decision from Evatt and the Australians up to that time and lays the blame primarily with Churchill, 'connived at by Roosevelt' and 'aided and abetted by Australia's representatives in Washington and London who did a grave disservice to their duty when they became involved in this campaign and withheld vital information from their political masters. Of those representatives, Day is unsparing in his criticism: 'As former or present conservative MPs, Page, Bruce and Casey proved ill-suited to serve the needs of a more nationalistic Labor government'.†

The centrality of Curtin's 'Look to America' has led to the popular view that politicians of that era could be divided into 'Australia first' and 'Britain first' camps. Yet the charge that Casey withheld information about the 'Beat Hitler First' policy from the Australian government does not hold up, as Bridge has shown. The Australian War cabinet saw the report of the ABC1 talks of January–March 1941, which decided the 'Hitler first' issue.‡ As Curran has pointed out, there was general agreement in Australia upon the importance of Britain to Australia's survival.§ Up until Pearl Harbor, it was not only Casey and his fellow UAP members who prioritised the need to win the war in Europe. Upon becoming Prime Minister in October 1941, Curtin did not change Australia's military strategy or question the commitment of troops to Britain. As late as November 1941, on the eve of Pearl Harbor, Curtin agreed to reinforcing the AIF in the Middle East.¶ In other words, it was not just conservatives, but Labor politicians too, who saw the

---

\* Alomes, *A Nation At Last*, p. 116.
† Day, *The Politics of War*, p. 326.
‡ Bridge, 'The Other Blade of the Scissors', p. 141.
§ Curran, *Curtin's Empire*, p. 131.
¶ Ibid., pp. 81–2.

good sense from Australia's perspective in 'saving Britain'.

Joseph Maiolo writes of a noticeable change of mood in Washington in the last months of 1941. Hull had become convinced that further negotiations with Japan were futile. Frank Knox, Political Head of the Navy, and Henry Stimson, Political Head of the Army, both former Republicans in the Hoover regime, were firmly of the view that hostilities with Japan were inevitable. Knox had been Republican Vice Presidential nominee in the Presidential election of 1936. Stimson had been Secretary of State in the Hoover Administration. It is significant that two experienced men from the conservative side of politics came to these conclusions about Japan.*

The advent of a Labor government in Australia in October 1941 initially gave Casey no reason to consider his future, after he was refused permission to return to Australia for consultation.† Curtin, the new Prime Minister wanted him to remain at his post in the United States.‡ Casey's relations with the new Minister for External Affairs, Evatt, however, were not amicable and Casey ultimately accepted the offer of the British Prime Minister, Winston Churchill, to become Britain's Minister of State in the Middle East, based in Cairo. Casey accepted this appointment despite knowing of Curtin's strong preference for him to remain in Washington.§

Few events in his long career attracted as much criticism from both his political opponents and, in the long term, writers and historians, as his acceptance of the Cairo appointment.¶ Curtin wanted Casey to remain as the Australian representative in the United States and his decision to accept Churchill's offer has been often portrayed as a snub to Australia in its hour of need. Curiously, some observers who were not impressed with his efforts during the two years he spent in the United States were critical of his leaving. The intensity of the debate about the posting to the Middle East

---

\* Joseph Maiolo, *Cry Havoc. The Arms Race and the second World War 1931–1941* (London: Arts and Humanities Research Council, 2010), p. 36.
† Casey Diaries, 9 October 1941 and 11 October 1941. Casey to Evatt, 16 October 1941; Evatt to Casey, 15 October 1941, cables, A981/225, NAA.
‡ Curtin to Churchill, 13 March 1942, *DAFP*, Vol. V, Doc. 409.
§ Curtin to Casey, 17 March 1942, cablegram, SW 16, A981, Great Britain 138, NAA.
¶ See Bridge, *A Delicate Mission*, pp. 12–13.

may be gauged by Churchill's response to Curtin's objections:

> Both principal Ministers I have consulted and Chiefs of Staff are agreed in wanting Casey for this most important post which requires military experience and knowledge of public affairs both ministerial and diplomatic. I had a whole evening in the train with Casey when I was in America and learned from him that he was very anxious for a change.*

Churchill went on to suggest that Curtin appoint Menzies to replace Casey in Washington, a suggestion that fell on deaf ears.

This was at a time when the war situation created unbearable tensions, pushing tempers to a knife edge. For instance, on virtually his last day in Washington, Casey noted:

> Splenetic reaction from Mr Curtin and from the Melbourne Herald about my accepting Mr Churchill's proposal. Mr Curtin is hard pressed – and in respect of him, I believe I have happened, by bad chance, to come between the hammer of his and the anvil of Mr Churchill.†

The sometimes acrimonious exchanges between Curtin and Churchill over the latter's offer to Casey of a senior Ministerial position in the Middle East in 1942 reveal a duality in Casey's personal relationships. Hudson observes that Casey never forgave Curtin for objecting to and attempting to stop him leaving Washington for the Cairo appointment. His unforgiveness extended to refusing invitations in later years to write about Curtin. Yet Hudson also sees a redeeming quality in Casey in that he never allowed his personal animosity to affect his official responsibilities. According to Hudson, Casey 'went out of his way' to sell Curtin and Evatt in high places.‡

So far as the Cairo appointment was concerned, Hudson's observations suggest that Casey should have realised that he was not qualified for the job, which according to Hudson, 'was awesome in its scope and complexity'.§ Casey's difficulties in the Middle East

---

\* Churchill to Curtin, 13 March 1942, DO 35/1009, 1, cablegram, 1 Winch 12, PRO.
† Casey Diaries, 20 March 1942.
‡ Hudson, *Casey*, p. 134.
§ Ibid., p. 138.

would do great harm to his reputation. The post was so complex that it is doubtful if any one person, no matter how experienced, could have juggled, successfully, the many competing interests that formed the area of every day responsibilities. On 8 March 1942 the American jurist, Felix Frankfurter, by now a close friend of Casey, was moved to commit to his diary:

> My sum total impression was that poor Dick Casey never in his life gave a thought to the position of the Jew in the world in general, or to Zionism in particular, that he suddenly is confronted with problems for which he has no background ... Casey not only knows nothing of the Balfour Declaration and of Palestine since then, but he doesn't even know that there is such a history or that people like me know it.*

Casey's difficulties in his new, Middle East role emanated principally from the British Foreign Office, whose officials regarded the Australian as an ignorant outsider who had usurped the Resident Foreign Office representative there. Yet it was not the case that Casey left the Middle East without accolades. When Lebanon declared war on the Axis powers in February 1945, and became a foundation member of the new United Nations, Casey would have been entitled to appreciate the comment of a London newspaper that 'the refreshing frankness of Mr R.G. Casey had a good deal to do with the agreement'.† The British Representative in Beirut, Louis Spears reported to London that Casey had turned out 'to be a real rock'.‡ In any event, Casey's efforts apparently satisfied Churchill, who, the following year, offered him the governorship of Bengal. The contrary view, that Churchill was simply removing an unsuccessful appointment cannot be discounted.

Despite his stellar career, Casey's reputation as a politician mostly revolved around the perception that he was a 'good man' well-liked by his colleagues and acquaintances but somehow superficial and lacking in political substance. As Hudson has put it, 'All his life, he tried to be a good man [and] like all men,

---

\* Joseph Lash (ed.), *The Diaries of Felix Frankfurter* (New York: Oxford University Press, 1975), p. 153.
† *Daily Mail* (London), 22 November 1943, quoted in Hudson, *Casey*, p. 153.
‡ Hudson, *Casey*, p. 140.

Casey could be inconsistent and foolish; he could be vain and self-seeking; in some intimate relationships he could be inept; especially as he aged, he could show lack of proportion in estimates of his own importance'.[*]

As evidence that Casey was 'a good man', Anne Henderson has described how, upon the death of Lyons in April 1939, Casey gave substantial on-going financial support to Enid Lyons and her large family, most of whom were dependent. Federal Cabinet, immediately after Lyons' death, chose Casey with his 'dignity and tact', as the appropriate person to ask the widow, Enid, where she wanted the late prime minister to be interred.[†] Hasluck, whose career was similar to Casey's to an astonishing degree, wrote of him, 'Dick Casey presented himself well. I am not sure how much of this was studied and contrived and how much was due to natural grace … either by early training or by nature, he found it congenial to be on parade and met people easily and without shyness'.[‡] Bridge identifies Casey's gifts as being a good listener, a loyal assistant, well-travelled and read, and an officer and a gentleman in the old sense of those words.[§]

The notion that Casey was 'a good man' is also taken up by Alan Renouf, former Australian diplomat, in his book dealing with the foreign policy of Evatt. Commenting on Casey's advising President Roosevelt of the impending visit to Washington of the new Australian Foreign Affairs Minister, Casey wrote that Evatt was 'an intense admirer of the United States'. Renouf called this comment 'weighty testimony as Casey was politically opposed to Evatt. Moreover, Evatt, after becoming Foreign Affairs Minister in late 1941, left Casey in no doubt of his animosity towards him. However Casey was always a fair man'.[¶] Indeed, Evatt's attitude to Casey, according to one memoir, may have been based on Evatt's

---

[*] Ibid., p. viii.
[†] Anne Henderson, *Enid Lyons. Leading Lady to a Nation* (North Melbourne: Pluto Press Australia, 2008), pp. 250–7.
[‡] Paul Hasluck, *The Chance of Politics* (Melbourne: Text Publishing, 1997), p. 83.
[§] Bridge, 'R.G. Casey's Contribution to Australian War Policy', pp. 80–90.
[¶] Alan Renouf, *Let Justice Be Done. The Foreign Policy of Dr H.V. Evatt* (St Lucia: University of Queensland Press, 1983), p. 83.

distrust of those members of 'the ruling class who were imbued with a sense of social superiority', including Menzies, Bruce and Casey. Yet the same memoir claims that, over the years, Evatt's opinion mellowed. Casey, as Foreign Minister, as a matter of courtesy, gave Evatt advance notice of what he planned to say in a foreign affairs debate in parliament.*

Similar attestations of Casey's generosity of spirit appear in the entry of Garry Woodward and Joan Beaumont in an anthology of Paul Hasluck's achievements. As they put it: 'The observation of the forms did not stand in the way of Casey taking a deep and often generous interest in his senior officers' personal circumstances'.† For Hudson, Casey was something of a virtuous anachronism. He describes Casey as 'a moral man…an oddly innocent man…an honourable man', but with notions of honour belonging in the early twentieth century rather than later.‡ Hudson notes in Casey what he describes as 'an Edwardian paradigm of secular gentlemanliness'.§

Yet Casey's popularity could be interpreted as a flaw. The United States's Consul-General to Australia in late 1941, Nelson T. Johnson, recorded a conversation with Evatt at a social gathering at Johnson's home shortly after the formation of the Curtin government, during which Casey became the topic of conversation. Evatt had expressed the view that Casey was a poor representative of Australia. Johnson noted that his polite remark to the effect that Casey appeared to have a good reputation and to have made a very wide circle of acquaintances in the United States brought a heated retort from Evatt: 'The trouble with Casey is that he tries to be so popular. All this popularity business is nonsense. What Australia needs in Washington is an unpopular man. It is the unpopular man who gets things [done] because he does not have to worry about what people think of him'.¶ It must be added that

---

\* Buckley et al., *Doc Evatt, Patriot, Internationalist, Fighter and Scholar*, p. 414.
† Garry Woodard and Joan Beaumont, 'Paul Hasluck and the Bureaucracy' in Tom Stannage, Kay Saunders and Richard Nile (eds.), *Paul Hasluck in Australian History, Civic Personality and Public Life* (St Lucia: University of Queensland Press, 1999), p. 149.
‡ Hudson, *Casey*, p. viii.
§ Ibid., p. x.
¶ P.G. Edwards (ed.), *Australia Through American Eyes, 1935–1945. Observations by American Diplomats* (St Lucia, University of Queensland

while Evatt was regarded in both London and Washington with reservations, bordering on hostility, Casey enjoyed genuine respect and widespread co-operation in both places.*

Clearly, Casey in Washington was employing what later became known as 'soft power', that is, winning hearts and minds by building a favourable opinion about, in this case, Australia. To the contemporary mindset, this proposition seems blindingly obvious. But in 1930s Australia, a nation that hitherto had had no foreign relations and no foreign service, international diplomacy, especially in regard to the United States, represented something new. If Casey's style did, in fact, add to his substance, it also made his substance more acceptable, certainly in Europe and Washington. He was not a quintessential Australian politician, a shortcoming that inhibited his career in Australia. Viewed in a positive light, Casey's style gave him easier entrée into senior levels in Washington and London, where his substance would be heard and noted and perhaps heeded.

Casey's personal characteristics were subjected to examination by a colleague, who had the opportunity to observe him in a different context to Evatt. Alan Watt, First Secretary at the Australian Legation in Washington during Casey's appointment there, described him as 'a man who learned more by personal contact and conversation than by reading documents and reflecting deeply upon their contents'.† This practice of employing personal contact in preference to studying and responding to the documentation, arguably at least, encouraged a more effective and possibly more rapid exchange of views.

The conclusion that can be drawn is that Casey was good with people or that he possessed what today might be described as emotional intelligence. The historian M.H. Ellis made the observation, not entirely valid, that Casey had talked, at some time with nearly every man of note or fame in the world in the preceding fifty years. It is easy to ridicule this claim but proving negatives is never easy. Moreover, Ellis argued that 'no man in Australia, few in the British-speaking world, have had such a variety of experiences

Press, 1979), p. 69, and David Horner, *High Command. Australia and Allied Strategy 1939–1945* (Sydney: Allen and Unwin 1982), p. 197.
* Bridge, *A Delicate Mission*, p. 12.
† Watt, *The Evolution of Australian Foreign Policy 1938–1965*, p. 301.

and been associated with so many and so various an assortment of offices and personalities ... he was accessible ... he was always working, always had his facts at his fingertips'.\* Implicit in Casey's practice was a belief that such exchange of views may well lead to a speedier resolution or agreement, rather than the more conventional exchange of diplomatic notes, possibly over an extended period. This is not to assert that oral negotiations 'over the negotiating table' invariably lead to a quicker resolution of the matter. Actual personal contact between the negotiating parties, however, brings into play those qualities of personality, body language, manner, a readiness to at least understand and recognise the other's position.

Casey relied heavily on 'the personal touch' in all his dealings, whether they be with his colleagues or in his diplomatic duties. He clearly felt the need to discuss and explore all aspects of an issue before reaching the point of conclusion where a policy position could be taken. Casey claimed to be at his best when he had a colleague with whom he was comfortable testing out ideas. This was the case during his first year in Washington when he worked hand-in-glove with Lord Lothian, the British ambassador. As Casey put it:

> My mind works best when I have some individual with whom I can argue out a problem – someone against whom one can fling one's arguments – and they come back at you – and vice versa. This is the way Lothian and I worked.†

Waters cites the example of how, when Casey was later Minister for External Affairs, he was at a loss as to how to proceed with a review of its organisation. His friend, Lester Mike Pearson, the Canadian Minister for External Affairs, was the type of person who could act as a sounding board to enable Casey to develop new policies. 'If only Mike and I could get alone somewhere and think it through', a solution could be found'. Casey explained that his senior departmental officers were adequate at this sort of discussion but that they were so pressed with day-to-day problems that they had no time for basic thinking. Casey admitted that he was no good 'at

---

\* Quoted in Gordon Greenwood, *Approaches to Asia. Australian Postwar Policies and Attitudes* (Sydney: McGraw-Hill Book Company, 1974), p. 465.
† Casey Diaries, 16 December 1940.

battling this sort of thing' through by himself and that he had to have somebody with whom he could bat the ball back and forth. Lest too much might be made of one dinner-table conversation, Waters makes the point that studying Casey's 'voluminous diaries' reveals little evidence of foreign policy being worked out on paper or through memoranda or departmental submissions. Rather, 'it is the private meeting, the personal exchange and the lunch or dinner conversation where Casey was at his best'.*

On the other hand, Casey was not often described as a deep thinker or significant driver of policy. Edwards, in his examination of the making of Australian foreign policy, concluded that Casey was not a major Australian policy-maker while in Washington. According to Edwards, Casey was 'charming, tactful and quick witted, but not a profound or original thinker on great issues. It could be said that throughout his career, he was more of a diplomat than a politician in the sense that he ably executed the policies devised by others'.† This view cannot go unchallenged. The whole thrust of this work sustains the view that Casey was not only a self-starter but an ideas man as well. The author recalls hearing an address by Casey as Governor-General at Sydney's Victoria Barracks. He described how he travelled everywhere with a small notebook in his pocket to note down any ideas he had, rather than run the risk of relying on his memory to implement them.

A recent work by Caryn Courtney claims that Curtin was more complex, determined and shrewd than previously imagined.‡ Casey's alleged lack of substance in the area of policy development would surely have constituted an impediment to his implementing Curtin's and Evatt's thinking in the area of Australian military and political strategies. Yet, Curtin was emphatic that he wished Casey remain representing him, and his External Affairs Minister

---

\* Christopher Waters. 'Cold War Liberals: Richard Casey and the Department of External Affairs, 1951–60' in Beaumont, Waters, Lowe and Woodard (eds.), *Ministers, Mandarins and Diplomats* (Carlton: Melbourne University Press, 2003), p. 93.
† P.G. Edwards, *Prime Ministers and Diplomats. The Making of Australian Foreign Policy* (Melbourne: Oxford University Press, 1983), p. 127.
‡ Caryn Coatney, *John Curtin. How He Won Over the Media* (North Melbourne: Australian Scholarly Publishing, 2016).

Evatt in Washington. In a different context, Millar claimed that Casey lacked the intellectual skill to out-argue Menzies. Given that Menzies has often been described as one of the best orators to grace the Australian political spectrum, Casey's inferiority does not necessarily denote a significant failing.* Yet, this inferior status of Casey vis-à-vis his leader had all kinds of negative consequences. Waters suggests that to be an effective Minister for External Affairs in Australia requires either a close and intimate working relationship with the Prime Minister, such as Evatt had with Chifley, or the stature and energy to take the initiatives without prime ministerial approval, such as Spender did in committing Australian land forces to the Korean War without Menzies' prior approval.† Yet, by all accounts, the relationship between Menzies and Casey was anything but close.

Here too, the evidence is far from conclusive when it comes to Casey's understanding of world events. Casey, for example, correctly warned Menzies against involvement in the ill-fated Suez Crisis of 1956. He was also an early advocate of Australia forging closer relationships with non-Communist Asia in the 1950s, relations that he fostered as Minister. These are examples of Casey as a perceptive and proactive thinker when it came to Australia's foreign policy requirements. Casey was a key player in the Menzies years, but was not a stereotypical conservative, nostalgic for empire.

Casey, as we have noted, was viewed as sophisticated, British and engaging. His 'people skills' that came naturally to him and which he employed to the full in the varied assignments of his long working life, created a lasting impression. The criticism that he was effectively a British agent in Washington does not stand up to any sort of scrutiny. Yet, Casey is not considered a heavyweight when it came to strategic thinking or planning. The suggestion contained in much of the literature is that Casey was a follower – a good 'lieutenant' as Hudson has put it – rather than a leader who could influence events. The achievements of Casey's Washington mission strongly challenge this picture of Casey as an amiable executor of orders given by others.

---

\* Millar, *Australia in Peace and War*, p. 359.
† Waters, 'Cold War Liberals', p. 94.

*Chapter Two*

# Casey, Australian Diplomacy and the American Challenge

Because the alliance between the United States and Australia, formalised through ANZUS in 1951, is the bedrock of Australia's post-war foreign policy, it is often forgotten that there was nothing obvious or natural about this alliance before Pearl Harbor. Casey's role in the United States had to be situated in the context of the triangular Australia–Britain–United States relationship before the war. What each nation perceived as its 'national interest' was more often a source of conflict than agreement prior to Pearl Harbor.

It is a cliche of international affairs that the concept of the 'national interest' is one that is common to all nations. Perhaps the best definition came from the British statesman, Viscount Palmerston: 'We have no eternal allies and we have no eternal enemies. Our interests are eternal, and those interests it is our duty to follow'.[*] Winston Churchill famously remarked that Britain does not have friends or allies, it only has interests; the French President Charles de Gaulle noted that nations have no feelings, only interests. The Australian academic Gary Smith defined national interests in basic terms as 'survival'.[†] For less powerful states like

---

[*] 'Lord Palmerston. Speech', House of Commons, 1 March 1848. Quoted in I.D. Vita, *The Making of British Foreign Policy* (London: Unwin Paperbacks, 1968), p. 11.
[†] Gary Smith in Gary Smith, Dave Cox, Scott Burchill (eds.), *Australia and the World* (Sydney: Oxford University Press, 1996), p. 24.

Australia, the implications of the great powers' prioritising of the national interest are alarming. In the words of David Day, national interest constituted:

> ... one of the realities of international relations that nevertheless seems to demand constant repetition for it to be appreciated. It is this, that in the final analysis great states will act only to protect their perceived interests regardless of treaties and understandings with lesser states.*

Casey understood the concept of the national interest; his practice of international politics placed him firmly in the 'realist camp'. Michael Wesley has defined 'Australian realism' in international relations in terms of three characteristics – experientialism, systemic pessimism and pragmatism. As we shall see, these three characteristics clearly apply to Casey's approach to international diplomacy.

Experientalism, according to Wesley 'has fostered an intensive focus on the particularities of Australia's international position – size, isolation, wealth, population, culture – and how these factors can help understand the ways in which Australia relates to the world beyond its shores'.† Australia has always participated in, but also viewed sceptically, multilateral organisations such as the League of Nations or the United Nations. Instead, the tradition of Australian realism is to look for pragmatic solutions to the existential threats facing Australia.

The crisis facing Australia in 1941–42 was not unexpected. From the first settlement in the late eighteenth century, there has existed in Australia a sense of isolation from 'home', meaning Great Britain, that was keenly felt. As Wesley has put it:

> Since European colonisation, Australia has always been a rich, isolated, *status quo* state. This has fostered a particular attitude towards the outside world, and imbued Australians' thinking about the world and their place in it with a distinctive character. It is only natural that a country's physical location and basic perceptions of itself and its

---
\* David Day, *Menzies and Churchill at War* (North Ryde: Angus and Robertson, 1986), p. 250.
† Wesley, 'The Rich Tradition of Australian Realism', p. 326.

surrounds will be the most profound shaper of how its thinkers perceive international relations.*

Although Britain's navy was the most powerful in the world, there remained the fear engendered by the isolation of the Australian colonies, and later the Federation, that Britain's seemingly unchallenged naval authority could not provide all the protection needed. Moreover, the colonies were dismayed by the application of British diplomacy to problems in the Western Pacific even before Federation. The colony of Queensland, perceiving itself to be the closest to the 'problem' areas northwards and fearful of foreign occupation of New Guinea, in 1883 annexed the Territory of Papua. The repudiation of the annexation by the British government and the German annexation of the north east of New Guinea heightened anxiety throughout the Australian colonies.

In the two plus centuries since the commencement of European settlement, Australians perceived several nations as constituting a serious threat to their security: France, Russia, Germany, China and Japan. The nearest neighbour, the Netherlands East Indies, was not considered in the same hostile terms because it was a colony of a friendly European power. These considerations lead to an understanding of why there has always existed in Australia a need, perceived but not always actual, for allies capable of rescuing Australia from conquest by a hostile European or Asian power. Robert Menzies graphically expressed this need in a phrase that has entered the canon of Australian core beliefs: 'No country in the world more than ours needs great and powerful friends'.†

Critics of this view argue that the perception of an ever-present threat is based upon an incorrect reading of the policy and posture of the 'other' nation, or else driven by political imperatives. Smith, Cox and Burchill suggest that Australia's cultural insecurity explains its attitude towards the prospect of external military threats. Recognising that Australia has never been invaded, they make the point that Australia has no traditional adversaries.‡

While the question arises as to what extent its security fears

---
\* Ibid., p. 325.
† Quoted in Souter, *Acts of Parliament*, p. 460.
‡ Smith et al., *Australia in the World*, p. 25.

were products of Australian cultural isolation and insularity – a settler-colonial outlook projected into fantasies about potential military threats – a sense of vulnerability to external attack and fears of racial contamination became enduring themes of Australian history. These notions spawned an array of beliefs and initiatives, ranging from local defence forces, including individual navies in some colonies. However, more astute minds believed that the new nation should set about establishing friendly international relations outside the ambit of the empire. There were notions and ideas emerging that questioned the conventional wisdom of leaving the matter of 'international relations' to London.

Australia took more than thirty years to develop its voice in international affairs. Shortly after Federation, the Department of External Affairs was created, but its responsibilities revolved principally around Australia's relations with Britain and the Pacific islands and it was eventually abolished in 1916, its functions distributed around other departments. As Hudson has pointed out, 'external affairs' did not mean then what it means now. In 1901, 'external affairs' simply referred to the imperial connection with London, not to connections with the world at large or even with the rest of the Empire. The 'external' relations of the embryonic Department of External Affairs was restricted to the Colonial Office in London.[*]

Deakin, the second Prime Minister, recognised that the national interest of the fledgling nation of Australia would be served by the adoption of a more proactive role in international affairs. Deakin, who had become Prime Minister and Minister for External Affairs for the first time in September 1903, set a standard of independence in international relations, specifically with the United States, that did not accord with the wishes of the British government. One of his early clashes with London over this issue occurred in 1907, while he was attending an Imperial Conference in London. Deakin proposed the creation of a permanent Imperial secretariat to give the self-governing colonies of the Empire an effective voice in foreign policy, defence and economic co-operation. The British government, not surprisingly, was opposed to conceding any

---

[*] W.J. Hudson, *Australian Diplomacy* (Australia: Macmillan, 1970), p. 1.

responsibilities for foreign relations to the dominions, no matter what their constitutions may or may not have said, but all lacking an ingredient that it, Britain, alone possessed, that is, the hundreds of years of experience in international relations that resided in Whitehall. Yet, Deakin was acting within the words, if not the spirit, of the Constitution and the reality that the Australian Constitution is a statute of the British Parliament, emphasised its arguing strength. Section 51, provides for the Commonwealth Parliament '... to make laws for the peace, order and good government of the Commonwealth with respect to ... (xxix) External Affairs'.

While the formal alliance between Britain and Japan that began in 1902 did little to reassure Australians that their island home in the South West Pacific had been made more secure, British politicians and military leaders saw the Anglo-Japanese naval alliance as a plus for the security of Australia. The alternative, from Britain's perspective, was for Australia to pay more for its own defence. When Earl Kitchener produced his *Memorandum on Australian Defence* in 1910, he predicted the possibility of British naval forces being fully engaged in European waters and not being able to come to the aid of Australia in its moment of need. Kitchener saw the solution in compulsory military service and a more concentrated Australian defence posture. The British Foreign Secretary, clearly repudiating the Australian hostility to the treaty, noted in January 1911 that 'the logical consequence of denouncing the Anglo-Japanese alliance would be that Australia and New Zealand would undertake the burden of naval supremacy in the China Sea. This, they are neither willing nor able to do'.*

In 1907, Prime Minister Deakin's interpretation of the new Commonwealth's responsibility took the novel form of inviting a visit by a significant American naval fleet then making its way around the world, a journey conceived by President Theodore Roosevelt to emphasise that the United States was indeed a power to be reckoned with. Ignoring what London would dictate as correct protocol, Deakin issued the invitation to the United States Consul-General in Melbourne, the State Department in

---

\* A.W. Stargardt, *Australia's Asian Policies: The History of Debate: 1839–1972* (Hamburg: Institute of Asian Affairs,1977), p. 122.

Washington and the American Ambassador in London, without first approaching the British Foreign Office or the Governor-General, Lord Northcote.* This was not an oversight, nor was it a deliberate snub on Deakin's part, but rather a clever diplomatic ploy. He reasoned, probably correctly, that both the Governor-General and the Colonial Office in London would reject any request made through the normal channels. By initially issuing invitations direct to various arms of the American administration, Deakin placed Britain in a position where a refusal became impossible, especially after it was made public that the American Secretary of State had accepted the invitation, at a time, when the whole matter was a subject of furious debate in London. Deakin's delight upon learning of the American acceptance of his invitations was captured by a journalist, who claimed that he was 'trembling with excitement', when he made the announcement. He wrote that Deakin saw the visit as recognition by 'the other Great White Power of the Pacific' that Britain, the United States and Australia would be united 'to withstand yellow aggression'.†

The Great White Fleet, as it became known, received a tumultuous welcome at its Australian ports of call, Sydney, Melbourne and Albany, the reasons being obliquely spelt out by Deakin in his address of welcome, when he referred to 'that unnatural treaty, the Anglo-Japanese treaty' as opposed to the similar cultural heritage and traditions shared by Australia and the United States.‡ Deakin was acknowledging both the hostility of many Australians to the Anglo-Japanese Agreement and a widespread desire for closer links with the United States, which was perceived as closer to Australia in outlook, institutions and lifestyle, more forward-looking than Britain and being more relevant to Australia's security as a Pacific nation. In an editorial, *The Age*, while advocating the creation of an Australian navy, took comfort from America, 'our friend and ally, navally dominant in the Pacific'.§

---

\* Gavin Souter, *Lion and Kangaroo. The Initiation of Australia 1901–1919* (Sydney: William Collins, 1976), p. 140.
† *Sunday Times* (London), 23 August 1908.
‡ J.R. Reckner, *Teddy Roosevelt's Great White Fleet* (Annapolis: Naval Institute Press Annapolis, 1988), p. 76 and Souter, *Lion and Kangaroo*, p. 143.
§ *The Age*, 17 March 1908, p. 8.

Initially, the United States was perceived as an Atlantic power. The late opening up of the western coast states and territories led to the realisation that the United States was also a Pacific power.

Yet, it is possible to make too much of the visit to Australia of the 'Great White Fleet'. In her oft-quoted article written in 1970, the historian Ruth Megaw claims that the visit was the first public opportunity which Australia had had of demonstrating her reaction to a permanent American presence in the Pacific. She claims, moreover, that the visit cast its shadow to a future American-Australian alliance which was not to eventuate until the Second World War but which was already present in a formless, embryonic fashion in many Australian minds in the early twentieth century.\* This, surely, is hindsight. It is true that public comment arising from the visit of the Great White Fleet emphasised the kinship with America based upon similarity of race, language, institutions and what might be termed the dynamics of a new nation. Australia was seen as a replica of the United States a hundred years earlier. However, it is also true that that closeness would have been laid to rest during the twenty long years of strict American isolationism following World War One. It must be admitted that the perception of the United States as a 'saviour' of Australia, should Japan embark on an expansion of her interests in the Pacific, was a popular one. Sadly, such views were often based on excessive optimism rather than an understanding of the real state of American politics.

Australian interest in more independent foreign relations diminished in the governments that followed Deakin's three ministries. The call by the then Opposition Leader, Andrew Fisher, in 1914 that Australia would aid Britain to 'her last man and her last shilling' reflected a patriotic fervour shown by many, but by no means, all Australians.† Michael McKernan suggests that 28 October 1916 could be Australia's Independence Day when the Australian people voted against conscription, refusing to give the government of Billy Hughes the power 'to compel young Australian

---

\* Ruth Megaw, 'Australia and the Great White Fleet 1908', *Journal of the Royal Australian Historical Society*, 56, June 1970, pp. 121–31.

† Colin A. Hughes, *Australian Prime Ministers 1901–1972* (Oxford: Oxford University Press, 1976), p. 45.

men to go to war on the other side of the world." He claims that it is significant that 'so many embraced their responsibility' and turned out to vote when it was not compulsory to do so, rejecting Fisher's 'last man and last shilling' call. Real politics meant that farms, factories, offices, banks and schools all needed to be manned.†
Thus we see ordinary Australians demonstrating independence and exercising an effect on foreign affairs. Although the impetus for an independent foreign policy was submerged during the Great War, it re-emerged immediately after. The British Dominions obtained direct representation at the Versailles Peace Conference in 1919 and Dominion ministers signed the Peace treaty on behalf of their respective governments. The Treaty was later ratified by these same Dominion governments. Moreover, the Dominions became full members of the League of Nations.

Australia's voice at the peace talks, due largely to the efforts of the Nationalist Prime Minister W.M. Hughes, was more influential than its relative size dictated, to the extent that Hughes argued with the American President, Woodrow Wilson, and played a small role in the writing of the League's Charter. Ironically, Hughes sided with Wilson in defeating an attempt by Japan to include, in the Covenant of the League, a declaration of racial equality. Hughes had perceived this as a threat to the White Australia policy, about which he was, in the words of Poynter, 'almost fanatical'.‡ Yet Hughes, like Deakin, was able to show that a small power like Australia could influence international decision making even if the decisions made after World War One created ever more formidable dangers in the Pacific.

Hughes believed that the former German colonies and protectorates in the Pacific were potential bases for an attack on Australia and persuaded the League to grant Australia a mandate over what was previously the German protectorate of New Guinea,

---

\* Michael McKernan, 'Independence Day' in Deborah Gare and David Ritter, *Making Australian History. Perspectives on the Past Since 1788* (South Melbourne: Thomson, 2008), p. 345.
† McKernan, 'Independence Day', p. 346.
‡ J.R. Poynter, 'The Yo-Yo Variations: Initiative and Dependence in Australia's External Relations, 1918–1923', *Australian Historical Studies*, Vol. xiv, 1970, p. 241.

enabling it to be joined with the existing Australian Territory of Papua.* The Pacific came under discussion again at the Washington Conference in 1921, when three treaties were signed, the Naval Treaty being the one most relevant to Australia's security. The terms of this Treaty provided for Britain, the United States, Japan, France and Italy to limit their naval strengths to specified ratios, that had the effect of the major powers reducing their tonnage of warships by about 40%. The Treaty also forbad the building of any new naval fortifications on the new Pacific mandates. While the ratios indicated that the Japanese navy would always remain smaller than either the British or American fleets, in fact, Japan emerged in a stronger position because her sphere of interest was limited to the Pacific, whereas Britain had responsibilities to guard an Empire that spanned the world. Britain's navy had to be spread thinly, while Japan could enjoy concentrating hers in just one, albeit large, ocean. Similarly, the United States needed to maintain fleets in the Pacific and the Atlantic. Thus Japan could become virtually dominant in the Pacific, a development that fed Australian disquiet.

The Anglo-Japanese alliance was not renewed at the Washington conference and instead Britain decided that its strategy for protecting its interests east of Suez was the building of a naval base at Singapore. In theory, a British fleet could be sent to Singapore in time to check any act of aggression on the part of Japan before Australia was endangered. The justification for Britain's building and maintaining the Singapore base was the crucial need for the Southeast Asia region to keep Britain supplied with vital materials, such as rubber and oil. Singapore was also the key to Britain's plans for defending Malaya, Australasia and India from Japanese aggression.

The Singapore strategy has been criticised as inherently flawed because the British navy was not strong enough to fight a multi-ocean war and because fleets of battleships were becoming less important, as the naval stalemate of World War One showed and the rise of air power confirmed. On the other hand, defenders of the Singapore strategy pointed out that fleets remained crucial,

---

\* L.F. Fitzhardinge, *William Morris Hughes*, Vol. 1 (Sydney: Angus and Robertson, 1964).

that naval tactics had improved since the Battle of Jutland, and that there was no real alternative to British sea power in terms of defending Australia. As Christopher Bell has put it:

> During the 1920s Britain possessed a comfortable margin of naval superiority over its rivals, and it might have maintained a large fleet in the Far East and still dominated European waters. This possibility was only undermined by the emergence of a triple threat from Germany, Italy, and Japan in the mid-1930s. These events were exceptional and unpredictable.*

Casey, a cautious supporter of the Singapore strategy, would have to face up to these very 'exceptional, and unpredictable' events in June 1940.

Bruce, a vastly different Prime Minister to Hughes, initially did not wish Australia to have an independent foreign policy but he later modified that position and propounded the view that the Dominions should have a greater influence in the development of the foreign policy of the Empire. A flaw in this argument is that the British Empire was made up of such scattered, disparate nation-states that it was almost impossible to conceive of a foreign policy that would be acceptable to them all. Casey, writing in 1938, perceived the difficulty: 'The basic problem is how the immediate and direct interests of the various parts of the Commonwealth are to be reconciled in practice with Imperial solidarity in the field of foreign affairs'.†

The Balfour Declaration of 1926 strengthened the autonomous direction of Australia vis-à-vis the Commonwealth. The members of the Commonwealth were to be regarded as equal in status and, in no way, subordinate to one another in their domestic or external affairs, although united by their common allegiance to the crown. The Statute of Westminster, passed by the British Parliament in 1931, gave legal form to the Balfour Declaration and resolutions passed by the Imperial Conference of 1930, and conferred on the

---

\* Christopher M. Bell, 'The 'Singapore Strategy' and the Deterrence of Japan: Winston Churchill, the Admiralty and the Dispatch of Force Z', *The English Historical Review,* June 2001, Vol. 116, No. 467, pp. 604–34.
† R.G. Casey, 'Australia's Voice in Imperial Affairs', in W.G.K. Duncan (ed.), *Australia's Foreign Policy* (Sydney: Angus and Robertson, 1938), pp. 48–9.

Dominions (that is, members of the Commonwealth), full powers to make laws. Although Australia did not adopt the Statute of Westminster until 1942, there were no reasons why Australia could not have been more innovative in establishing relations outside the Commonwealth. A proper interpretation of the relevant clause in the Constitution finally came in 1936, when two justices of the High Court, Evatt and McTiernan, held that the Federal government was utterly free to deal with foreign states.*

Writing about the 1920s and 30s, P.D. Phillips argued that 'Australia certainly was content to do without a foreign policy of its own'.† Yet Bruce attempted to create a small Australian foreign service with its own ambassadors. Rejecting his earlier arguments, Bruce brought Allan Leeper, an Australian-born officer of the British Foreign Office, to Australia to advise on the organization of the External Affairs Office that had been re-established in the Prime Minister's Department. It was Leeper who recommended the creation of the Liaison Officer post in London, to be occupied by Casey (1924–31).‡ Casey proved to be a valuable source of information to the Australian Cabinet, information that otherwise may have remained hidden from local eyes. Before Casey, the Colonial Office was the main source, and, according to Hudson, delivered all material by sea-mail.§ However, cables would have arrived expeditiously.

There were myriad possibilities of conflict between Australia and Britain, separated as they were by half the globe. Britain, traditionally, was vitally concerned with Europe, both from a trading point of view as much as by security considerations. Australia, on the other hand, judged its interests, especially its security interests, to be totally in the Pacific region. Nevertheless, Bruce persisted with the notion that Britain should consult Australia in formulating foreign policy.

Between 3 March 1927 and 23 September 1935, the Federal

---

\* Hugo Wolfsohn, 'The Evolution of Australia in World Affairs', *Australian Outlook*, March 1953.
† P.D. Phillips, 'Australia in a Changing World', in Duncan, *Australia's Foreign Policy*, p. 13.
‡ Poynter, 'The Yo-Yo Variations', p. 248.
§ Hudson, *Casey*, p. 20.

Labor caucus did not pass a single resolution on foreign policy.* The last of Australia's 'commissioners' in Washington, Herbert Brookes in 1929, aware that both the onset of the world-wide Depression with the concomitant need for reduced government expenditure and the installation of a new Labor government in 1929 made his position less than tenable, saved Prime Minister James Scullin embarrassment by resigning the following year. Thus, the structure that Bruce had created in the External Affairs Department withered after his departure and had to await the arrival of a new government led by Joseph Lyons and his United Australia Party for some kind of revival. Bruce would play a part in this revival, when Lyons appointed him High Commissioner to Britain in 1933, a post he retained until 1945.

The uneasy relationship of Australia with Britain that had characterised the nineteen twenties persisted into the nineteen thirties. The basis of it lay in the two different ways in which Japan was perceived, Australia believing Japan to be a threat, Britain believing that Japan could bring a measure of stability to Pacific affairs. There was certainly an element of wishful thinking on London's part with Britain reluctant to commit naval forces to the Pacific and nominating Japan as a proxy. Casey was one of many Australian leaders who breathed a sigh of relief when Japan turned north to invade Manchuria in 1931; Casey wanted Japan to have a 'free hand' in Manchuria to lessen its appetite for a southward invasion. There is an irony here in that one of the constant refrains Casey heard in Washington in 1940–42 from the likes of Secretary of War, Henry Stimson and Under Secretary of State, Sumner Welles, was that British and Australian appeasement sowed the seeds of Japanese empire building in China. Casey was quick to respond that the Americans shared the blame for offering no guarantee of support for firmer British action.

Appeasing Japan and Germany became a staple of the Lyons' government and of Casey's engagement with international politics.† In the first of several of his forays into foreign relations,

---

\* Edwards, *Prime Ministers and Diplomats*, p. 67.
† Carl Bridge, 'Appeasement and After', *Australian Journal of Politics and History*, 2005, p. 374.

Lyons appointed a Minister for External Affairs, J.G. Latham, the first time since 1916 that the portfolio was not held by the Prime Minister. In 1934, Latham led a mission to Tokyo hoping to lessen tensions and achieve some kind of understanding with an increasingly aggressive Japan. Although he expressed sympathy for Japan in its dispute with China over Manchuria, Latham declined a Japanese offer to exchange diplomatic representatives, claiming that Australia was not yet ready to establish its own foreign service. However, on Latham's recommendation, a trade commissioner was appointed to Tokyo.\* This mission to Tokyo achieved little beyond laying on Lyons the mantle of belonging to the 'appeasement camp', an appellation that later assumed a distinctly pejorative connotation and one which appeared to ignore the widespread desire to do whatever was necessary to avoid another major war.

Reflecting somewhat forlorn hopes that the United States would become a security blanket for Australia in the event of Japanese aggression, Lyons was favourably inclined to the establishment of some kind of diplomatic presence in Washington. Moffat, the Consul-General to Australia, drew Lyons' attention to the practical difficulties in Australia needing to communicate with Washington by going through London. Moffat also had difficulties in understanding Australia's reluctance to sever its close, or what he perceived as subservient, ties with Britain.† Lyons went only some of the way in acting on Moffat's suggested creation of a legation in Washington, electing instead to appoint, in 1936, an Australian Counsellor to the British Embassy in Washington, an appointment floated by Bruce four years previously. Lyons agreed to London's insistence that the officer appointed be 'subject to the authority of the British Ambassador, who has the right to see all communications sent to the Commonwealth Government'.‡

Lyons, in London in 1937 for the Imperial Conference, raised the idea of a Pacific Pact, binding nations committed to promoting regional understanding and peaceful settlement of

---

\* Edwards, *Prime Ministers and Diplomats*, p. 90.
† J.P. Moffat Diary, 6 February 1936, Moffat Papers, Vol. 37. N.H. Hooker (ed.), (Cambridge, Mass: Harvard University Press, 1959).
‡ Lyons to S.M. Bruce, 2 February 1937, letter, A981 EA Department 152, NAA.

disputes, a suggestion that drew little support. Lyons envisaged a pact embracing all the Pacific nations, including the United States and Japan plus those European powers with an interest in the Pacific, Britain, France, the Netherlands and Portugal. In mounting his argument to the conference, Lyons referred to a conversation with President Roosevelt in July 1935, during which the American president had expressed his readiness to enter into an agreement with Japan, or with any other country to secure the preservation of peace.* At this time, 1935, relations between Japan and the United States were deteriorating rapidly and it is likely that Roosevelt's reply, if quoted correctly, simply reflected a non-specific desire for an easing of tensions between the two nations, without any intention of Lyons' suggestion being acted upon. Certainly, no documentation can be found to substantiate Lyons' claim.

In rejecting Lyons' plea for a Pacific Pact, the British Foreign Secretary, Anthony Eden, claimed that it would simply repeat what was already in the Kellogg Pact of 1928. It was at the Imperial Conference that Casey, who was there as a member of the Australian delegation, emerged as a strong advocate of greater Dominion participation in the formulation of British foreign policy and, according to Waters, emerged as spokesperson for the 'radical' appeasers.† Casey's contribution could well be seen as an attempt to demonstrate that the Dominions could contribute to the formulation of what might be termed 'Commonwealth Foreign Policy', an aim already identified as part of the thinking of Lyons' predecessor, Bruce. This was also the conference where the Australian delegation learnt that it would take between 53 and 70 days for a British fleet to make the journey from European waters to Singapore, a revelation that added to the woes of the Australians.‡

Casey's appetite for appeasement was certainly as wholehearted as anybody's in the late 1930s. His aim was to ensure that Britain was

---

* There is no record of this conversation in the Prime Minister's Department files, or with the Lyons papers held in the National Australian Archives. The only known reference is contained in Dame Enid Lyons, *So We Take Comfort*, pp. 241–3.
† Waters, *Australia and Appeasement*, p. 146.
‡ Minutes of Meeting, 2 Whitehall Gardens, London, 1 June 1937, *DAFP*, Vol. 1, Doc. 33, p. 107.

not once more entangled in a continental war and therefore unable to defend Australia if required. After the German reoccupation of the Rhineland in 1936, Casey welcomed the speedy dismantling of the shackles imposed upon Germany at Versailles.* Casey argued that rather than defend Czechoslovakia against the German menace, 'it would be very much fairer to the smaller countries, and particularly those in Central and Eastern Europe' if they were told the truth of the inevitability of a Greater Reich.† Strategically, Casey wanted Britain to do everything possible to woo Mussolini away from Hitler and therefore re-establish Italy as a British and not a German ally.‡ This was hugely important in terms of the balance of naval forces in the Mediterranean, and, therefore, Britain's capacity to offer credible deterrence to Japan in the Far East. Waters makes the point that there was general recognition that the terms imposed upon Germany after 1918 were too harsh and that it would be only a matter of time before Germany commenced a re-building program to restore her powerful position in Europe.§ The appeasement policies followed by British Prime Minister, Neville Chamberlain, most of the British Cabinet, and virtually the whole of the Australian ministry were natural consequences of that recognition. There was certainly no offer of help from the United States during the 1930s. Casey, understood all of these international currents as well as, and probably better than, any other Australian politician.

Among the Australians, it was only Billy Hughes, Minister for External Affairs and a contributor to the Versailles Treaty, who argued for tougher action to stop German expansion. Even Hitler's brazen takeover of the remainder of Czechoslovakia in March 1939 did not put an end to a faith in appeasement in Australia, with Menzies, for example, arguing strongly that Poland was not worth going to war over. With the benefit of hindsight, it is clear that they failed to realise that Hitler would renounce his assurances and become the evil force that would dominate Europe for six years. Yet there are good reasons for

\* Curran, *Curtin's Empire*, p. 68.
† Paul Twomey in Bridge, *Munich to Vietnam*, p. 24.
‡ Waters, 'Casey. Four Decades', p. 183.
§ Waters, *Australia and Appeasement*, p. 146.

thinking that appeasement in the 1930s was a sensible, perhaps the only approach, short of war, that could have been taken.

Hughes was not the only one wishing to take a firmer stand. A notable 'anti-appeaser' was Percy Spender. In 1937, he won, on ALP preferences, the seat of Warringah over the incumbent, Archdale Parkhill, Minister for Defence, campaigning on the lack of preparedness for Australia's defence.* As a newly elected member, Spender did not have an immediate effect on government views. Rather, time did that.

The final Cabinet decision to establish Australian Legations in Tokyo and Washington was taken in March 1939. Lyons sought endorsement from London but, before he could make a public announcement, he was dead. The government parties spent the next eighteen days in acrimonious debate over the leadership, Menzies emerging as the eventual winner of a coalition government riven by bitter and deep-seated differences. In his first public announcement after becoming Prime Minister, Menzies announced the establishment of the Washington, Tokyo and other posts, appointments that, in the past, he had opposed. The fact that the appointments were a Cabinet decision left him little choice. Menzies sent Casey to Washington, Latham to Tokyo, William Glasgow to Ottawa, and Frederic Eggleston to Chungking. Another of Menzies' acts was to move Hughes from the External Affairs portfolio, replacing him with Henry Gullett.

American isolationism meant that there was little American sympathy for Britain and even less for its erstwhile imperial outposts. The British Ambassador Lothian told Foreign Minister Halifax in November 1939, that 'there was not I think, any particularly strong feeling in the US for Australia and New Zealand'.†Australian representation in Washington was an obvious and urgent need. Megaw argued, validly, that the exchange of ministers between Australia and the United States was not driven by policy considerations but rather brought about by fears of Japan.‡

---
\* David Lowe, in *Australian Dictionary of Biography*, Vol. 18, p. 445.
† Lothian to Halifax 10 November 1939, quoted in Tom Frame, *Pacific Partners* (Sydney: Houghton and Stoughton, 1992), p. 36.
‡ Ruth Megaw, 'Undiplomatic Channels: Australian Representation in the United States, 1918–1939', *Historical Studies*, Vol. 15, No. 60, p. 630.

Certainly, the proposal came at a propitious time. The worsening international situation raised the traditional Australian fears about the need for acquiring supportive allies.

Casey's actual appointment to the United States was announced publicly by Menzies on 8 January 1940. The exchange of diplomats was not consummated for another six months when Clarence C. Gauss presented his credentials as United States Minister to the Governor-General in July. According to Menzies, 'the American Minister to be diplomatically accredited to Australia, the first such appointment, will become for all Australians the living embodiment of a gesture of friendship and recognition by the United States'. True as this expression may have been, it simultaneously expressed the intense ambition of the Australian government for the United States to occupy a central role in Australian security.

In his justification for establishing the office and exchanging diplomatic ministers with the United States, Menzies stated that he expected Australia 'to play an effective part in the development and strengthening of peaceful contacts between all Pacific Powers'. In answer to the obvious question, why the United States but not Japan, or rather why not the United States and Japan, Menzies was unequivocal: 'I say ... quite frankly that Australia attaches importance to have [sic] the friendship of the United States and is prepared to do much to improve it'. The question of diplomatic representation with Japan, he said, was 'under immediate consideration'. Menzies was so anxious to make an appointment to Tokyo that he had asked Bruce, in London, to seek the King's approval to do so.* Even before reaching Buckingham Palace, the plan was nipped in the bud by R.A. Butler, Parliamentary Under Secretary of State for Foreign Affairs. Because of the high levels of tension between Japan and the United Kingdom, especially what Butler called 'economic warfare' and supply of raw materials to Japan, the appointment of an Australian representative in Tokyo could be seen as evidence that Australia was dissatisfied with Britain's handling of the situation or even a 'break in Empire diplomatic and economic fronts'.†

---

\* Menzies to Bruce, 25 January 1940, cablegram, 13, A2937, Legations, NAA.
† Bruce to Menzies, 5 February 1940, cablegram, 92, A2937, Legations, NAA.

In a message sent to the Australian Counsellor at the British Embassy in Washington on 8 January 1940 for release to the American media, Menzies lavished praise upon Casey:

> Not only a distinguished representative of his own country uncommonly well qualified to fill the distinguished office ... one of the most influential members of the Australian government ... the highest qualities of capacity, energy and patriotism.

As for Casey's mission, Menzies emphasised the common civilisational bonds of the two countries:

> we have the same general ideas of government; we attach the same supreme importance to the liberty of the individual; we have in common the conviction that the proper object of all governments is to forward the happiness of ordinary men and women, and not merely of a chosen few. And we are better able to exchange our ideas and to forward our ideals by joint effort because we speak the same language and share the same literature.*

Menzies, whose oratorical and literary skills were recognised equally by his political enemies as much as by his ardent supporters, did not normally descend into such flowery language. At times, there seems to have been a note of desperation in the message.

Reflecting the growing concern at the deteriorating international situation, Menzies defined diplomacy as he saw it. The business of diplomacy is not a mere business of dexterity in negotiation. Its real purpose is to remove misunderstandings, not to create them. Its real justification is peace'.† Behind the fine words, the tasks confronting Casey were formidable. Essentially, Casey and Menzies were relying on Roosevelt to bring the United States into a closer orbit of opposition to the German war machine.

The question confronting Casey in the Washington appointment was not whether to seek greater American aid for Britain, or to concentrate on involving the United States in Pacific

---
\* Menzies to Keith Officer, Australian Counsellor at British Embassy, Washington, 8 January 1940, cablegram, unnumbered in *DAFP*, Vol. III, Doc. 7.
† Ibid.

and Southeast Asian security affairs, specifically those affecting Australia. Clearly there was a need to do both. The survival of Britain had as its corollary the survival of British naval, military and air forces and the possibility that, eventually, Britain might be in a stronger position should Australia become involved in hostilities with Japan.

There was the risk that Casey would be seen as pushing the 'Empire line', that is seeking access to American resources, men, materiel and money in order to preserve the British Empire, a fear aired constantly in the United States following the end of the First World War. Casey had to convince a sceptical American government and population that the national security of the United States did not allow them the comfort and luxury of standing on the sidelines.

*Chapter Three*

# Casey in the United States: Roosevelt's 'the washing of the hands'.

In taking up his appointment, Casey hit the ground running. The *New York Times* wrote,

> Richard Casey, Australia's first Minister to the United States, said today that Australians, partly with the aid of American supplies, were making a gigantic effort to help Great Britain in the war'. According to this account:
>
> Mr Casey who arrived here last night, said that Australia through manufacture and purchase, was gathering together 2,500 training planes with which to build up a corps of tens of thousands of aviators.*

Casey's first written report to his Minister, Henry Gullett, dated 9 March 1940, advised that although he had been confined to bed for a week with influenza, he had presented his credentials to the President, called on Secretary of State Hull and begun the 'long and wearisome business of formally calling on each of my [sixty] diplomatic colleagues'. Recognising the important role of Trade Commissioners, Casey visited the Office of the Australian Trade Commissioner [Mr Macgregor] during his early three day visit to New York. This first report signalled the manner in which Casey was to approach his responsibilities:

> I have of course, seen a good deal of Lord Lothian, the British Ambassador, and the senior members of his staff – as well as

---
\* *New York Times,* 22 February 1940, p. 4.

the senior members of the State Department and a selection of other people of consequence in this capital ... I have spent three days in New York ... lunched with Messrs. Morgan Stanley and Company, with the publisher and senior staff of the *New York Times*, and with the President and senior officers of the Radio Corporation of America ... have made contact with J.P. Morgan and Company and with the Anglo-French Purchasing Mission – as well as a number of influential private individuals in New York with whom I was previously acquainted. I have had what I think I may describe as a good reception by the press in this country.

In the same report, Casey set out what could be described as operating guidelines:

the Australian Legation was established solely for good relations between the two countries.

it will studiously avoid being regarded as a war propagandist.

he [Casey] will emphasise the similarity in outlook and bearing of the American and the Australian peoples.

he will emphasise the complete independence of Australia in all matters, domestic and external, whilst at the same time stress the voluntary and willing co-operation of Australia as a loyal member of the British Commonwealth.*

Casey reported to Gullett that public opinion was bewildered about the war. However, he had quickly become aware of widespread Anglophobia. The view was widespread that Britain had cynically let down the Czechs, Poles and Finns. His interpretation at one point struck a note of gallows humour: 'If we [Britain and the Commonwealth] are winning, the Americans will sit back and be sceptical and – irritating and know-all – but if we're losing, they'll become worried but much more helpful'.†

A short time later, Casey noted to McEwen, who replaced Gullett as Minister for External Affairs, resentment against the war in general, because of a discerned attack on American exports. The British blockade restricted American exports to much of Europe,

---

\* Casey to Gullett, 9 March 1940, Papers of Richard G. Casey. MS 6150. Vol. I, Box 24, NLA.
† Casey to Gullett, 14 March 1940.

while Britain's need to increase defence spending, reduced her purchases of consumer and similar manufactured goods from the United States. This view was compounded by what Casey observed as a forgetfulness about the reasons for the war:

> When a war has been waged for six months, neutrals tend to forget its real origin and causes. They see it, in this instance being waged largely with economic weapons and numbers of people are drawing the conclusion that, for this reason, it had an economic origin. The Allies and Germany are, in reality, fighting for markets – what has America to do with this sort of struggle, except to protect their own export trade?[*]

Indeed, solving an economic issue was Casey's first major task. Casey may have believed that his major role in the United States revolved around such security considerations of Britain and Australia arising from a mutual fear of Japan, but awaiting his arrival in Washington was a referral from High Commissioner Bruce, seeking Casey's assistance over the 'thorny subject' of wool.[†] It is proposed to examine this in some detail, because, firstly, it was Casey's initial major challenge in the United States and secondly and more importantly, it illuminates the extent of Casey's prowess in achieving a satisfactory result in a clash of interests between Britain, the United States and Australia.

Casey had a unique opportunity to understand Japanese intentions in the years leading to 1942. The two ambassadors that represented Great Britain during the time of Casey's posting in Washington (Lothian and Halifax) both gave him full access to all their incoming and outgoing messages, including Sir Robert Craigie's reports from Tokyo. In addition, Casey's close relationship with S.M. Bruce, the Australian High Commissioner in London, enabled Casey to pick up the general policies of Whitehall and Downing Street. Because of his long spell in London in the 1920's Casey was always regarded as an unofficial member of the UK Foreign Office. He received intelligence of the greatest value. So, it is not surprising that he was asked to be involved in the 'thorny subject' of wool.

---
\* Casey to McEwen, 26 March 1940, letter, RGC4, NLA.
† Bruce to Casey, 1 March 1940, letter, A3300, 73, NAA.

Conflict had arisen between Britain, Australia and the United States over the question of wool sales to Japan. Australia wanted to sell as much wool as possible to Japan, then still a neutral. The Ministry of Economic Warfare, in London, fearful that Japan was passing on Australian wool to Germany, wanted restrictions placed on these Australian sales. Britain's deep interest in the matter was perhaps exemplified by the existence of a Committee for Sale of Empire Wool Abroad, under the chairmanship of Lord Essendon. One such restriction was limiting contracts to 'very small quantities and ... extremely short periods'. Specifically, supplies should be limited to a month by month arrangement. The Menzies cabinet, under pressure from Country Party members, considered such restrictions to be unreasonable. The Australian view was that Japan's need for wool was too great for any to be on-sold to Germany. More importantly, any restrictions or conditions placed on Australian sales to Japan could jeopardise the whole marketing relationship.

In a long cable to the UK High Commissioner in Australia, Anthony Eden, now Dominons Secretary, explained that Britain was anxious to avoid creating difficulties with the United States in the area of withholding exports to Germany.* London, at that time, was negotiating with Washington in drawing up a schedule of these vital commodities. The American position was strongly opposed to allowing any exports of wool to Japan. Britain believed that despite the cost to Australia, it would support the American position to deprive Japan of Australian wool, in the expectation that the Americans would support British proposals to halt vital exports to Germany.† While this two-way arrangement clearly served the interests of both Britain and the United States in preventing exports to both Germany and Japan, it was an arrangement thrashed out in the context of Britain's long-term plan to foster good relations with the Roosevelt Administration. Australia's trading interests would have been seen in London as largely irrelevant when placed beside Britain's perception of the threat posed by revanchism in Germany.

Bruce told Menzies that he would instruct Casey 'to put his

---

\* Eden to Whiskard, High Commissioner, 17 February 1940, cablegram, in *DAFP*, Vol. III.
† Bruce to Menzies 17 February 1940, cablegram, 41, A981, Trade 68, iii. 66 127, NAA.

back into getting results' while telling Casey: 'the matter is now to a great extent, in your hands'.* It was clear that Bruce had high hopes of Casey presenting a strong case to Washington for Australia to continue to sell wool to Japan, with as few restrictions as possible. Casey's diary shows that over three days at the end of March, he held talks with Hull, and two influential advisors, Assistant Secretaries, Stanley Hornbeck and Adolf Berle. He also conducted discussions with the American representative of the British Ministry of Economic Warfare, who was familiar with the current state of the Administration's thinking. Arising out of all these negotiations, Casey, on 25 March 1940, was able to inform Menzies that the State Department had agreed that wool could be sold to Japan on a three-monthly basis, rather than a monthly basis, provided it was not sold on credit.† Casey's assurance to Menzies certainly indicated a more flexible approach by Washington. Casey's well-known reluctance to speak of his own achievements prevents a complete understanding of how this flexible approach came about. It may be inferred, however, that Casey was, in some way instrumental in obtaining a compromise agreement from Britain and the United States on a matter of equal and joint importance to both countries. The fact remains that Bruce and Menzies, on the basis of Casey's apparent early success, may have felt justified in the choice of Casey for the Washington appointment.

This early foray into American politics also shed light on Casey's realism that was on display throughout his time in the United States. Some of his countrymen saw the world rather more naively. In January 1940, Dr Ian Clunies Ross, Australian member of the International Wool Secretariat in London, compiled a report, emphasising the importance of the relationship of Australia 'to the United States'. Clunies Ross saw Australia's security problems in the Pacific and 'the possibility of establishing a better understanding of Britain and her problems in the US, through the interpretation of those problems by Australia'. However, his reasoning that followed those arguments were themselves woolly. Clunies Ross saw in the United States 'a latent fund of interest in and sympathy

---

\* Bruce to Menzies, 16 February 1940, letter, M103, January–June 1940, NAA.
† Casey to Menzies, 25 March 1940, cablegram, 48, A3195.1.1996, NAA.

for Australian social ideals and character'. Accusing 'Australian opinion of the United States and its people as too often influenced by ignorance ... and the fact that Australians are the heirs to that attitude of condescension and superiority too frequently shown by the English', he yet concluded that Americans felt sympathy for and appreciation of Australia and her people. He described this attitude to Australia as 'remarkable' in view of the little conscious effort that had been put into its development.* Bruce, in London, enthusiastically dispatched the report and its wishful thinking to Menzies and to Casey.

Casey was under no such illusions about American sympathy for Australia. Indeed, this early triumph was completely overshadowed by confirmation from Roosevelt to Casey of where Australia stood in American perceptions. In what can be described only as the ultimate bad news, Casey's reports during his first weeks in Washington contained the first clear indication of where the American government stood in relation to any threat to Australia. Perhaps aware of the dolorous import of the message, Casey buried it in a prolix account of his discussion with the President when presenting his credentials. Roosevelt had described how some years earlier he had asked his Cabinet what the attitude of the United States would be in a variety of situations, an attack on Canada, an attack on a South American nation and lastly an attack on Australia and New Zealand. The opinion of the Cabinet was in favour of coming to the aid of Canada and those South American countries that were either in or above the northern part of the Continent, such as Panama, Mexico or Guatemala, but less likely if the attack involved one of the more distant South American Republics. Australia and New Zealand however, warranted no American response. The Roosevelt Cabinet believed that the element of distance denoted a declining interest on the part of the United States, to such an extent that that it was impossible to make any public reference to those countries, Australia and New Zealand, either directly or indirectly.†

This was a confirmation, if one were needed, of Roosevelt's

---

\* Dr I. Clunies Ross, 22 January 1940, memorandum, AA:M104.1940, Item 8, NAA.
† Casey to Gullett, 9 March 1940.

doleful message given to Bruce nine months earlier and recorded by him on 4 May 1939, but apparently not passed on to Menzies or, for that matter, to Casey. In this memo, Bruce described how he had raised with the President the degree of anxiety he had found in Australia, not only in the government but among the people, about the future actions of Japan in the Pacific region. Bruce reported to the President that he was constantly asked about the attitude of the United States towards any southward moves by Japan. Roosevelt simply repeated the account of the Cabinet decision that, in the words of the US Attorney General, Australia was 'a hell of a way off'.*

Roosevelt's comments to Bruce in this same interview throw further light upon this phenomenon. The President recounted how, in initially announcing that the United States would respond to any attack on Canada, public opinion had immediately expressed shock, but that after some thought, they had concluded that it was the right decision and had accepted it. However, the President believed that the American people would not take the same supportive view to a similar statement regarding Australia. On this basis therefore, American intervention should Australia be attacked was out of the question. Bruce summarised his discussion with Roosevelt in the following terms: 'Nothing said to me constituted any binding undertaking as to what the United States action would be in the event of developments in the Pacific …'.†

It remains unclear why Bruce did not pass on this message to Menzies. Equally unclear is why Bruce, who was always close to Casey, appears not to have warned him upon learning of Casey's elevation to the Washington post. Casey, upon meeting the President for the first time as Minister Plenipotentiary, ideally should not have been in the position where he was ignorant of White House thinking on the very matter for which he had been appointed.

In some respects, the admission that the President gave Casey was more definite, with less room for change than the President's

---

\* S.M. Bruce, 4 May 1939, Note of Conversation with F.D. Roosevelt, President of the US, M104, Item 7(4), NAA.
† Ibid.

advice to Bruce, nine months earlier. In explanatory comments, Roosevelt conceded to Bruce that the United States would be 'vitally concerned' should Japan make any move that would 'take her south of the Equator'. This was clearly not a commitment, but at least, it signified that the United States might reconsider future actions in the Pacific region if Japan indicated any aggressive intentions.[*] Roosevelt's talk to Casey included no such promises. It was, according to Casey, unequivocal in its determination for the United States not to get involved in aiding Australia. The reverse situation, the ability of Australia to aid the United States, had not yet occurred to the American President.

The significance of Roosevelt's unequivocal 'washing of the hands' message to Casey lies in its timing, presenting it to Casey at the very beginning of his engagement with the United States. No matter what hopes Australia may have held for American aid should the need arise, the President wanted to make it quite clear that the present view of the Administration eliminated the possibility. However, recognising the despair that his advice would create in Canberra, the President gave an assurance that he would create an opportunity for Casey to discuss the matter with him further.

For the remainder of his term in the United States, this worrying message of American indifference to Australia could well have haunted Casey, as he attempted to turn around public opinion, Administration thinking and American naval and military strategy. As stated in the introduction to this book, Casey was not given to introspection or rather, to disclosing his innermost thoughts, but it is not difficult to imagine that the full import of Roosevelt's message must have weighed heavily upon him. Yet, so far as can be traced, he never referred to it again in either official communications to Australia or in personal correspondence, beyond recognising the overwhelming strength of isolationism in the US Congress and the Roosevelt Administration. Perhaps, in psychological terms, he either repressed the message or alternatively, simply did not admit this clear indication of Administration thinking into his own thinking process, because it represented the very thing he had been

---

* Ibid.

commissioned to change. To accept it would be an admission not so much of defeat but of a pursuit of a hopeless cause.

It is generally recognised that Casey would have faced enormous difficulties in working in Washington. Years later, Keith Waller, Ambassador to the United States during the Johnson years, described one aspect of these difficulties: 'Australia has always been at a disadvantage in the United States in having no constituency. There is a Polish vote, a Scandinavian vote, a Jewish vote, an Irish vote, but no single constituency which is in any way, dependent on the votes of an Australia-oriented section of the community'.* For most Americans, Australia was all but invisible.

Casey understood, correctly, that it was the State Department where much of the hostility towards Britain and ignorance about Australia was generated. In his initial meetings with Berle and Hornbeck, respectively, Assistant Secretary of State and Far Eastern Adviser to the Secretary of State, it was confirmed to Casey that American reluctance to become involved in any sort of conflict was not necessarily the considered opinion of either the President or the Administration, but rather a reflection of public opinion. Hornbeck made the point that in the United States, more than any other country, public opinion made itself felt on government policy, and that it was practically impossible for a President or his Administration to 'put over' a policy of which a majority of the people disapproved. President Wilson, he said, found that out. This was no doubt a reference to Wilson's unsuccessful attempt to bring the United States into the League of Nations. President Roosevelt gave more lead to the people than any president for many years, but even he had to frame and adjust his policy to enable him to get Congressional approval. Casey quoted Hornbeck's graphic description of Roosevelt's gamesmanship: 'He often flew kites and if he found that he couldn't steer north, he altered his course to north-east'.† In an earlier letter to McEwen, Casey recognised Roosevelt's need to dissemble:

---
\* Sir Keith Waller, 'A Day in the Life of An Ambassador', in W.J. Hudson (ed.), *Australia in World Affairs* (Sydney: George Allen and Unwin, 1980), p. 394.
† Casey to McEwen, 27 March 1940, letter, RGC3, NLA.

> The President ... until the Presidential election in November ... will have to repeat ad nauseam that he is determined to 'keep this country out of a European war' in terms that will carry the requisite amount of conviction and at the same time allow him adequate freedom of action.*

Casey was thus able to conclude that in the scope and range of his responsibilities, influencing American public opinion would be no less important than influencing the policy makers.

The United States' refusal to join the League of Nations and Australian resentment at high American duties on the import of Australian wool contributed to a perception of the United States as a less than friendly power and in one sense, a rival. Nor was the relationship between the United States and the British Empire as a whole, much stronger. The depth of the chasm between these two English-speaking nations is perhaps illustrated by a remark attributed to Churchill in 1927 that war between the two countries was not 'unthinkable'.† Kershaw argues that the isolationism that had taken hold in the United States at the end of the First World War became still further engrained during Roosevelt's first term. He has noted that:

> The impact of [that] involvement on American society had been profound. Fifty thousand American soldiers had lost their lives in a conflict which, to many, had not been their country's concern ... most Americans felt that this must on no account, ever be allowed to happen again.‡

Many of the politicians referred to as isolationists often preferred the term 'non-interventionists' as signifying, for instance, a desire for the United States to object to Japanese aggression and atrocities by instituting boycotts of Japanese products. Far from being a simple withdrawal from international discussions and negotiations, the non-interventionists saw themselves as active participants, not interfering in the affairs of other nations but, at the same time, steering the United States on a particular path that

---

\* Casey to McEwen, 26 March 1940, letter, RGC4, NLA
† Mark Stoler, *Allies in War. Britain and America Against the Axis Powers 1940–1941* (London: Hodder Arnold, 2005), p. 3.
‡ Kershaw, *Fateful Choices*, p. 188.

would result in a more peaceful world.

'We are not isolationist', claimed Roosevelt, 'except insofar as we attempt to isolate ourselves completely from war'.* The original Neutrality Act, signed by the President in August 1935 arose largely from an attempt by the Administration to assist Abyssinia after Italy's invasion, a proposal that aroused much hostility in the Congress. This first Act provided for an embargo on the sale of armaments, but not including oil, to all belligerents in any war between, or among, two or more foreign states. Frequent amendments to the Act meant that there were virtually five Acts between 1935 and 1937. It would be correct to conclude that the strengthening of the Neutrality Acts in April 1937 marked the zenith of the isolationist doctrine in the United States. Secretary of State Hull later described the 1920s as a 'crucial period', when 'the country had gone wildly in favour of isolation, nationalism and peace at any price'. In the 1930s nothing had changed: '... the isolationist sentiment was so overwhelming that there was almost total opposition to any armaments building, however necessary in the light of world conditions'.† In the 1930s, the United States experimented with the use of diplomatic and economic sanctions to discourage military aggression, and with legislation to keep the United States out of European and Asiatic wars.‡ Hull resumed his efforts further, 'to advance the economic and peace proposals' he had long been advocating: 'Economic recovery and military disarmament seemed to me the two most vital and outstanding factors for peace and business recovery'.§

The later amendments to the Neutrality Act inhibited attempts to assist the Allies. Roosevelt's proclamation of 5 September 1939 imposed an embargo on the exports of arms to all belligerent nations and led Menzies to protest to the President. Menzies stressed the difficulties Australia would face in obtaining 'vital supplies', including civil aircraft for training purposes, while, at the

---

\* Robert A. Divine, *Roosevelt and World War II* (Baltimore: Johns Hopkins, 1969), p. 9.
† Cordell Hull, *Memoirs* (New York: Macmillan, 1948), pp. 124, 288.
‡ Ibid. Rexford G. Tugwell, *The Democratic Roosevelt* (Baltimore: Penguin, 1957), p. 4.
§ Hull, *Memoirs*, p. 105.

same time, no corresponding disability would be inflicted 'upon our enemy'.* Roosevelt's reply dumped the whole blame on the Congress. As the President put it:

> Earlier this year I endeavoured to bring about the repeal of the embargo provisions of our neutrality legislation…Congress finally decided to postpone the consideration of this matter in spite of the considered recommendations of the Secretary of State and my own efforts.†

Charmley has noted that:

> Historians are still divided about Roosevelt's real intentions between 1939 and 1941. The *orthodox* interpretation has a President whose heart was in the right place, that is, anti-Hitler, but who, through [according to taste] fear of Congress, or a recognition of political realities had to proceed cautiously.‡

On the other hand, Heinrichs noted, 'Franklin Roosevelt, who entirely lacked an isolationist mentality, worried about the drift of world affairs, but not to the point of sacrificing his domestic objectives'.§ Burns considered the President 'beguiled by public opinion'.¶ According to Burns, the President 'floated helplessly on a floodtide of isolationism' and, as a consequence, was 'as a foreign policy maker, during his first term, more pussy-footing politician than political leader'.** As Rock has put it: 'It has been abundantly demonstrated by American diplomatic historians that the isolationist element in Congress was both large and vocal and that Roosevelt, the consummate politician, was ultra sensitive to its bellowing'.†† According to Lowenthal, Roosevelt was torn between

---

\* Menzies to Officer, Washington, 7 September 1939, cablegram, 28, AA1972/141. Box 6, NAA.
† Roosevelt to Menzies, 16 September 1939, letter, AA. A1608, A41/1/5, NAA.
‡ John Charmley, *Churchill's Grand Alliance. The Anglo-American Special Relationship 1940–57* (New York: Harcourt Brace & Company, 1998), p. 16.
§ Waldo Heinrichs, *Threshold of War. Franklin D. Roosevelt and American Entry into World War II* (New York: Oxford University Press, 1988), p. 7.
¶ James Macgregor Burns, *Roosevelt. The Lion and the Fox. 1882–1940* (New York: Harcpurt Brace, 1956), pp. 32–3.
\*\* Burns, *Roosevelt. The Lion and the Fox*, p. 262.
†† Rock, *Chamberlain and Roosevelt*, p. 307.

his 'instinctive caution and fear of isolationist sentiment, and his desire to act as a leader of the democracies'.*

As a consequence, Roosevelt was largely reactive and forced into a series of tactical manoeuvres as those under him applied pressure for more or less support for those countries resisting the aggression of Germany, Italy, and Japan. Nonetheless, Casey was optimistic that the President would educate the American people, 'that isolationism is not necessarily the best policy in their own interests'.† Casey's judgment of the political situation as it affected Britain's and Australia's interests led him to sympathise with Roosevelt: 'It is a tragedy that the Presidential and Congressional elections happen to be this year. It is not the President's fault that America is not doing more'.‡ This was a simplistic conclusion and ignored the President's failure to provide strong leadership to a country crying out for guidance and an explanation of the woeful situation developing on the other side of the Atlantic.

Casey's description of his first impression of Roosevelt bordered on the rapturous. As Casey described the President to McEwen:

> The President is a most remarkable man. Crippled and almost completely immobile, he has a personality, character and intelligence of a remarkably high-order. It is impossible to enter his presence without being conscious of being with a great man.§

Conjecturing on the likelihood of Roosevelt seeking a third term, Casey suggested that the German leadership believed that if anyone could 'get America into the War against them, then Roosevelt can'. Roosevelt, he argued, was Germany's great potential enemy. Accordingly, he believed that Germany was unlikely to commence a great assault on Britain before the Democratic Party Convention in mid-July, lest such an assault create a wave of sympathy in the United States for the Allies, converting into a certain nomination

---

\* Mark Lowenthal, 'Roosevelt and the Coming of the War. The Search for United States Policy, 1937–41', *Journal of Contemporary History*, Vol. 16, No. 3, July 1981, pp. 413–40.', p. 418.
† Casey to McEwen, 8 May 1940, letter, RGC10, NLA.
‡ Casey to McEwen, 23 April 1940, letter, RGC6, NLA.
§ Casey to McEwen, 26 March 1940, NLA.

of Roosevelt. Such an outcome, in Casey's thinking, 'would be a great blow to Germany'.* In this prediction of Hitler's war plans, he proved to be wide of the mark, but Casey's assessment of Roosevelt's importance to the Allied cause was sound.

There was, for Casey, no alternative to Roosevelt. Republican presidential candidates had no appeal as far as Australia was concerned: 'They are not very inspiring. I have met them all'.† Offering an outsider's view of the Presidential Elections, Casey was scathing:

> Most of those who have Presidential designs throw their hats into their ring [or their diapers as Secretary for the Interior Ickes said of young Mr Dewey], months before the Convention and undertake highly organised nation-wide speech-making tours, accompanied by 'build-ups' in the Press by wireless and on films. It is a little discouraging, after reading some of the Sunday newspapers and illustrated weeklies, to meet some of the candidates privately. The strength of character, he-man qualities and high statesmanship that one is led to expect from the press build-ups are frequently quite difficult to discern.‡

Casey reported that all the possible Republican candidates for President had expressed themselves publicly for Isolationism, varying only in degree. While Robert Taft would ultimately prove himself 'sound from our point of view', Casey reported that Governor Dewey held a 'particularly cheap and nasty Isolationist line'. It is ironic therefore, that the Republican who eventually lined up against Roosevelt in November, Wendell Willkie, lost support among Isolationists because he was perceived as too pro-Allies. Casey became a great supporter of Willkie after the election and wanted him to fly the American flag in a tour of Australia and Singapore.

With all the Republican contenders firmly committed to non-intervention in the European conflict, Roosevelt was certainly Britain's best hope. Roosevelt could have thus been excused for reasoning that, on this basis, it was imperative that the United States, under his current Administration, did nothing to suggest

---

* Casey to McEwen, 14 March 1940, letter, RGC2, NLA.
† Ibid.
‡ Casey to McEwen, 26 March 1940, letter, RGC4, NLA.

that it was considering an active role in the European conflict and thus face possible defeat. This optimistic view gradually became unsustainable for Casey, who was increasingly alarmed by American inaction as the threat to Britain grew.

After receiving Roosevelt's baleful report at their first meeting, Casey would have better understood an American policy that deliberately excluded Australia from consideration of material support. In this respect, he would have been mirroring the views of Chamberlain, who, not long before, had expressed the view that if Britain 'got into trouble', she could expect no help from the United States. Indeed, 'it is always best and safest to count on nothing from the Americans but words'.*

Nonetheless, Casey had reached the prescient conclusion as early as April 1940 that an 'incident' in which American national honour was affronted 'might well set fire to public opinion and lead to an early and active participation in the war'.† It is unlikely that Casey envisaged the scope of the 'incident' that would engulf the United States at Pearl Harbor, but Casey clearly wanted to ensure that the greatest possible advantage could be taken from any unexpected event. Casey, aware that conflict would certainly break out in the Pacific, knew that the United States would be reluctant to participate, leaving Australia doomed with Britain unable, and the United States unwilling to help. Casey had to pin his hopes on an 'incident' that would make it impossible for the Americans to ignore the need to become involved. Casey's task therefore, would be to help the Americans develop a new sense of the usefulness, even the vital importance, of Australia. This was a political task and not something that could be left to naval and military attaches. Casey would have to take the initiative.

---

\* Cited in Rock, *Chamberlain and Roosevelt*, p. 48. Chamberlain wrote this in a letter to his sister, Hilda, on 17 December 1937, TNA, NC 16/1/1032.
† Casey to McEwen, 23 April 1940, letter, RGC6, NLA.

*Chapter Four*

# Spring 1940: From Phoney War to the Fall of France

Upon arriving in the United States, Casey was presented with an interesting array of challenges in his quest to both bring Australia to American notice and to influence public opinion about Britain's urgent need for greater American support. One consolation for Casey was that, from the outset of his American post, he was welcomed by the American administration, a welcome taken up by the American media. The *New York Times* reported that 'Australia has given her best in sending us Richard G. Casey'.* In an earlier report, the same journal had emphasised the 'increasing importance of Australian-American commercial and other relations', without any reference to common defence or strategic considerations.† Elsewhere, the issue of common security interests did receive attention. The *Washington Post* in a lengthy editorial welcoming the simultaneous announcement in Washington and Canberra of the establishment of diplomatic relations between the two nations did discuss the defence interests of both:

> Because of the war and the continuing crisis in the Far East, questions of mutual concern to the US and the Australian Commonwealth have greatly increased in number and importance ... The importance which the Canberra government attaches to the newly created post of Minister to Washington is seen in the appointment of a high official, Richard G. Casey...‡

---

\* *New York Times*, 21 February 1940. The *NYT* first broke the news on 25 December 1939, p. 1, a leak that the P.M.'s Dept. described as 'intelligent anticipation'.
† *New York Times*, 25 December 1939, p. 1.
‡ *Washington Post*, 9 January 1940, p. 6.

These different American perceptions of Casey's role pointed to the central issue for Australia – how to translate 'questions of mutual concern' into some form of American commitment to the Allied cause.

Casey arrived in Washington during the period known as the Phoney War. Re-entering the rarefied world of diplomacy at a much higher level than his previous London role, Casey confronted a world beset with conflicts and threats of conflicts. The first battalions of the Australian Sixth Division set sail for the Middle East and arrived in Suez in February, thus beginning the flow of the Australian Army to the other side of the world. In the period between his arrival in March and the invasion of France in May, Casey worked tirelessly. He needed to improve his understanding of the American political scene, to work out who his friends and enemies were in diplomatic circles in Washington, assess American military capacity, and advocate for stronger ties between the United States, Britain and Australia.

Early in his mission, Casey had discerned where the centres of influence lay. Obviously, the Oval Office of the White House was central to United States policy formulation but the decisions and directions that flowed out of the Oval Office had emanated from a vast array of sources that flowed into it. Tracking these inflows and exercising his own influence upon them thus became the focus of Casey's attentions.

Hudson identifies the challenge confronting Casey as 'achieving personal acceptance by powerful men'.* Yet because of Casey's reputation for an inability to win over Cabinet colleagues and his seeming inability to garner support within his own party, there must have been doubts about whether he would be capable of either achieving personal acceptance or of influencing American attitudes. Yet Hudson offers an interesting interpretation of how he was perceived in the United States. The very characteristics that had been detrimental to his successful progress in the Australian political milieu, that is, a sense of urgency that he was unable to communicate to colleagues in the context of what Hudson describes as 'the laconic phlegm of Australian society' and a frustration

---

* Hudson, *Casey*, p. 116.

with the more routine, conventional political ethos, were seen in the United States, not as nervous tautness but rather as 'attractive liveliness'.* Hudson also makes the point that by adopting means and methods peculiar to the American environment, that is, courtship of the press, personal propaganda and cultivation of contacts, Casey easily blended in with his American hosts.

In one of his early messages to the minister, after arriving in Washington, Casey described Adolf Berle 'as a man of considerable influence', and 'in-growing and introspective, very intelligent and stubborn, very critical of the English'. On the other hand, Casey believed him capable of being 'nursed along so far as we are concerned'.† This would be no easy task. According to Reynolds, Berle 'believed that America had the strength, particularly economic, to determine the peace and also the moral right, unlike the British, whose foreign policy seemed to him, not only inept but consistently self-interested'.‡ In a letter to Canberra, Casey sketched a brief background:

> He is the third man in the State Department, being inferior in status only to Cordell Hull [Secretary of State] and Sumner Welles [Under Secretary of State] ... his appointment is political a nominee of the President ... not a career man ... a man of pronounced ability and a recognised force in the State Department.§

Berle was, in fact, a member of the 'Brains Trust', a small group of men whom Roosevelt had gathered together, mainly from academia, before his election in 1932. In the inner circles of the Roosevelt White House, there were two classifications of those around the President, informal perhaps but brutally valid, 'B.C.' and the others. 'B.C.' meant those who had joined the Roosevelt camp before the Democratic Party Convention in Chicago selected Roosevelt as the Presidential candidate, hence 'Before Chicago'. Their numbers were small and generally comprised Roosevelt's personal staff. Their loyalty to FDR was unquestioned. Perhaps the

---

\* Ibid., p. 117.
† Casey to McEwen, 26 March 1940, letter, RGC3, NLA.
‡ David Reynolds, *The Creation of the Anglo-American Alliance*, p. 256.
§ Casey to McEwen, 26 March 1940, letter, RGC3, NLA.

most important was Louis Howe, who teamed up with Roosevelt in the 1920s and who has been described as his 'closest working associate'.* But seemingly just as close and vital was Harry Hopkins, who has also been described as 'Roosevelt's closest adviser'.† Casey early recognised the influential place occupied by Hopkins in the Roosevelt 'family'. Hopkins was to become an important contact in Washington for Casey.

The second group, those who had joined the Roosevelt bandwagon after the nomination, included the Brains Trust. They had a philosophical commitment to Roosevelt and a belief in Roosevelt's ability to provide national leadership. Also present was an expectation to actively participate in that leadership, an expectation that might be ambition or simply an altruistic desire to serve the nation at a time of crisis. The Brains Trust occupied senior influential positions, served as speech-writers and gave Roosevelt a 'broad education in economics'.‡

Berle, who had been professor of corporate law at Columbia Law School, Professor Raymond Moley of Columbia University, Professor Rexford G. Tugwell of Columbia University, William C. Bullitt, a former diplomat who had been Roosevelt's 'observer' in Europe and two men from the world of finance, James P. Warburg and Charles W. Taussig, made up this inner group.§ Although the Brains Trust was said to have been disbanded once Roosevelt won the 1932 election, its members continued to wield a powerful and pervasive influence. In 1933 the complexity and volume of events, both domestically and internationally were beyond the grasp and understanding of any one person. It was essential therefore that the President surround himself with informed, committed advisers, upon whom he could rely.

The decision-making process that operated in the Roosevelt White House has been the subject of much examination and

\* Kenneth S. Davis, *Invincible Summer. An Intimate Portrait of the Roosevelts Based On the Recollections of Marion Dickerman* (New York: Atheneum. 1974), p. 16.
† Magnus Magnusson (ed.), *Chambers Biographical Dictionary* (Edinburgh: R. Chambers, 1992), p. 732.
‡ Donald R McCoy, *Coming of Age* (New York: Penguin Books, 1973), p. 201.
§ William Manchester, *The Glory and the Dream* (London: Michael Joseph, 1974), pp. 49, 51.

speculation. As one commentator has put it: 'Those who knew Roosevelt best, agreed that he was a man infinitely complex and almost incomprehensible'.* Or, as Reynolds has put it, Roosevelt was prone to 'casual administrative methods'.† It seems that Roosevelt took advice from as many sources as possible, but the eventual decision may frequently have been the initial one grounded in his own conclusions. However, even if they were sometimes sounding boards, Roosevelt's inner circle had the advantage of personal contact with the President.

Although only Assistant Secretary of State, Berle appears to have had more access to the President than Hull. In identifying the powerful position that Berle occupied in the Roosevelt Administration and then targeting Berle, Casey set himself a formidable, but logical goal. At their very first meeting, it was clear that Berle regarded Casey as simply an antipodean representative of Whitehall, a judgment Casey did everything possible to demolish. From Casey's perspective, the plan to modify the isolationist and anti-British views of Berle were of paramount importance.

There are two aspects of Casey's determination to establish some sort of relationship with Berle. Firstly, Casey's early identification of Berle as a target for 'nursing' recognised Berle's closeness to Roosevelt. In a work devoted to the family life of the Roosevelts, one author describes how Berle, in correspondence to Roosevelt during the pre-Presidency years, always began his letters with the salutation, 'Hail Caesar'.‡ This practice persisted after Inauguration, suggesting a respectful intimacy between the two men. Berle was given wide latitude in the day-to-day working of the White House, because of the special relationship he had with the President. His position as Assistant Secretary of State did not require him to report to the Secretary of State. Rather he reported directly to the President, apparently causing Roosevelt some embarrassment: 'Get hold of Berle and tell him to be darn careful in what he writes me because the Staff see his letters and they are highly indiscreet',

* James MacGregor Burns, *Roosevelt. The Soldier Of Freedom. 1940–1945* (London: Weidenfeld and Nicolson. 1971), p. 602.
† Reynolds, *Creation of the Anglo-American Alliance*, p. 236.
‡ Davis, *Invincible Summer*, p. 112.

wrote Roosevelt to an aide. Lest he offend Berle, Roosevelt then added to the memo, 'tell him a little later on I want him to come down and lunch with me'.*

A study of his diaries that recorded his innermost musings on a wide range of topics reveals that Berle, in his various conversations with foreign diplomats, unsurprisingly, was not revealing Administration secrets. That is, Berle's messages to those outside the White House were frequently at marked variance with the views he was committing to his diary. The diaries therefore constitute a far more reliable guide to understanding and interpreting the Roosevelt Administration. For Berle, Casey was an ideal source of intelligence. Berle was able to take back to the Oval Office Casey's thinking, which of course represented not only a strictly Australian view but, Whitehall's, also. Clearly, it suited Casey's purposes for Berle to see the Australian as a valuable source of information.

An examination of Berle's diary shows that he was in fact torn between his Anglophobia and the stark realisation of the fact that a Europe of the dictators was an ever worse prospect for the United States. In other words, Berle represented a large section of American opinion in that he was anti-German, anti-Russian, and anti-British. Berle had already reached some conclusions about the participation of the United States in the conflict as early as the first few months of the European war. His diary entry for late November 1939 includes: 'The British and French might well be worn out and in that case, we shall have to enter the war'. Berle also believed that, were Germany and the Soviet Union to combine to become dominant, 'we should have to become a militarist nation'.†
Berle's apparent indifference to the immediate crisis confronting Britain was qualified. On 5 December 1939, he wrote, with his pleasure undisguised:

> The change in public opinion here has been remarkable. The Russian invasion of Finland seems to have stopped everyone in their tracks … the pacifists of last month are urging all

---

\* FDR to General Edwin Watson, 11 February 1937, Berle Papers PSF, Box 94, Roosevelt Memorial Library.
† Adolf Berle Diary, 29 November 1939, Berle Papers, p. 94, Roosevelt Memorial Library.

kinds of measures against Russia. Plainly the neutrality of this country is not as solid as it was a week ago.*

Berle often expressed unhappiness that the United States might have 'to defend the British Empire'.† Indeed, the suspicion that Britain was attempting to engage American participation in defending the Empire was a constant theme in Administration discussion. As referred to elsewhere in this thesis, a widely held view in the United States, not just restricted to the isolationists or non-interventionists, was that the American involvement in the First World War had been costly in men and materiel with no discernible advantage to the United States beyond sharing the burden of assisting in the preservation of Britain's colonial interests. Casey took it upon himself to unburden Berle and others of such fallacies.

When Casey arrived in the United States, the domestic situation had improved dramatically, but the international situation was deteriorating rapidly. Casey does not describe his reaction when, at their first meeting, Berle asked him if Australia had considered what it would do in the future if Britain were beaten or even if, as a result of the war, Britain were unable to extend 'adequate defence' to Australia.‡ Berle emphasised that the question came not from official sources but he was simply interested for his own information. Clearly, the defeat and occupation of Britain by Germany was seen by Roosevelt's advisers as a possibility. The terms of the question, not 'what would Australia do' but rather 'if Australia had considered what it would do' in such circumstances carried an implication of Australian unpreparedness.

Casey's raison d'être in Washington revolved around those very eventualities, but at that point, probably for tactical reasons, he was reluctant to lay open his awareness of the peril that Australia would face. He replied that Australia had hardly dared to consider such possibilities. Moreover, Australia had such close and important links with Britain, in trade, finance and defence that he had no right to anticipate that any other country would provide the

---

\* Adolf Berle Diary, 5 December 1939, Roosevelt Memorial Library.
† Ibid.
‡ Casey to McEwen, 27 March 1940, letter, RGC3, NLA.

essential background and connections that Britain provided. He did concede, 'speaking frankly', that some in Australia hoped that should the nation find itself in that situation, 'the United States would not be indifferent to a threatened change in the status quo in the Pacific'. Such a development, Casey emphasised, 'was only a hope ... dependent on the state of public opinion in America at that time'. This exchange with Berle preceded the revealing interview with the President, when Casey learnt that the Roosevelt Administration had already considered the possibility of Australia coming under threat of invasion and had decided that no American assistance would be granted.

Berle gave no assurances and, in fact, did not refer to the Cabinet decision, simply limiting his comments to a general agreement of the reliance of government on public opinion. He told Casey that, in any event, he did not believe that Japan's deep involvement in China allowed her to contemplate any 'southward adventure'. Finally, the Far Eastern policy of the United States was the most considered and developed of all their regional policies.[*] Berle's question to Casey revolving around the possibility of Britain being defeated or so engaged in the European conflict as to be unable to assist Australia, hinted at discussions about the break-up of the British Empire.

Despite the senior position he held in the White House firmament, Berle held dogmatic views that failed to reflect an understanding of the history of important issues. Casey was quickly made aware of a residual, historical antagonism towards Britain that had its beginnings in the American Revolution and the war of 1812–15. According to Berle, the British burned the White House in 1812 for no reason except spite. The fact that Berle would bring up this old, old encounter indicates the depth of his animosity towards Britain. Berle also referred to unpaid war debts although he did concede to Casey that 'it was sheer ignorance to believe that you could demand payment of war debts and at the same time, steeply raise American customs tariffs against all foreign goods. The two were mutually antagonistic'.[†] Casey often noted how hard it

---

[*] Casey to McEwen, 27 March 1940, letter, RGC3, NLA.
[†] Casey to McEwen, 26 March 1940, letter, RGC4, NLA.

was to change the American perception that the British Empire was by definition a bad thing. As Casey noted to his diary: 'The British Empire, in the minds of many Americans, was 'the British Vampire'.'* Casey was left in no doubt that Berle was one of those Americans who held such views.

Berle's understanding of the factors that ended the Great War in 1918 betrayed the Administration's determination not to commit forces to a European war. As the Battle of Britain raged, Berle reflected upon the end of the last war in which the United States fought alongside Britain:

> The World War really ended because the many races and groups in Europe rose up and threw off their German and Austrian masters. If this war comes to an end, it will be by somewhat the same process; I doubt if we are going to put several million men on the European plain to reconquer the continent; I doubt if the British can do so; I doubt if the blockade, galling as it will be, can accomplish anything really effective; the ultimate reconquest will be psychological and political.†

Yet, the world situation as it existed in 1940, where there was a real possibility that Germany would achieve a status of overwhelming power vis-à-vis the rest of the world, was way beyond the situation in 1917–18. These predictions, based as they were on dubious foundations, proved wide of the mark. Internal revolts certainly occurred in both Russia and Germany, but these were, at best, simultaneous with the breakdown of fighting. On the other hand, Berle's emphasis on internal revolts reflected American and British strategic thinking. Even in 1941, there was no real thought of a large American landing in Europe. The plan was a blockade, support for internal revolts and bombing. Roosevelt hoped to avoid formal American entry into the war.‡

Casey believed that American reluctance to become more involved in Britain's plight could not be modified while the Administration's senior figures, exercising much influence, such

---

\* Casey Diaries, 22 November 1940.
† Adolf Berle Diary, 21 October 1940.
‡ Reynolds, *Creation of the Anglo-American Alliance*, p. 213.

as Berle, remained indifferent, even hostile. Berle's constant references to the United States being embroiled in a war to save 'the British Empire' infuriated Casey because it ignored the fact that the British Empire was not a series of undeveloped nations that were exploited simply to add to Britain's wealth but included Canada, Australia, South Africa and New Zealand that contributed significantly to the world's food supply and equally to the world's energy resources. Nonetheless, Casey was surely correct when he noted that 'it will be of good value for me to see as much of him as possible' and that towards that end, 'I have of set purpose created opportunities of meeting him'. Berle's response showed signs of friendship, 'although he is by temperament, rather without warmth in his personal relations'.

Casey seems to have enjoyed his jousting with Berle, but needed patience given that Berle was fond of rehashing old arguments. If Berle could be 'turned' or 'nursed', there was no outward sign yet of a changed outlook. Hornbeck may have seemed the more appropriate contact for Casey, but it was a key decision on Casey's part to concentrate on Berle who was personally close to the President.* No doubt, this facilitated Casey's access to the Oval Office. Berle himself would never acknowledge any departure from his long-held positions. While the British accused the United States of failing to stand up for a dying democratic world, Americans often expressed dismay at British cynicism. In June 1941, as Barbarossa was about to be unleashed, Berle was still denouncing British cynicism and naked self-interest. His diary reads,

> The British meanwhile, are not showing even the remotest signs of statesmanship. In a conversation with Welles, the other day, Halifax proposed trying to 'appease' Russia by recognizing her seizures of the three Baltic republics, intimating that he did not care very much for the Baltic peoples ... had a less high opinion of them than he did of the Finns. Considering that the British were largely instrumental in setting up the Baltic republics at the close of the last war, this is a reversion to the old Foreign Office practice which specialised in polite dishonour when it served their interests.†

---

\* Casey to Minister, 27 March 1940, Secret RGC3, Vol. 1, Box 24, NLA.
† Adolf Berle Diary, 6 June 1941.

On an outing with Berle and his wife in July 1941, Casey was told by his host that the United States was 'anti-German' but not 'pro-British'. Among the sins cited by Berle were the 'orgy of slanging of the United States' undertaken by British politicians such as Churchill and Chamberlain on the 'Uncle Shylock theme' after World War One. According to Berle, it was the British who cynically made friends or enemies of Russians or Finns depending upon their self interest and nothing more. These were the arguing positions that Casey encountered and grappled with in his frequent dealings with Berle.

It must be acknowledged that Casey's encounters with Berle brought Casey into Berle's network. The complex but blossoming relationship between Casey and Berle was in evidence as the Phoney War came to an end. On the evening of 11 May, Casey reported on 'a long talk' with Berle that day, discussing whether the German invasion of the Netherlands and Belgium, which had begun the previous day, would bring the United States closer to joining the war. That this was a matter of high policy suggests that Casey could have only considered that Berle was senior enough and influential enough to have a significant input into White House thinking.* It was just as significant that Berle was prepared to discuss such a vital matter with a junior diplomat. There was exhibited in this exchange a clear indication of Casey's growing stature in Washington.

Roosevelt and Halifax met the same evening after the Casey/Berle talks, when the President told the Ambassador that he had reason to believe that, following the German invasion of the Netherlands, Japan was contemplating intervention in the Netherlands East Indies. The President refused to reveal his source but Casey learnt of the President's remarks immediately.† Casey could only have been overjoyed at the President's advice, representing as it did an acknowledgment of Japan's serious intentions in the Pacific, an argument that was crucial to Casey's 'mission' to seek greater American interest in the Pacific region. Casey's activities as disclosed in his diaries at this time reveal an

---

\* Casey to McEwen, 11 May 1940, cablegram, 77, A3196 I. 3153, NAA.
† Casey to Dept. of External Affairs, 12 May 1940, cablegram, 82, A3195. I.3176, NAA.

almost obsessive pursuit of his responsibilities in representing Australia and a certainty that Japan would initiate some kind of hostilities in the Asia/Pacific region. Casey hoped that Berle would relay his concerns to the President.

Casey and Berle traded information and barbs not only over history and wartime strategy, but the shape of the post-war world. Berle's specialisation was planning a post-war world where Britain had given up its empire and the United States played the leading role in the peace.*

Casey became a part of that conversation. Berle came to perceive Casey as influential, perhaps excessively so. The American thought it best to keep Casey in his embrace rather than at arm's length. Casey subsequently became a sounding board for Berle and a participant in the discussions about the post-war world. For instance, Berle in November 1940 recorded in his diary:

> a little dinner at home for the Argentine head of the Central Bank, Prebisch, a brilliant man of under 40; Felipe Espil, the Argentine Ambassador; Dick Casey, the Australian Minister; Ronald Ransom; and myself. This was exclusively a party to leave reality behind ... *we planned and re-planned a new world*.† [My emphasis.]

Berle came to value Casey's counsel, and perhaps his company. After the dinner with the Argentinian banker and ambassador, Casey was moved to note...'the main interest lay in the fact that Berle had invited the Australian Minister to come in on such a discussion'.‡

The relationship that Casey had built with Berle gave Australia a voice in American planning that it would not otherwise have had. In June 1941, Berle asked Roosevelt for permission to begin tentative outlines of the post-war order and the President agreed, emphasising that such a study must not be revealed outside the Oval Office.§ Berle included Casey in the study. That Berle sought Casey's presence on what the President insisted was a confidential

---
\* Reynolds, *The Creation of the Anglo-American Alliance*, pp. 256–7.
† Adolf Berle Diary, 28 November 1940.
‡ Casey Diaries, 28 November 1940.
§ Reynolds, *The Creation of the Anglo-American Alliance*, p. 256.

study illustrates Berle's growing high opinion of Casey. If the purpose of the study were to ensure that the United States did not make the same mistakes as Berle believed it did in 1919, the presence of Casey, a representative of the Commonwealth, became even more significant.

Casey cultivated and prized his easy access to Berle and his colleagues at the State Department, Dean Acheson and Stanley Hornbeck, each an Assistant Secretary of State. Hornbeck, like Berle, proved a useful source of information and comment. On 27 March 1940, Casey described Hornbeck to McEwen as 'a man of consequence and authority'.* From Hornbeck, Casey soon learned the depth of anti-Japanese sentiment in the United States. According to Casey, Hornbeck claimed that:

> The Japanese believe that they were the salt of the earth, and their mission on earth was to spread Japanese culture, commerce, and authority. All Japanese parties and sections believe this. There were, in this respect, no 'moderates' in Japan, everyone believed it.†

Hornbeck, in June 1940, vented to Casey his gloomy conviction that Japanese governments had had a policy since 1894 of adhering to an agreement only for so long as it suited them and, according to Hornbeck, Japan had broken every agreement that it had entered into.‡ Casey found this snippet interesting, if not necessarily correct. Casey, like most Australians, was anxious to avoid war with Japan, to buy her off with concessions if possible, or encourage her to advance in a direction away from the equator. Americans like Hornbeck were opposed to appeasing Japan and saw the Chinese as doing the work of sapping Japanese strength.

Casey's relationship with Hornbeck may not have been as close as his relationship with Berle, but it appears to have been conducted in a franker manner. Casey recounted a long discussion he had had with Hornbeck on the evening of 25 June in which both 'got a little heated', culminating in Casey telling the American that in relation to Roosevelt's refusal to take a more belligerent stance

---

\* Casey Diaries, 27 March 1940.
† Casey to McEwen, 27 March 1940, letter, RGC3, NLA.
‡ Casey Diaries, 25 June 1940.

against the Axis powers while still continuing to encourage the Commonwealth, 'someone else does the exhorting and we do the fighting'. Casey continued that the Commonwealth, in supplying military aid to China, was running the risks of war with Japan, whereas the United States, by doing no more than stationing a fleet in the Pacific, was taking no risks whatever. Casey noted that, despite the heated words, they nonetheless parted friends.[*]

With Dean Acheson, the hawkish third Assistant Secretary, Casey enjoyed a far more informal, even personal relationship. Acheson was much more likely than Berle to sympathise with the British cause. Acheson's scope of responsibilities in the State Department did not include any of the areas which Casey perceived as being relevant to his own responsibilities. Yet, the two became quite close in a friendship conducted in Washington but not what might be described as 'official Washington'. By May 1941, Acheson's friendship with Casey had reached the point of Acheson coaching Casey in how to use the new Lend-Lease program, potentially to effect a new trade treaty, while American 'vested interests', usually in 'full cry', were distracted by the war.[†] The Casey diaries reveal that their contacts became more frequent after Pearl Harbor. Perhaps the degree of their friendship and mutual trust may be gauged by the fact that when Casey was posted to Cairo in early 1942, the Achesons offered to mind the two Casey children and did so for several months.[‡]

It is possible to reach a completely contrary interpretation of Casey's apparent success in the United States vis-à-vis his singular lack of success in Australia. Put simply, it may well have been that Casey relied more on style than substance, a cliché expression that nonetheless remains a viable explanation. Yet, it must also be recognised that the sophisticated, battle-scarred politicians surrounding, indeed inhabiting, the White House (including the 'Before Chicago' crowd) and the upper levels of the Administration were able to discern the difference between style and substance.

---

[*] Ibid.
[†] Casey Diaries, 12 May 1941.
[‡] The source here is the author's interview with Jane Macgowan, Casey's daughter, 21 September 2011.

After only a few months in Washington, Casey considered himself sufficiently accepted within the Roosevelt Administration to hold frequent, unscheduled talks with senior people such as Hornbeck and Berle. Indeed, a cursory examination of Casey's diaries and cablegrams reveals striking evidence of Casey's extraordinary sociability: multiple lunches, formal dinners, parties where he met and conversed with persons such as Vice President Henry Wallace, Hull, Welles, Berle, Hornbrook, Henry Morgenthau and Navy Secretary Frank Knox. It would be likely that a newspaper publisher from a non-partisan publication, such as the *New York Times*, might also join in at some point. These were not fleeting encounters but discussions, usually pre-arranged and not infrequently, conducted over a dinner table. Casey was an extremely busy man, at the height of his powers and his days so full that, by his own admission, not all of his discussions were recorded in the diaries.

It was not unusual for Casey to spend an active day in Washington, talking to a variety of people whom he would consider as worth talking to, hold a dinner party at the Legation attended by those who might be regarded as persons of influence and then board a plane or train for a visit to some city, to begin a round of meetings and talks early the next day.

Casey appears to have made few records of his (no doubt, frequent) telephone conversations or casual, unscheduled encounters with people who came within the orbit of his activities, confirming the fact that his diaries do not constitute a complete picture. Nonetheless, his diaries suggest astonishing energy and successful networking with his principal American targets. Casey's indefatigable pursuit of contacts, mentors and persons occupying positions of power, so quickly after arriving in Washington, all point to the fact that Casey was capable of not only creating his own luck but was able to discern exactly where he could put such good fortune to the most effective use.

Diplomacy was the world that Casey knew best.

He rapidly became aware that the United States would never embark on a major policy shift unless it had the support of the American people. It thus fell to Casey to tell the American people where their interests lay, a task normally outside the responsibility of a foreign diplomat. It is a matter of record that Casey was able to judge just how far he could go on this delicate course. Disputing a proposal made by Clunies Ross that American public opinion could be formed by using the same techniques employed to sell 'a commodity', Casey emphasised that while changing a physical or a buying habit may be achievable, 'it is quite different and much more difficult to set out to change an attitude of mind'.

Casey saw a grave risk that the American people 'are all too apt to place [such material] in the category of propaganda'. He claimed that a great suspicion of propaganda, in any of its forms, existed in the United States at that time, a suspicion strengthened by a widely-spread and deeply felt fear of being dragged into another European war.

It is possible to discern Casey's ability to use and exploit the media by referring to a letter he wrote to Prime Minister Bruce in December 1924, shortly after taking up his position as Bruce's representative in Whitehall:

> I think that if you at any time wanted to get anything in the Australian press by cable from here – it would be very simple for you to cable me in cipher what news you wished expressed and for me to have the cable agencies quietly inspired, preferably through a third party.*

This demonstrates that even at that stage of his career, he had developed a technique to achieve press coverage that was close to manipulation. He further honed his skills in managing the media, as he began his mission in Washington. Casey embarked upon a carefully thought out program to exploit the American media, press, radio and newsreels. As Casey described his task:

> I believe that all references to Australia in the American press are to the good. I want to see them get used to seeing the name 'Australia' in their papers – and to foster the picture of a young and virile nation composed of a people like themselves, developing a land the size of their own, and at the same time, defending their freedom and independence against the forces of aggression.†

---

\* Hudson, *My Dear P.M. R. G. Casey Letters to Bruce 1924–1929*, p. 11.
† Casey to McEwen, 16 April 1940, memorandum, Washington 89/40

Casey understood the importance of not lecturing the Americans but rather of giving the American media something of interest to report: 'It will be one of my objectives to ensure that as many references to Australia as possible appear in the daily press ... since I have been in this country, there have been widespread press references to my appointment and to the new Legation, together with photographs and good reports of my speeches and movements'.*

Casey planned to bring Australia to the notice of the American people in a non-threatening way, avoiding 'the taint and taunt of propaganda'.† He engaged a public relations adviser, Earle Newsom, whom he found useful and helpful. Casey could not disguise the fact that he was Australia's official representative in the United States and that Australia was Britain's ally in the war against Nazi Germany.‡

However, guided by Newsom who knew how far he could press his ideas, Casey managed the legal minefield and avoided transgressing US sensitivities about foreigners pushing their own point of view or illegal war propaganda. However, when he perceived the Australian Department of Information, stepping over the fine line in August 1940 with a plan to spend US$300,000 on advertising, Casey consulted the State Department and the plan was dropped.§ Casey set himself the task to steer a middle course, speaking freely about the Australian war effort and the reasons that Australia was in the war, 'whilst studiously avoiding any suggestions as to what Americans should do about the war.

In his first few months in Washington, he addressed a large number of newspaper executives and journalists in Washington, a

---

Confidential, A981, USA 79.1, NAA.

\* Among Casey's deposit of papers held at the National Library, the collection of press clippings from the American years is well nigh overwhelming. See MS 6150. Box 39, NLA

† Casey to McEwen, 16 April 1940, memorandum, Washington 89/40 Confidential, A981, USA 79.1, NAA.

‡ For a full account, see Griffen-Foley, 'The Kangaroo is Coming into Its Own', pp. 1–20.

§ Casey to Murdoch, 22 August 1940, Casey to Newsom, 27 August 1940, Casey to Murdoch, 3 October 1940, AA3300/1940/66, NAA, cited in Bridge, *A Delicate Mission*, p. 8.

gathering of the Economic and Social Institute Labor Camp, the National Foreign Trade Convention in San Francisco (audience eleven hundred), the Overseas Press Club in Washington, a Businessmen's Lunch in San Francisco and a further evening address for twelve hundred executives, the Commonwealth Club in Washington, the New York Herald Tribune Forum in New York, the Washington Torch Club, the University of Utah, the Twentieth Century Club in Hartford, Connecticut, the Harvard Chapter of American Students Defence League in Harvard, the East Asiatic Society at Harvard Club in Washington, Meeting of Law, Banking and Business Men in Miami. His record of radio talks and interviews, beginning in April 1940, is equally impressive. Indicating an intensive study of the reactions of the American press to his activities, he reported to McEwen: 'No less than 1,400 inches of single-column press references have appeared in the principal newspapers of America ... apart from Australian news cabled from Australia, that is, it represents press references to Australia that would not have appeared had the Legation not been created'. Casey told McEwen that this press publicity had resulted in his being 'the target' for a wide range of correspondents (*sic*) 'mainly serious and worthwhile communications on a variety of subjects, both seeking and giving information'.\* Casey opined that 'the success of our endeavours here will be measured by the increased references that we can get in the American daily and periodical press ...'.

As the Allied position deteriorated rapidly in June 1940, Casey decided that decisive action was called for but he was acutely aware that any overt attempt to win American support for, let alone participation in the European conflict, was anathema. To take on these powerful shapers of opinion was to court disaster:

> One's mind has to accept the fact that the reality that has to be faced is American public opinion. I believe that no one other than Americans can say or do anything that is going appreciably to speed things up – and an incautious word or even what might be interpreted as going an inch too far might get wide and devastating publicity.†

---

\* Casey to McEwen, 16 April 1940.
† Casey Diaries, 5 June 1940.

Despite Casey's own reservations about the danger of speaking out, a few days later in New York City he addressed a wide selection of organizations. These included No.1 Wall Street, the Union League Club, the Dutch Treat Club (a private charity body made up of prominent Wall Street figures), India House, making 'a total of about 400 leaders of thought in New York'. Privately, he met and talked to Willard Chenery, editor of *Colliers Magazine*, Henry Mertz, editor of the *New York Times*, J.M. James, managing editor of the *New York Times* and Jacob Sulzberger, publisher of the *New York Times*, Colonel Patterson, owner of the *New York Daily News*, the highest circulation tabloid, and Lowell Thomas, journalist, explorer and film maker. On the same visit Casey also had a long talk with Dorothy Thompson, commentator and journalist.[*] Thompson enjoyed a reputation comparable to Michelle Grattan in Australia.

An examination of the speeches he made reveals that Casey had developed various themes which he repeated in different parts of the country. For instance, one which he delivered frequently was to explain why Australia was at war when it was not threatened. This involved an explanation of Australia's membership of the British Commonwealth, a desirable end in itself, as it corrected some of the misunderstandings around Australia's status. Australia was no longer a British colony.

Casey discerned 'a curious dualism' in the United States – the regard and respect which thinking Americans held for Britain, tempered by jealousy and something of an inferiority complex'.[†] He soon detected a similar dichotomy of views among the major American newspapers, with the *Chicago Tribune*, *Daily News* (New York) and *Times-Herald* (Washington) invariably adopting what he termed 'an anti-British' view.[‡] Casey's tactic was to flood the press with information about Australia, making himself the subject of the story if necessary. Casey, helped by Newsom, over time became something of a celebrity. Evidence for this is that a speech he gave at the California Institute of Technology in June 1941 received attention from newspapers on the East Coast. [§]

[*] Casey Diaries, 13 June 1940 and 17 June 1940.
[†] Casey to McEwen, 26 March 1940, letter, RGC4, NLA.
[‡] Casey to McEwen, 23 April 1940, letter, RGC7, NLA.
[§] Reported in *Republican*, Springfield Mass, 16 June 1941; *New York Sun*,

Casey showed increasing assertiveness and a heightened appreciation of how polling created public opinion in a conversation over lunch with Dr George Gallup, founder of the American Institute of Public Opinion and virtual creator of public opinion polls. Casey persuaded Gallup not to proceed with conducting an opinion survey. The subject was to be Americans' attitude to a statement by Hull, following the invasion of The Netherlands, that Dutch colonies in the South West Pacific must not be allowed to fall into Nazi hands. In a report to his minister, describing the events, Casey considered that it would be dangerous to risk getting an unfavourable reply to such a question from public opinion in the United States at that time.

Australia did not have public opinion polling in the 1930s, but Casey was quick to work out that opinion polls did not just measure opinion, but 'created' it.[*] Casey was sceptical at first but acknowledged that most Americans believed in opinion polls because, despite their small samples, they were proving very accurate in predicting the actual results of elections. At one level, this was something of a relief. Casey, hoping for a Roosevelt win, recognised that, by running for a third term, Roosevelt was taking a risk. He was comforted by the fact that a Gallup Poll, released on 14 April 1940 showed Roosevelt on a 53% approval and possible Republican candidate, Senator Vandenberg on 42%.[†] At another level, the results were sobering; more than 90% of Americans wanted the United States to stay out of the war.

Roosevelt's recognition of the opinion poll as a key factor in determining what the American public wanted and didn't want, impressed Menzies, who perceived that characteristic as a positive, politically. According to Menzies, Roosevelt was, in effect, 'a master politician, judging public opinion accurately, never getting too far ahead of it, never impatient'.[‡] Casey, however, with his long

---

16 June 1941; *Portland, Maine Express* 16 June 1941; *Journal*, Lewiston, Maine, 16 June 1941; *Boston American*, 16 June 1941; *Lewiston Evening Journal* 16 June 1941; *New York Enquirer*, 26 June 1941 plus 12 other papers. See MS 6150, Box 39, NLA.

\* Casey to McEwen, 6 May 1940, letter, RGC9, NLA.

† Ibid.

‡ Robert Menzies, *The Measure of The Years* (London: Cassell, 1970), p. 6.

experience of the British and Australian systems of government found the reluctance of the Roosevelt Administration to get too far ahead of public opinion a departure from what he believed to be effective leadership. Unlike Menzies, Casey was not impressed with the purely political skills exercised by the President.

Casey would often reflect upon the enormous influence of public opinion on American decision makers, indeed a greater influence than existed in other democracies. All politicians were able to use the media, print and radio, and talk to established American pressure groups, farmers, manufacturers, newspaper publishers and editors, radio executives and broadcasters. Casey needed an edge over his rivals and found it in his ability to fly his own aircraft to meet his audiences. This both facilitated his activities and made him into something of a celebrity, which in turn, enhanced his standing and reputation in a nation that loved celebrities. It is necessary to remember that Casey was a wealthy man and the costs of entertaining these important Americans could not have been met from the salary and allowances that came with the appointment as Minister.

There was not a great deal about the American political system that earned praise from Casey. In 1940, he noted that the President has 'full information' but achieves very little because he has 'practically no power over the Congress'. To make matters worse, 'representative government doesn't exist in this country'; instead, 'Leader writers and columnists largely shape public opinion – admirable people, no doubt but without public responsibility'.\* Casey was no more pleased that, in the United States, newspaper publishers, who were usually the proprietors, set the political stance of their papers.

Casey recorded that he had had lunch with Henry Luce, the founder and publisher of *Time* magazine and Furnas, publisher of the *Saturday Evening Post* on 25 June, itself evidence of his networking skills. Luce was so deeply entrenched in the philosophy of the Republican Party that nothing that Roosevelt did or said could be viewed favourably. As one commentator put it: Luce's fealty to Republicanism came a close third after God and country

---

\* Casey Diaries, 7 June 1940.

and indeed, all three were related to in the continuum of his ideals'.*

Casey may have heard unreliable rumours from Luce and others in the Republican camp. Indeed, Casey recorded an early impression of Harry Hopkins a day after meeting with Luce when he noted, at the height of the Battle of Britain, that Hopkins was '[contrary to the usually unreliable Republican tittle-tattle] very much on our side and willing and eager to discuss practicable means of overcoming the defeatism and pessimism that is sweeping over the USA as to Britain's chances'.† Yet Casey, unsurprisingly, nominated Luce 'as a force to be reckoned with'. In one of his discussions with Casey, Luce shared his opinion that in any partnership with the United Kingdom, it was the United States, the future world leader, that would be the senior partner.‡

During the Battle of Britain, Casey knew that he had to tread carefully, lest he draw the ire of more hostile columnists:

> I have given a lot of thought to what I can usefully say publicly since I have been in this country. I have consulted selected Americans who are well disposed and have political sense. There is a great deal that I can say – and I have been saying it in public speeches and in my NBC broadcast. There is however, a limit beyond which one must not go. An inch over the limit and one runs the risk of being 'written down' by some ill-disposed columnist with a big following. I can tell them the point of view of Australia about the war and what we believe is behind the war – but I must be extremely careful not to lay myself open to the charge that I am telling the American people publicly what to do and advocating intervention in the war.§

Casey then listed the bodies he had spoken to in the terms just described. The list was impressive: National Press Club, Washington; University Club, New York; Economic Club New York; English Speaking Union, Washington; Overseas Writers, Washington; International House, Chicago; Women's Press Club, Washington;

---

\* John Kobler, *Luce. His Time, Life and Fortune* (London, 49 Poland Street: Macdonald Publishing, 1968), p. 177.
† Casey Diaries, 26 June 1940.
‡ Casey Diaries, 28 September 1941.
§ Casey Diaries, 5 June 1940.

American Society of International Law, Washington; English Speaking Union, Chicago; Daughters of British Empire, Chicago: English Speaking Union, Milwaukee; National Broadcasting Company. However, as events in Europe worsened, Casey noted, '... the limits to what I can say have progressively advanced'.*

To maintain the positive image of Australia, Casey found it necessary to wear the public 'mask' that Hudson and Spender referred to. Casey's private descriptions of the American public often reflected his utter disdain as well as his own prejudices. As Casey put it, 'The Irish question is not dead. There are large numbers of Irish in America, who hate Britain ...'† Two senior American cardinals, O'Connell and Dougherty, strongly opposed the United States' entry into World War One.‡ Casey drew attention to a report compiled by the British Library of Information in New York about the political inclinations of Roman Catholics in the United States. The report concluded that, while strongly anti-Nazi, American Catholics continued to be strongly Isolationist. Casey's belief in the importance of this finding is contained in the following comments to the Minister:

> There is no doubt, of course, of the importance of turning Catholic opinion, which is very influential in this country, in the right direction... the suggestion has been made to me that the Australian bishops, many of whom are of Irish origin, might be induced to address an appeal to the hierarchy of the United States asserting as vigorously as possible, the view that the Allies are defending everything which makes the continued practice of religion possible and that every religious authority should rally in their support.

Casey believed that Catholic isolationism was so strong as to be almost anti-Allies, thus leading him to justify his suggestion by emphasising very strongly the wide-spread failure in Catholic circles in the United States to appreciate the true character of the present struggle. Casey was forthright to the point of proposing

---

\* Ibid.
† Casey to McEwen, 26 March 1940, letter, RGC4, NLA.
‡ Charles Callan Tansill, *Back Door to War. The Roosevelt Foreign Policy 1933–1941* (Chicago: Henry Rigney Company, 1952), p. 600.

how the Catholic bishops should publicise their statement.*

Yet if the Irish came in for harsh stereotyping from Casey, this was nothing compared to the scene that Casey claimed confronted him in Florida the following winter:

> Miami beach succeeds in representing in concentrated form almost all the things that I most dislike. It is highly artificial ... and the human element most revolting ...large numbers of rich and offensive Jews – and generally fat, unhealthy and unintelligent people who overdress and sit about and eat and drink and gamble, stay up half the night ... ostentation, silly gossip, physical and mental sloth – vulgar and senseless display of wealth ...†

The problem was not just the Catholics and Jews, but vested interests everywhere, especially the businessmen, in the United States who were working against an American commitment to the war.‡ Above all there were the isolationist politicians, 'small minded, provincial, without any conception of the issues involved or their implications for the future of mankind'.§

The wild card affecting both the European and Pacific theatres of any future war was the Soviet Union. Aware of the pivotal role that the Soviet Union held in the balance of global power, Casey made contact with Konstantin Umansky, the Soviet Ambassador, although he had learnt that the Ambassador was a 'notoriously unreliable' person.¶ However, Casey duly reported to Canberra that the Russian had assured him that the Soviet Union did not propose to intervene any further in the war and that her attack on Finland in the Winter War of November 1939–March 1940 was based on the strategic need to defend Leningrad. Situated only a few miles from the eastern end of the Gulf of Finland, Leningrad, according to the Ambassador, was in an impossible defensive position. Negotiations with Finland had broken down and thus invasion was the only remaining course of action. At that time, the Soviet attack on Finland was regarded by Britain (and Australia) as aggression of a

---

\* Casey to McEwen, 14 June 1940, letter, RGC11, NLA.
† Casey Diaries, 5 January 1941.
‡ See, e.g., Casey Diaries, 27 December 1940.
§ Casey Diaries, 5 June 1940.
¶ Casey to McEwen, 23 April 1940, letter, RGC7, NLA.

kind similar to the German invasion of Poland. Despite assurances given by the Soviet Ambassador that his country 'did not propose to intervene any further in this war, with which Russia was not further concerned', Casey remained suspicious of actual Soviet intentions.* Ideally, Stalin would be drawn into a war against Japan, unlikely though this prospect appeared.

The Winter War between the Soviet Union and Finland offered some prospect of stirring interest in the European war, at least in certain parts of the United States. As Casey noted to his diary, there were 'the large number of Scandinavians in the Middle West influencing the historic Middle West tendency to isolationism'.† Casey was aware that the fate of Finland and the threat to Norway, Sweden and Denmark was causing both rage and fear. Early in his mission, Casey undertook a speaking tour of the Mid-West including Chicago, Madison, Milwaukee and Minneapolis. The importance of public opinion there was made clear to Casey when the worsening situation developing in Europe caused him to reconsider his plans. As he put it to his diary: 'My inclination was to abandon most if not all the visits but I am now told authoritatively that this would cause some resentment ...'.‡ Among those he consulted, Berle and British consular officials, who both recommended that he proceed, the principal reason given – again illustrating the extent of Casey's being perceived as an effective spokesman for Allied interests – was that 'no-one from our side had been in the northern Middle West for a long time' and it was thought necessary to 'show the flag'.§

That the Mid West was the isolationist heartland was not accidental. A substantial segment of Wisconsin's population was descended from German migrants, while other Middle West states such as Minnesota had similar northern European settlers. Few wished the United States to become embroiled in a conflict in Europe, from where they themselves, or their ancestors, had fled. Casey occasionally made these visits flying in his own aircraft and this factor alone aroused levels of interest that initially had

---

\* Ibid.
† Casey to McEwen, 26 March 1940, letter, RGC4, NLA.
‡ Casey to Canberra, 20 May 1940, cablegram, 93, NAA.
§ Casey Diaries, 1 May 1940.

been stirred by Casey's demeanour. For many Mid-Westerners, he fitted the perception of an international diplomat in manner, dress, speech and the particular charm that both he and his wife, Maie, exuded. As Hudson suggests, it is possible that the very qualities that created something of a barrier in his political relations in the Australian context, perhaps summed up succinctly in the phrase, 'the Australian Anthony Eden' worked in the very opposite direction in the United States.

Casey's thirst for useful information led him to engage in what might be described as unconventional practices. Information was Casey's stock-in-trade. Early on, he was very cautious about what information he divulged and to whom. He was obviously receiving information from the British Embassy, but was unsure about the limits of what he could relay to Canberra. Reporting to McEwen on 23 April 1940 about the enthusiastic British response to an American request that its ships might be refitted at Singapore, Casey warned:

> I need hardly say that the above is of absolute secrecy. My source of information is completely reliable, but both my informing you of this and the information itself must never be mentioned – if I am to preserve my position here.[*]

As if regretting that he shared the information, Casey concluded by warning that 'you do not read too much into the above' as the request may have reflected military exigencies rather than having a political significance.

Casey became bolder over time. In a brief note in his diary, written in early June 1940, he made the revelation that he sent copies of his reports to Australia to Bruce in London. The off-hand manner in which Casey discloses this practice suggests that he perceived nothing amiss in it:

> It is necessary to put down the background of affairs of the last week or so in order to knit together the cables that I have sent to Australia and repeated to SMB [Stanley Melbourne Bruce]. For the first two or three days of the invasion of Holland Belgium, I experienced a feeling of depression and foreboding but this passed and after that I spent a fair

---

[*] Casey to McEwen, letter, 23 April 1940, RGC7, NLA.

proportion of my time in putting heart into people – Allied and neutral.*

It is conceivable that the practice was in accordance with Australian diplomatic procedures existing at that time. It is also conceivable that within the new Australian diplomatic service, there were no policies or procedures laid down on matters such as this. Casey's reports, copies of which he was sending to Bruce, were headed 'Secret', denoting a clear indication of their status and the restricted circulation applying to such documents. There is no indication on the messages Casey was sending to the Prime Minister or the Minister for External Affairs that a copy was being simultaneously forwarded to Bruce in London. A more benign interpretation would be that both men regarded the practice simply as an exchange of information. Both were Australian public servants, serving their country abroad. It was only natural that each saw the need to learn as much as possible about the momentous events that were unfolding every day.

Moreover, the advising of Bruce by Casey was not a one-way transaction. Casey noted in his diary: 'I see Lothian almost every day and I see the cables that are passing direct (or through Lothian, or through Kennedy) between Winston and the President'.† If Casey can be criticised for passing on information to a colleague, then it is possible for the same criticism to be levelled at Lothian, the British Ambassador for passing on this correspondence to Casey. Indeed, Casey told McEwen that he showed Lothian his letters 'to check my own impressions'.‡ Finally, it must be remembered that the year was 1940, that France was in the process of capitulation and that Britain and the Commonwealth were totally alone. In such a time, an air of desperation would not be impossible. For the players in that conflict, knowing as much as possible would be a paramount consideration.

Yet Casey's knowledge was evidently far from perfect. After Pearl Harbor, Casey was moved to note that one reason why the situation was now so perilous was the poor flow of information

---

\* Casey Diaries, 5 June 1940.
† Casey Diaries, 15 June 1940.
‡ Casey to McEwen, 4 April 1940, letter, RGC4, 1940. NLA.

between London and the Dominions over issues such as reinforcing Singapore. According to Casey:

> A fundamental factor in the war situation of today, and the last year or so, is that we [the British peoples] have failed rather badly in the business of keeping in touch with each other – the old problem of bad liaison. We in Australia have failed to establish and maintain adequate appreciation of what had been going on in the minds of the British War Cabinet …*

Casey himself could hardly be accused of failing to make efforts to facilitate just such an exchange of information. On occasions, the information confirmed Casey's and Australia's worst fears. Another matter of vital concern to Casey was the state of American readiness for war, should its leaders decide to intervene on the Allied side. Casey well understood that the British navy was the point of connection between the security of Britain, the United States, and Australia. Casey's networking skills in pre-War Washington enabled him to receive briefings and to participate in discussions that might otherwise have been denied him. For instance, the Naval attaché at the British Embassy, Captain Curzon-Howe explained to him that, in early 1939, 'practically the whole American fleet, concentrated at Norfolk, Virginia had been sent to the Pacific region'. Casey noted that the United States had insufficient ships to maintain appropriate strength in both the Atlantic and Pacific Oceans. The transfer meant that only four old battleships remained in the Atlantic. Approved by the President, the transfer reflected an American fear of Japan's intentions.† Casey also detected a growing realisation in the United States that the Royal Navy was primarily responsible for safe-guarding the Atlantic and indeed, the continued existence of the British Navy was the *sine qua non* that made American isolationism possible.‡ While the secret agreement between the Admiralty and the United States Navy of May 1939 allowed American ships to take command of the western and southern Atlantic, should war break out between Germany and the United States, there was no similar agreement for the Pacific

---
\* Casey Diaries, 6 January 1942.
† Casey to McEwen, 27 March 1940, letter, RGC3, NLA.
‡ Casey to McEwen, 23 April 1940, letter, RGC6, NLA.

where the United States studiously avoided committing itself to defending Britain's empire.

There was much to be concerned about in the statistics of the American armed forces, gathered by Embassy staff in Washington and conveyed by Casey to Canberra in May 1940. This report was the first indication that Casey, since arriving in the United States, was able to assess American offensive capability. He undoubtedly considered that the disposition of American aircraft carriers and war ships in the Pacific vis-à-vis the Atlantic conveyed an appreciation by Washington of the primacy of the Pacific. He reported that of the entire American fleets of fifteen battleships, 37 cruisers and six aircraft carriers, twelve battleships, 29 cruisers and four carriers were based either on the Pacific coast or at Pearl Harbor.* This disposition arose from a strategic plan by the US Army and Navy and was based on the hypothesis that the United States would join the European colonial powers in defending their common interests in the western Pacific against attack by Japan.

While the naval strength quoted by Casey might appear to be numerically satisfactory, at least in peacetime, it was seriously inadequate to cope with any prolonged period of hostilities. The strength of the Army, the Army Air Force and the Naval Air Force was, in Casey's estimation, 'less than satisfactory'.† Casey's judgments were much too benign. The armed forces of the United States in 1940 were so inadequate that the security of the nation and indeed the security of the western world were jeopardized. *The Official History of the United States Army* states that, from 1918, the armed forces of the United States underwent an almost continuous weakening for a decade and a half. In 1919, the total strength of the Army was 846,498. It dropped dramatically until, in 1939, it was 188,565. Twelve months later, as the deterioration of international relations assumed such critical importance, the number increased to a paltry 267,767.‡ The emasculation of the armed forces extended beyond personnel. The equipment remaining at the end of the

---

\* Casey to McEwen, 6 May 1940, letter, RGC8, NLA.
† At that time, the United States did not possess a separate Air Force.
‡ Mark Skinner Watson, *United States Army in World War II. Chief of Staff: Prewar Plans and Preparations* (Washington, D.C: Historical Division, Department of the Army, 1950), p. 16.

Great War became increasingly obsolescent: there had been some support for directing resources to a strong Navy on the grounds that it was 'the first line of defence, the only really necessary line of defence for the time being'.* As Casey put it to McEwen on 8 May 1940, not much could be expected, given 'the strength (or lack of it) of the three American fighting services. It is not a pleasant picture. Clearly the help that America could give quickly if and when she comes in would be largely moral'.†

Casey saw reason for real concern at a statement by the Assistant Secretary of War that despite the efforts to build up the Army's resources, 'some fifteen months would elapse after Mobilization Day before even a million men could be adequately supplied with the more critical items of ordinance equipment … we could raise two or three million men but we could not furnish their weapons and supplies in less than two years'. There was here a dual problem in that not only were the Americans not particularly interested in Australia, the country that so many hoped would prove the salvation perhaps of Britain and certainly Australia, lacked the capacity to do so.‡

It is clear that Casey made good use of his first months in Washington to push back against Washington's blindness when it came to Australia and Australian interests. Roosevelt was the target, but the strategy was to influence American decision making by working on those individuals, such as Berle, and key opinion makers in the media and polling, to whom the President might listen. Here Casey was not just hard-working, but clearly effective.

---

\* Watson, *United States Army*, p. 15.
† Casey to McEwen, 8 May 1940, letter, RGC10, NLA.
‡ Matloff and Snell, *The United States Army in World War II*, section titled 'The Study – War with Japan', p. 1.

*Chapter Five*

# Summer 1940: Casey's Battle for Britain

A criticism that has been made of Casey is that he was single-mindedly obsessed with saving Britain when he should have pursued the narrower focus of pushing Australian interests.

The reality was more complex. Casey did focus upon saving Britain during the summer of 1940 when invasion seemed a real possibility. Yet he justifiably argued that Britain's salvation was vital to both American and Australian interests. Moreover, it was because he was arguing for American aid to Britain that Casey was able to establish himself in Washington as a diplomatic force to be reckoned with.

Within three months of Casey's arrival in Washington, it seemed that Britain was about to be invaded and probably defeated. In summary, the situation Casey faced at the beginning of his term, bleak as it may have been, grew immeasurably worse during the following six months of 1940, his first six months in Washington. In January, France and Britain seemed strong enough to resist any German adventures, the Low Countries and Scandinavia had not been attacked by the Wehrmacht, Italy had not joined Germany in any military sense either in Europe or North Africa and the Soviet Union's relations with Germany remained enigmatically neutral while it attempted to cope with Finnish resistance to the Soviet invasion.

By the end of June, however, France, the Low Countries, Denmark and Norway had been overrun by German forces, continental Europe was virtually being governed from Berlin,

Italy had joined Germany to form the Axis, with substantial forces in North Africa, while Finland had been forced to capitulate to the Soviet Union, a defeat seen as detrimental to the Allies. The suddenness of the French capitulation on 17 June is well illustrated by the assurances given to Menzies by Lord Caldecote, the UK Dominions Secretary, a few weeks before, as late as 29 and 30 May that, 'we should not like it to be thought that we regard a French collapse as imminent or as other than a possibility' and that 'there is no reason to assume that anything is radically wrong with the French Army'.*

The month of May 1940 was the crucial time when the full enormity of Britain's isolation as the sole combatant in the conflict with Hitler, the only nation still standing, became vividly real. Moreover, following the collapse of France, the question of whether Britain would fight on against the overwhelming superiority of Germany or succumb to a negotiated peace was debated passionately and forensically at the highest levels in London. Britain's leaders were deeply divided as they faced the helplessness of being the sole remaining obstacle to the creation of a Nazi Europe.† The world awaited the launch of the German war machine on a Britain that was clearly unready for a fight for survival.

Churchill became Prime Minister on 10 May 1940; a coalition government was formed against the background of German troops pouring into Belgium and The Netherlands. Despite the inevitable Cabinet re-shuffle, there was not complete confidence in Churchill as leader. Two days earlier, Sir Alexander Cadogan, Under Secretary and Permanent Head of the British Foreign Office, speculating on who would take over if Chamberlain resigned, wrote in his diary, 'Winston useless'.‡ One Parliamentarian wrote: 'The Tories don't trust Winston ... there seems to be some inclination in Whitehall to believe that Winston will be a complete failure and that Neville

---

\* Caldecote to Menzies, 29 May 1940, cablegram, 172 in *DAFP*, Vol. III, Doc. 304 and Caldecote to Menzies, 30 May 1940, cablegram, 174 in *DAFP*, Vol. III, Doc. 315.
† John Lukacs, *Five Days in London, May 1940* (New Haven: Yale University Press, 2001).
‡ *Cadogan Diaries*, 8 May 1940, p. 277.

[Chamberlain] will return'.* Nor was there complete unanimity in the new leadership team. Lord Halifax, now Foreign Secretary, was still entertaining the possibility of negotiating with Hitler.

Lukacs has documented the intense debates and arguments that characterised those four days of debates and arguments which were confined solely to the War Cabinet. Elements in the cabinet, led by Halifax, sought for several days in late May to devise some kind of accommodation with Hitler, which, while saving Britain from the destruction that had been inflicted upon other parts of Europe, would turn Britain into a vassal state, perhaps even retaining a puppet king (the name of the previous king, now the Duke of Windsor was mentioned in that context) but essentially governed from Berlin. As early as December 1939, Halifax had told the cabinet that if the French dropped out, 'we should not be able to carry on the war by ourselves'.†

The motivation driving Halifax was not a willingness to accede to the demands of Hitler as such, but rather an ardent desire to avoid the bloody and destructive consequences of a German invasion and a fiercely fought battle within the British Isles. The memories of the death and destruction of World War I were too vividly implanted in his memory. Churchill, in resisting the very concept of negotiating with Hitler, either directly or through an intermediary such as Mussolini, anticipated that Hitler's demands would be so great, including the handover of Gibraltar, Malta, the British Fleet, the naval bases 'and much more', that resistance leading to defeat could be no worse: 'We should become a slave state, through a British government which would be Hitler's puppet, which would be set up'.‡ The historian, Ian Kershaw, argues that Britain's decision, in May 1940, to 'stay in the war', that is, to resist the expected German invasion and to mount a repulse to Hitler's ambitions:

> was far from being the obvious, even inevitable, decision that some subsequent events [and some persuasive historical writing] have made it seem. The War Cabinet seriously

---

\* Lord Davidson to Stanley Baldwin, 11 May 1940, letter, quoted in Lukacs, *Five Days*, p. 14.
† Cited in Lukacs, *Five Days*, p. 126.
‡ Hugh Dalton. *The Fateful Years: Memoirs. 1939–1945* (London, 1957). Cited in Lukacs, *Five Days*, pp. 4–5.

deliberated the choices for three days, with a new prime minister still tentatively feeling his way, the British army seemingly lost at Dunkirk, no immediate prospect of help from the United States and a German invasion in the near future presumed to be very likely.*

Not only was this crucial debate not revealed publicly at the time, Churchill, in writing his history of the Second World War deliberately omitted all references to it and in fact, reported the opposite: 'Future generations may deem it noteworthy that the supreme question of whether we should fight on alone never found a place upon the War Cabinet agenda. It was taken for granted and as a matter of course by these men of all parties in the State, and we were much too busy to waste time upon such unreal, academic issues'.† As Reynolds has pointed out, this assertion is strictly correct but seriously misleading. There were no items on the Cabinet minutes headed 'Surrender' or 'Negotiated Peace', but while Churchill wrote that he and his colleagues were much too busy to waste time on such unreal, academic issues, Reynolds asserts that 'those issues had seemed all too real in May 1940' and that 'the way he concealed the debate is the most significant cover-up in *Their Finest Hour*'.‡

It is uncertain how much Casey, in Washington, was aware of the day-by-day arguments during the crucial week of 24 to 28 May 1940 and what he knew was most likely to come from Bruce, who was close to Chamberlain and Halifax, but often at loggerheads with Churchill. Edwards makes the point that Bruce and Casey frequently discussed proposals before submitting them jointly to Canberra.§ In a 'Most Secret' message to Menzies, on 16 May, less than a week after Churchill's ascendancy to the prime ministership, Bruce wrote that the 'Present War Cabinet showing more initiative and vision than predecessors in preparing to meet situation when it arises'.¶

---

\* Kershaw, *Fateful Choices*, pp. 7–8.
† Winston Churchill, *Their Finest Hour* (London: Cassell and Co, 1949), p. 157.
‡ David Reynolds, *In Command of History. Churchill Fighting and Writing the Second World War* (London: Allen Lane, 2004), p. 169.
§ Edwards, *Prime Ministers and Diplomats*, p. 127.
¶ Bruce to Menzies, 16 May 1940, cablegram, 331, A3195. 1.3299, NAA.

The Australians had their reservations about political developments in London. Just a few months earlier, Menzies had savagely criticised Churchill. Obviously deeply opposed to Churchill's strong opposition to any kind of negotiations with Hitler, Menzies told Bruce: 'I cannot tell you adequately how much I am convinced that Winston is a menace. He is a publicity seeker; he stirs up hatreds in a world already seething with them and he is lacking in judgment ..."*

Casey, though, came to see the positive side of Churchill, telling his diary that the messages that came from London to the President 'are clearly dictated by Winston himself as they are in his unmistakeable style – and are very good'.† Casey was clearly impressed with Churchill's determination to fight and the pressure he was attempting to pile on the Americans. More importantly, Casey must have appreciated how highly he was regarded in Washington and London to be given access to the correspondence between Churchill and Roosevelt.

Lukacs, in attempting to describe the motivations of Churchill in those crucial days, quotes some of the Prime Minister's utterances which go some way towards delineating the choices that Casey would have perceived: 'In these British Islands that look so small upon the map, we stand, the faithful guardians of the right and dearest hopes of a dozen states and nations now gripped and tormented in a base and cruel servitude'.‡ Churchill saw Hitler and his Reich as incarnating something evil and dangerous and saw himself as saviour not only of Britain but of much else besides – essentially, of all Europe.

Churchill addressed Parliament on 28 May, in which he spoke of 'the world cause to which we have vowed ourselves', and again a few weeks later [14 July], when he declared that Britain was fighting 'by ourselves alone, but not for ourselves alone'.§ The real import of this message might be summed up in the conclusion that Lukas

---

\* Menzies to Bruce, 22 February 1940, letter, M103, NAA. See also *DAFP*, Vol. III, Doc. 71.
† Casey Diaries, 15 June 1940.
‡ Churchill in a broadcast to the United States, quoted in John Lukacs, *Five Days*, p. 213.
§ Lukacs, *Five Days*, p. 213.

reached: 'At the end of May 1940 and for some time thereafter, not only the end of a European war but the end of Western civilisation was near'.\*

This worsened situation invites the question, how did this unexpected and rapid deterioration impinge upon Casey's perception of his role in Washington? Did the frightening prospect of a German invasion of Britain lead him to conclude that his efforts should best be directed at attempting to convince the Americans of the monumental importance of doing everything possible to rescue the last bastion of Western democracy in Europe from subjugation by the Nazis? Or did he adhere to his commission to make Australia's voice heard in the corridors of Washington and to make the United States aware of the strategic importance of the Pacific region?

In the summer of 1940, Casey clearly chose not to stick to a narrow interpretation of his brief of representing an Australia confronting nothing more than a possible threat from Japan, but instead broadened his efforts to help represent a United Kingdom facing almost immediate invasion by a real and superior foe. Casey's encounters in Washington and his clearer understanding of the global situation led him to reason that the immediate threat was not to Australia but to Britain. The threat to Australia from Japan was still just that, a threat and one which was not universally perceived as grave. There was certainly a common thread running through Churchill's messages to his Australian counterpart at this time, that a Japanese attempt to threaten Australia was not likely.† In the face of this, Casey could hardly make his first priority the gaining of American assurances to assist Australia in such an unlikely eventuality. Moreover, a German victory over Britain would have dire consequences for Australia because of the probable loss of the Royal Navy. Although no one could predict the fate of the British fleets, there was uncertainty that Britain would go to Australia's aid if invasion occurred.

As France collapsed, Australia attempted to persuade Roosevelt to give more American aid to Britain. According to Edwards, it was

---

\* Ibid., p. 217.
† Stanley, *Invading Australia,* p. 68

Bruce in London, in consultation with Casey in Washington, who suggested the appeals that Menzies made to Roosevelt for assistance in May–June 1940.* On 26 May Menzies cabled Casey asking him to 'present' to Roosevelt a heart-felt request for American participation in the major disaster unfolding in Europe. Much of Menzies' reasoning had already been canvassed by Churchill in his entreaties to the American president but Menzies' command of language was no less arresting than his British counterpart and deserves quoting, at least in part. Having asked for practical help for Britain in terms of military equipment, Menzies tugged at American heart-strings over its relationship to Australia:

> But quite plainly, and I know that you would wish me to speak plainly, without the most prompt material assistance from the United States there must be grave danger of a state of affairs rapidly developing in which the power of Great Britain to defend liberty and free institutions is destroyed and in which, we, your English-speaking neighbours on the Pacific Basin, must find our own independence immediately imperilled ... There is in Australia a great belief in your friendliness and goodwill. We feel that we are fighting for immortal things which you value as we do. On behalf of my own people I beg for your earnest consideration and swift action.†

Like Curtin's 'Look to America' plea the following year, Menzies emphasised Australia's dire vulnerability. To be fair, Menzies used his message also to emphasise the self-interest of the United States in not allowing Britain's world-wide influence to be diluted. Menzies, a few days earlier, had written to Churchill, strongly urging him to approach the American president in similar terms.‡ Churchill's reply was almost dismissive: 'Every form of intimate personal appeal and most cogent arguments have already been sent to Roosevelt ... If you and the other Prime

---

\* Edwards, 'R.G. Menzies Appeals to the United States', pp. 64–70.
† Menzies to Roosevelt, 26 May 1940, cablegram, unnumbered, A1608. A41/1/5 (ii), NAA. Menzies to Casey, 26 May 1940, cablegram, unnumbered, copies to P.M.s, Canada, New Zealand, and South Africa, AA: A1608. A41/1/5 (ii), NAA.
‡ Menzies to Churchill, 22 May 1940, cablegram, unnumbered, FA: A3196, 0.3135, NAA.

Ministers feel able to follow up our appeal by a personal appeal from yourselves, this would be very welcome to us'.*

For all his attachments to Britain, Menzies was realistic enough to read the signs and these told him that in the event of Australia being threatened in the Pacific region, Britain, fighting for survival, would be unable to offer Australia anything in the way of military or naval support. Yet Menzies struggled in his efforts to find an argument as to why the United States should offer to save Australia. His subsequent appeal of 14 June 1940 to Roosevelt betrayed an ever increasing note of desperation:†

> The friendship of Australia as an integral part of the British Empire is of importance to the United States. The British and American people have too much in common and may I add, too many precious ideas at risk and, of importance to the United States in this turbulent world, not to realise that, whatever their organic relations might be, they are exercising similar functions and that safety and development of each is of profound importance to the other.‡

It is conjectural whether Menzies actually believed that arguments about the shared heritage of Britons, Australians and Americans would carry any weight in Washington. He was acutely aware that Churchill had made similar appeals to Roosevelt and yet, for the last six months of 1940 Britain had faced the distinct possibility of invasion, while the United States virtually looked on, Roosevelt prevented from assisting because of the November elections.

The relevance of the Churchill/Halifax debate to Casey's responsibilities lies in the reality that Washington, in fact, was the focus of Britain's only real hope of holding off Hitler. Casey saw his position as especially vital in the business of networking because, while the average American is 'a free and spontaneous creature', by contrast 'the average member of the British Diplomatic service is a rather shy creature, the product of the British Public School system,

---

\* Churchill to Menzies, 24 May 1940, cablegram, M29, FA. A3195.1.3546, NAA.
† Menzies to Roosevelt, 26 May 1940, A1608. A41/1/5 (ii), NAA.
‡ Menzies to Roosevelt, 14 June 1940, cablegram, unnumbered, *DAFP*, Vol. III, Doc. 380.

and definitely not a good and quick mixer'.* Casey implied that he, by contrast, was a very 'good and quick mixer'. He was happy to serve alongside Lothian as, in Lothian's phrase, 'the second blade of the scissors'.†

Casey offered his advice freely and occasionally struck a note of optimism as he looked for an effective strategy to lever the United States into the war. Early in June, Lothian suggested to him that they (Lothian and Casey) should advocate a conference in London to discuss what action should be taken if the worst happened, meaning the capitulation of Britain. Casey expressed strong opposition. He argued that in the absence of actual knowledge of what the United States would do, such a conference would be of no use. Further, if the United States did 'come in', there would be a complete change and re-appraisal of strategy.‡

Hull later revealed that Roosevelt's decision to run for a third term was an immediate consequence of Hitler's conquest of France. He explains it thus: 'Up to that time, the President, in personal conversations with me and with some Democratic Party leaders had indicated his expectation and wish that I should be his successor'. According to Hull, Roosevelt's decision 'was an immediate consequence of Hitler's conquest of France and the spectre of Britain standing alone between the conqueror and ourselves. Our dangerous position induced President Roosevelt to run for a third time'.§

A week after the invasion of France, Casey told Canberra that events of the past few days had profoundly shaken American complacency: '[The] whole country, particularly Washington, is extremely nervous and depressed at realisation of their own unpreparedness and the United Sates may be menaced by trend of events in Europe'. Yet, while Casey detected a growing belief that while the United States should give Britain all possible assistance, there was no groundswell of opinion for the United States to become a participant in the war. Casey, shrewdly, warned that Australia should avoid making any criticism in the press

* Casey Diaries, 22 June 1940.
† Casey Diaries, 14 October 1940.
‡ Casey Diaries, 5 June 1940.
§ Hull, *Memoirs*, Vol. I, p. 855.

or elsewhere of American 'tardiness'. Nor should Australia give any indication that the United States should offer assistance to Australia. In the context of the American elections, Casey reported that many candidates believed that to speak out what he (the candidate) believes is the truth would cost him the Isolationist vote.* His reading of the mood of the American people however, detected a denial of the awesome prospect of the United States remaining the only democracy on the globe.†

Both Casey and Lothian shared the same combination of anger and bewilderment when it came to understanding the Administration's refusal to mobilise the American people. Lothian reported to London in May:

> The United States is still dominated by fear of involvement and incapable of positive action ... the war is steadily drifting nearer to them and they know it ... they are not pacifists [but] are highly belligerent by temperament ... the President would like to take action vigorously on the lines of his own principle 'Everything short of war' ... all the other candidates, especially the Republicans, none of whom are familiar with international affairs, are paralysed by fear of being charged with a desire to get the United States into war ... they are completely mesmerised by fear of the great god, 'the American Electorate'.‡

Or as Casey put it: "Self-interest' is the only lever – and it was not clear to me (or to Lothian) ... how to arouse this motive'. The 'motive' to activate this American 'self-interest' would have to be the preservation of the British fleet.§ The Roosevelt administration could only have been alarmed by a message from the American Ambassador in France, William Bullitt, that Britain's reluctance to dispatch more aircraft to France in the last weeks of the German invasion of that country was explained by the possibility that Britain would use the Royal Air Force and the Royal Navy as bargaining points in future negotiations with Germany.¶ According

---

\* Casey to Dept. of External Affairs, 17 May 1940, cablegram 88, NAA.
† Ibid.
‡ Casey to McEwen, letter, 8 May 1940, letter, RGC10, NLA.
§ Casey Diaries, 5 June 1940.
¶ Hull, *Memoirs*, Vol. I, p. 744.

to Charmley, Roosevelt believed that no matter what happened to Britain, such as a negotiated peace, the British Fleet must be kept from German hands, and become part of the United States fleet.[*] The prospect of the largest navy in the world falling under control of Germany would have catastrophic consequences for the United States.

The view in Washington was that a negotiated settlement between Britain and Germany was more likely than an invasion. Roosevelt's long-held opposition to colonialism and, in particular, the British Empire, led him to believe that to achieve that result, Britain would have to accept some form of governance from Berlin. Under no circumstance would Roosevelt consider American troops undertaking any adventure that would have the effect of propping up the British Empire.

A serious flaw in Roosevelt's argument lay in defining 'the British Empire'. The United States' longest border was with an integral component of the Commonwealth, Canada, which, in American eyes, stood for 'British Empire'. Roosevelt had already indicated that any attack on Canada would almost certainly bring an armed American response. Moreover, the Bahamas and Jamaica, both members of the Commonwealth, were close neighbours of the United States and it is difficult to believe that any European takeover of such close neighbours would be viewed benignly in Washington. In any event, these islands were within the ambit of the Monroe Doctrine.

For Casey, Roosevelt's position was not clear and in some ways, inconsistent. He believed that, privately, Roosevelt was far more interventionist than he appeared and that simply following public opinion was not the complete explanation. Roosevelt's failure to provide leadership of the American people would have disgusted Casey who firmly believed that leaders should lead, not follow, in this case following public opinion that was plainly ignorant and or dismissive of the worsening world situation. Lowenthal has advanced an explanation of Roosevelt's position as a series of fits and starts, whose interconnection the President himself denied at the time:

---

[*] Charmley, *Churchill's Grand Alliance*, p. 16.

These policy decisions could be grouped into three broad consecutive periods. Each of these periods was dominated by a thematic unifying search for a type of policy ... which shaped what he wanted and what he hoped to avoid. Each of these periods was ill-defined at the outset and was abandoned through the pressure of events, requiring the beginning of yet another search.\*

Casey suspected that the American failure to rearm may have constituted a more practical reason for Roosevelt's inaction, telling his diary on 5 June 1940 that 'It may be that the President realises that, even if they intervened in this war, they have virtually no fighting services to fight with-outside the Navy that is virtually stuck in the Pacific'. Even so Casey hoped that not only would American prestige boost the Allied cause but that 'they could send a few divisions, a few dozen destroyers, a fair tonnage of merchant shipping, a few squadrons of aircraft, and could help with equipment far faster than they are doing as neutrals'.†

Casey admitted to himself the next day that his speculations amounted to no more than 'wishful thinking'.‡ Of course the question has to be posed of what might the Americans have done? Immediately after the capitulation of France, the sending of a substantial contingent of American troops to Britain or the greater involvement of American naval units in the Atlantic, specifically to protect merchant ships carrying food and other essentials to Great Britain, would have been achievable without the necessity of a formal American declaration of war. There would have been political risks involved however, especially in the stationing of American troops in Britain. It certainly was not going to happen in Roosevelt's re-election year.

Casey's ire was accentuated by a letter from Roosevelt to Menzies, sent through the Australian Legation and which was a reply to the pleading letter that the Australian Prime Minister

---

\* Mark M. Lowenthal, 'Roosevelt and the Coming of the War' in Walter Laqueur (ed.), *The Second World War. Essays in Military and Political History* (London: Sage Publications Ltd, 1982), p. 50.
† Casey Diaries, 5 June 1940.
‡ Casey Diaries, 6 June 1940.

had sent to the President a few days earlier.* Roosevelt was effusive but resolute in re-affirming the traditional American stance of non-participation in countering the spread of Nazism rapidly engulfing Europe. The letter was dated 23 June, two days after French representatives signed the formal surrender documents at Compiegne, thus leaving Britain standing alone. Roosevelt put things this way:

> I have given your message my full and most careful consideration ... I do not fail to appreciate the dangers to the United States and to the world implicit in an Allied defeat ... America's sympathies lie with Allied governments ... to the Premier of France, I send my assurances of my utmost sympathy ... in like manner and subject to the same limitations, I want to assure you that so long as the peoples of the British Commonwealth of Nations continue in the defence of their liberty so long may they be assured that material and supplies will be sent them from the United States in ever increasing quantities and kinds.†

Casey, in a reflective mood on 2 July 1940, asked himself if nations ever went against their 'material interests'. The two examples of this occurring, he claimed, were the abolition of slavery and the free ride that British naval power offered to 'North [and South] America and Australia, South Africa and New Zealand'. According to Casey's figures, the Australian taxpayer spent less than one pound per head on its defence compared to more than three pounds per head for the British taxpayer.‡ Whether British altruism – as Casey claimed – was the reason might be debated, but Casey's general point that the British navy carried the burden of defence in the Atlantic was difficult to argue against.

All the representatives of Britain and Australia, Casey foremost among them, pressed the point that it was the Royal Navy which made the Monroe Doctrine viable. According to Casey, the American leadership knew the truth of this proposition, even if they would not declare it. As Casey put it in

---

\* Menzies to Roosevelt, 14 June 1940, A3196. O.3829, NAA.
† Roosevelt to Menzies, 23 June 1940, cablegram, 133, A3195.I.4695, NAA.
‡ Casey Diaries, 2 July 1940.

a letter to McEwen on 4 April 1940:

> Lord Lothian maintains [and he believes that the President and others in high places here agree] that for generations until quite lately, it was the British Fleet and not the American Fleet that maintained the Monroe Doctrine.*

The Doctrine was promulgated in 1823 and yet it was not until 'relatively lately' that the United States possessed a fleet of any great significance, a fleet capable of enforcing some kind of limited American hegemony over the two American continents, North America and South America. Even in 1940, the United States was unable to maintain significant fleets in both the Atlantic and Pacific Oceans. In other words, according to Casey's reasoning, the United States was unable to defend the two American continents both on the Atlantic and Pacific sides.† The only practicable arrangement therefore was for Britain to look after the Atlantic and the United States, the Pacific.

The corollary raised the question, why did the United States stand aloof from the grave threat facing Britain and pretend that the European conflict was of no consequence to American security? Casey became increasingly displeased at the President's almost obsessive interest in the future of the British Fleet, denoting to Casey that while Roosevelt was unprepared to give Britain meaningful support and assistance, he was most anxious to acquire the entire Royal Navy should Britain capitulate. From Casey's perspective, the Americans appeared at times almost as vultures circling the carcass of the British Empire. In a diary entry, Casey referred to a discussion with Roosevelt on 28 May 1940: 'I did not, at the time, appreciate the significance of what he had to say about the urgent importance of the preservation of the British Navy at all costs'. ‡

According to Casey, American concern about the British fleet reflected a realisation that it was the same British fleet that had been protecting the United States for years and that if the British fleet were to disappear, the Americans would have to set about defending

---
\* Casey to McEwen, 4 April 1940, letter, RGC5, NLA.
† Ibid.
‡ Casey Diaries, 5 June 1940.

themselves, which Casey said was 'unthinkable'. Casey quoted with approval an observation by Mark Sullivan, a journalist and friend of Roosevelt whom Casey cultivated: 'We have a national policy – the Monroe Doctrine. We think this policy has been enforced by the United States Navy. But it was never we who enforced it. It is the British Navy that kept European nations from seizing lands in the Western hemisphere. The British Navy prevented them, [thus] enforcing the Monroe Doctrine for us."

Casey had circulated a 'draft' hammering the point that for the Americans to take over the responsibilities required by the Monroe Doctrine in the Pacific, it would need to ensure the security of naval bases in the North Atlantic. Up until now, the Americans had relied upon the British to perform these tasks. Casey's drafting of these 'talking points' for columnists confirmed not only his growing confidence in his powers of manipulation, but also his grasp of strategic issues on both the Atlantic and the Pacific sides of the world.

Casey was irritated above all by the complacency of the Americans. On 2 July 1940, in one of his bleakest assessments, he told his diary that:

> There is no spirit in the American people today and they'll have to go through hell in the next ten years to produce some spirit. Their only concern now is safety and self preservation.[†]

Indeed, Casey's diary entries are scathing of the United States and Americans to the point where the reader would likely conclude that he was as anti-American as Berle was Anglophobic. A diary entry from July 1940 was typical of his acute sense of American betrayal of a good cause:

> The spectacle is a humiliating one of a great nation twittering with indecision and inaction, willing to wound but yet afraid to strike even in its own defence – tangled in the toils of domestic political manoeuvring at a vital moment – realising that the British are fighting their fight – yet giving inconsequential assistance – cursing Germany and yet yapping at Britain.[‡]

---

\* Casey Diaries, 4 July 1940.
† Casey Diaries, 2 July 1940.
‡ Casey Diaries, 12 July 1940.

Casey became increasingly forthright in July 1940 as he did his best to agitate the policy makers. When Under Secretary of State, Sumner Welles, speculated about the fate of the Royal Navy in the event of a successful German invasion of Great Britain, Casey retorted that the navy would not surrender but probably immolate their ships in attacking German ports, a view that Welles protested was illogical. 'People aren't logical in such circumstances', Casey persisted, adding that they would change their minds only if there was some eventual chance of the United States entering the war.\* Casey knew that Welles, and Roosevelt if they were relayed to him, would find these words provocative.

Hull told Casey in June 1940, as the full extent of the German mastery in Europe became evident, that he was under no illusions 'as to the seriousness of the situation or of its implications for America'. He confessed to Casey that he had persisted, to the point of boredom, in rubbing into Congressmen and Senators what a German victory would mean for the United States and that the United States would be obliged to do all its negotiations with other countries through Berlin or Tokyo.† Casey left this interview with Hull by claiming that he could see no satisfactory end to the existing situation unless the United States declared war and 'came in with us'. If this were to happen, however unpleasant the next few months would be, he believed that the situation could be retrieved by the throttling of Germany through the blockade. Casey records that Hull made no direct reply to this other than he hoped and prayed that Britain could 'last out for the next four or five months'.‡

Hull noted the desperate persistence of Casey in June 1940. Casey told Hull that he (Casey) and S.M. Bruce, the Australian High Commissioner in Britain, were 'emphatically' of the opinion that Germany would conquer Britain and that he would be extremely interested to see the United States declare war on Germany. Casey reasoned that as the United States was doing everything possible to sell equipment and supplies to the Allies, a declaration of war was an obvious corollary and that the effect

---

\* Joseph P. Lash, *Roosevelt and Churchill 1939–1941. The Partnership That Saved the West* (London: Andre Deutsch, 1977), p. 143.
† Casey Diaries, 6 June 1940.
‡ Ibid.

morally of such a declaration would be very great. Hull promptly replied that it was 'unthinkable' in the present situation'.*

Yet, curiously, Casey's challenging Hull over America's determination to remain out of the war does not sit with his remarks in a letter to McEwen of 5 June: 'It needs all the self-command one possesses not to be bitter and recriminatory towards this country'.† Certainly, this latter comment fits the perception of his reluctance to express a view that would not be kindly received by his listener, a reluctance that, on the basis of the two instances quoted above, he obviously sometimes foreswore.

In the dark summer of 1940, Casey reflected not just on American inaction, but Australian mistakes. In retrospect, he regretted that Australia had neglected participating in what he termed, 'international affairs', leaving them to Britain to handle, instead concentrating on domestic affairs and domestic politics. When such matters were discussed, 'the ignorant prejudices of individuals had a field day to the exclusion of calm deliberation. We grasped the shadow and let the substance go'.‡

In his daily dealings with the Administration, Casey maintained a formal, gracious demeanour. Privately, his diary discloses a deeply held anger and frustration at the reality that Britain stood utterly alone and her survival was very much in doubt. Unable to contain his exasperation with American foot-dragging, Casey committed to paper, a lengthy, considered statement, which he wrote for his own personal satisfaction and kept in his diary without sending it to anyone:

> I have been at a loss to know what attitude to take. They [the Roosevelt Administration] are apparently quite un-moved, or perhaps it is more correct to say that they steadily] refuse to take any action designed to awaken the American people to the grim days ahead, at the prospect of France and then Britain being over-run. One can almost hear them say to themselves, 'Well, well, fancy Britain going down – too bad'.

The President is the only person who could set American public

---

\* Hull, *Memoirs*, pp. 775–6.
† *DAFP*, Vol. III. pp. 387–91.
‡ Casey Diaries, 11 June 1940.

opinion on fire and he apparently won't do it. His broadcast speech on Sunday evening (26 May) was flat, full of domestic politics and given at a time, in fact, at the exact moment, when he might have given a high lead to the country.[*]

Casey speculated on the situation that would confront the United States in the event of Britain's capitulation or defeat: 'They might even have to stand up to the German and Italian fleets...or what would be left of them. They might even be asked by the South American republics how they proposed to see that the Monroe Doctrine was maintained'. He also quoted with approval, an argument mounted by the American journalist and commentator, Walter Lippmann:

> This country chose deliberately not to support an organised peace – and it chose deliberately not to take measures to prevent the war – and it chose deliberately not to take measures to support the resistance of the Allies. We have now to pay for the consequences of our deliberate choice. The price will be heavy. Let us pay it like men.[†]

Casey also offered an analysis of the slogan that was frequently heard, 'Every help to the Allies, short of war'. 'It is curious', he wrote, 'that no one stops to think what this expression actually means. *It reflects a realisation that we are fighting a war in which they are almost as interested as we are – and yet we can be killed, we can bear the grievous burden of cost – and they will sell us their armaments* [Casey's emphases].'[‡] These comments mirrored remarks made privately by Lord Chatfield, British Minister for the Co-ordination of Defence, that Americans would 'fight the battle for freedom to the last Briton, but save their own skins'.[§] Casey, reflecting upon a strike by waterside workers in June 1940 noted that politics 'brings something not much better than scum to the surface ... the best and most able people avoid politics.'[¶] While the United States strenuously opposed any involvement in the European

---

[*] Casey Diaries, 5 June 1940.
[†] Casey Diaries, 11 June 1940.
[‡] Casey Diaries, 12 June 1940.
[§] Cited in Reynolds, 'From Munich to Pearl Harbor', p. 73.
[¶] Casey Diaries, 10 June 1940.

conflict, it was likely that if Britain concluded a negotiated peace with Germany, leaving Germany undefeated and triumphant in Europe, Britain would be vehemently accused in the United States of 'selling democracy down the ocean', implicitly placing the United States in greater danger.

In a discussion at the State Department, James Dunn, one of Hull's political advisers, told Casey on 16 June, that the Pacific Fleet would be transferred from the Pacific to the Atlantic. Roosevelt, George Marshall, Chief of US Army and Harold R. Stark, Chief of US Navy, contemplated moving the Pacific fleet from Pearl Harbor to the Atlantic after the fall of France. Casey noted to his diary that he took up this 'wild idea' with Berle three weeks before and thought he had won the argument. Of course, any strengthening of the American Navy in the Atlantic would have provided some limited measure of protection of the convoys taking armaments and food to beleaguered Britain. On the other hand, weakening the American Pacific Fleet would have created alarm among those Pacific and Southeast Asian nations, mainly colonial and totally unable to defend themselves from Japanese attack. Australia and Britain favoured retention of the Fleet in the Pacific, arguing that the Royal Navy would always be in superior numbers to the German and Italian navies, thus freeing American ships to concentrate on the threat from Japan.

As Casey saw the problem, strengthening the American naval presence in the Atlantic at the expense of the Pacific 'would sacrifice vital interests in the Far East without corresponding advantages elsewhere'.[*]

According to Casey, Dunn conceded that the President could have done more in establishing American resolution to participate in the defeat of Hitlerism.[†] Casey inquired of Dunn why the President had never informed the American people that the Monroe Doctrine could be fully enforced only with the participation of the Royal Navy: 'Columnists etc said it, but until the President said it, it would not be believed by the mass of the people'.[‡] Dunn claimed simply that the President could not say that. His reasoning was that

---

[*] Casey Diaries, 4 July 1940.
[†] Casey Diaries, 16 June 1940.
[‡] Ibid.

it would have the opposite effect on the American people to what was intended, specifically, that there would be greater clamour for more ships to be built. Of course, this was precisely the effect that Casey sought. In any event, Britain's sinking of the French fleet at Oran on 3–4 July finally eased the pressure.*

It was the loss of France that caused Casey, temporarily at least, to discard his mask and goad the likes of Hull, Welles, and Dunn to do more to put pressure on Roosevelt to enter the war. Yet, having often vented his personal and undiplomatic anger, Casey recorded to his diary: 'I impress on everyone in sight that it is essential, in our own interests, not to show any bitterness. One's mind has to accept the fact that the reality that has to be faced is American public opinion. 'He recognised Hull's view that American public opinion was moving, but, to him, 'most irritatingly slow'.† Casey had to overcome his sense of outrage and get down to work to make the United States see where its self-interest lay.

Yet for all this effort to impress upon the Americans the importance of saving Britain, it would be wrong to conclude that Casey during the Battle of Britain lost sight of his mission of trying to 'save' Australia. The intense discussions that occurred in May between those holding Churchill's view and those prepared to negotiate in some way or another with Hitler were conducted against a background of the United States remaining seemingly indifferent to Britain's fate. The American position was doubly frustrating to the Australians in that American sympathy for the Chinese nationalist cause meant that the danger of the United States provoking some sort of precipitous reaction on the part of Japan was ever present.

The early months of 1940 saw a short-lived easing of tensions between Britain and Japan, which enabled the transfer of two bomber squadrons from Singapore to the Middle East, arousing Australian alarm. The tranquil atmosphere in Anglo-Japan relations evaporated with the fall of France, when Japanese aggression re-asserted itself with the demand for the withdrawal of British troops from Shanghai, the closure of the Hong Kong frontier and

---

\* Reynolds, *Creation of the Anglo-American Alliance*, p. 135.
† Casey Diaries, 5 June 1940.

the termination of British assistance to Chiang Kai-shek through the Burmese frontier.* Japan, hitherto hesitant in its dealings with Nazi Germany, now sensed that the European empires and the United States itself were vulnerable. Casey's balancing of British and Australian interests was made easier by the fact that, in the summer of 1940, Britain's goal was to encourage the United States into 'tougher diplomatic, naval and economic measures that would deter Japan from war'.†

Casey never lost sight of the importance of learning what the Americans knew about Japan's intentions and preparations. He told McEwen on 8 May 1940 that:

> I have tried to get information here as to what is going on in the Japanese Mandate [Marshall and Caroline Islands] but the State Department has very little information. It is thought extremely probable that Japan has prepared landing fields and harbour facilities for war purposes.‡

As Casey told Canberra early in his Washington appointment, protocol demanded that he call upon the sixty resident Ambassadors and Ministers, some relevant to his country's interests but most, not. He was mostly unimpressed with what he found. Casey's diary note for 15 June 1940 confirmed his awareness of how much the British and Australian cause depended on him personally:

> It is a curious thing, but I am the only Dominions Minister who is playing any part in the war business in Washington. Neither Christie [Canada] nor Close [South Africa], nor of course, Brennan [Irish Free State] have had, so I am told, any business or communication with the State Department or anything in any important connection related to the war. It rather confirms one's previous belief that the other Dominions' Legations are 'prestige' posts and nothing more.§

Casey therefore had to be discerning if he were to make useful contacts and understand better the strategic situation facing Australia.

---

\* Caldecote to Menzies, 26 June 1940, A981, Far East 31. II, NAA.
† Reynolds, *Creation of the Anglo-American Alliance*, p. 135.
‡ Casey to McEwen, 9 May 1940, A981, Far East 31. I, NAA.
§ Casey Diaries, 15 June 1940.

Among those with whom Casey connected was the Netherlands Ambassador, Alexandre Louden, who, recognising the threat common to Australia and the Netherlands East Indies initially approached Casey, seeking talks.* The discussions between Casey and Louden initially revolved around a statement issued by the Japanese Foreign Minister, Hachiro Arita, on 15 April 1940 affirming that Japan's interests lay in a continuation of the trade arrangements then existing between the Netherlands East Indies and other nations of the region, especially Japan. It said that 'the Japanese government was deeply concerned ... at any aggravation of the war in Europe that might affect the status quo of the Netherlands East Indies'.

The State Department speculated that the statement was either a warning to both sides, Germany and Britain, to leave Japan alone, or on the other hand, creating a justification for sending its own forces south.† Hull warned against any nation intervening because, as Hull put it: 'Intervention in the domestic affairs of the Netherlands or any alteration of their Status Quo by other than peaceful processes would be prejudicial to the cause of stability, peace and security not only in the region of the Netherlands Indies but in the entire Pacific area'. He reminded Japan of the notes exchanged as long ago as November 1908, confirming their policy to maintain the status quo in the Pacific region, reaffirmed by both nations as well as Britain and France in the signing of the (Washington) Treaty in 1921, specifically respecting the rights of the Netherlands and their 'insular possessions' in the Pacific.‡ Hull described the Netherlands East Indies as 'very important to the international relationships of the whole Pacific Ocean' and that many countries, including the United States depended upon the NEI for essential commodities.

Casey expressed disappointment at Hull's statement but it was 'still most useful'. It at least recognised an American interest in the southwest Pacific, the region of primary relevance to the security of Australia. It was an early introduction for Casey to

---
\* Casey to McEwen, 4 April 1940, letter, RGC5, NLA.
† Herbert Feis, *The Road to Pearl Harbor* (Princeton: Princeton University Press, 1971), pp. 51–2.
‡ Cordell Hull, 17 April 1940, Press Release, included in Casey Diaries, RGC3, NLA.

the complexity of the American-British-Dutch relationship. The British preference was for a united front of the 'ABD powers' aimed at dissuading Japan from any further aggression in Southeast Asia. Britain needed oil from the NEI and as much help as possible to support Singapore. There would be no guarantees from the United States, however, because an attack on Dutch or British possessions would not in itself engender the American public to support a war against Japan.* The fate of the NEI was a priority for Casey who put it most starkly on 2 July 1940 when he claimed that 'the destiny of the Netherlands East Indies [was] inseparable from the destiny of Australia'.†

Casey argued the case, long before it was widely accepted, that to think of the war as comprising various compartments that could be dealt with in isolation would be a major error. The Pacific could not be left 'to the wolves'.‡ Australia was not remote from the unfolding conflict, but vitally connected. In conversation with Casey in April 1940, Under-Secretary Welles read out a long list of the naval strengths of those nations that might be considered 'potentially opposed' to Japan ... Britain, Australia, France, the United States and the Netherlands. Naval craft from these nations, according to Welles, were in or close to Singapore, the Philippines and Hong Kong. No doubt impressed with the combined firepower of these warships, Casey assured Welles that the Australian government was attempting to make Darwin into a fleet anchorage, some sort of complementary naval station to Singapore. For Casey any military use that the Americans might have in mind for an Australian harbour was a welcome development.

More sobering was the belief expressed by Hornbeck that Japan had no limitations on its ambitions to expand its sphere of influence and to fulfil its 'mission on earth to spread Japanese culture, commerce and authority'. Moreover, he believed that Australia and the Netherlands East Indies fell within the ambit of Japan's eventual aims, even if Japan was presently 'bogged down' in China. Hornbeck was far from reassuring on the matter of Japan

---

* Reynolds, *Creation of the Anglo-American Alliance*, pp. 232–3.
† Casey Diaries, 4 July 1940.
‡ Casey Diaries, 18 June 1940.

actually invading Australia when he noted that he did not believe that Japan would have the opportunity to launch 'a big southward jump' in the direction of the Netherlands East Indies during the present war. Casey reported to Canberra Hornbeck's view that 'it is one matter to seize and another to hold'.* There could have been no comfort in these words in Canberra.

One task Casey set himself was to attempt to discover if isolationism was relative, that is, would the United States enter the war more easily in the Far East Pacific region or in Europe? This was a legitimate activity for a diplomat but, given the sensitivity of the Roosevelt Administration to what it defined as propaganda, there were risks of Casey jeopardising his close relationships with senior American officials by examining and discussing such a highly political issue. Casey pondered his options in a long letter to McEwen on 8 May 1940. He concluded that Australia's desire 'to curb Japanese ambitions' was reflected in United States policy, but whether Japanese aggression would bring the United States to a 'force of arms' was the great unknown. Casey stated that 'it was my own impression' that the bulk of the United States Navy would remain in the Pacific rather than the Atlantic. The latter would continue to be the responsibility of the Royal Navy. This was proved to be mostly true although one quarter of the American fleet would ultimately find its way to the Atlantic. Casey also took solace in the fact that 'just as Australia was anxious about Japan, so must Japan be anxious about the United States'.† As for practical steps that the Australians should take. 'Britain and Australia should do all they can to help America 'express herself' in the Pacific'. This meant that in relation to 'the Pacific islands the United States wants to use', Britain and Australia 'should be very liberal in this matter and let America use what Islands she wants'.‡

The issue that proved virtually insoluble from the outset was whether to adhere to the British line of appeasing Japan or whether to join the Americans in displaying sympathy for the Chinese cause.§ From Hornbeck, Casey learnt that American opinion

---
\* Quoted in Casey to McEwen, 27 March 1940, letter, RGC3, NLA.
† Casey to McEwen, 8 May 1940, letter, RGC10, NLA.
‡ Ibid.
§ Hudson, *Casey*, p. 123.

strongly sympathised with China in the war against Japan: there was no sympathy for appeasement of Japan, yet no readiness to offer guarantees to Britain or Australia in the event of further Japanese aggression. Hornbeck in his conversation with Casey on 25 June 1940 assured the Australian that Japan was not ready 'to do anything about Australia'. It infuriated Casey that Hornbeck was full of praise for Chinese resistance, but did not recognise that it was Britain and Australia that were risking war by supplying China through Burma, while the Americans debated whether to abandon the Pacific altogether by moving their fleet to the Atlantic. Casey wanted the Americans to commit to negotiations that would at the very least put at stake American commercial relationships with Japan.*

This was a delicate balancing act even for someone as nimble as Casey. Australia was in a difficult position given that it had to do all in its power to avoid confronting Japan without firm American guarantees. Gaining some reliable commitment to Australia from the United States in the event of war with Japan was the goal, albeit a very distant goal in the first half of 1940. Confirming the tenebrous prospects facing Australia, the Chief of the Australian Naval Staff told the War Cabinet on 18 June, that in the event of an Anglo-Japanese War, without American support, there would be no point in attempting to hold Darwin. Further, that if British naval forces and bases in the Far East were defeated and captured, Japan could bring Australia to terms by sea power alone without the need for invasion.† On 28 June 1940, Australia learnt that the loss of the French fleet meant that Britain, temporarily at least, could not reinforce Singapore.‡ It was vital that the American fleet remained in the Pacific. As Casey told his diary on 26 June 1940:

> I have been much concerned in recent days with trying to hammer out proposals for what we should do in the Far East, in view of great change in situation arising out of French fleet position and obviously uncertainty of US government as to whether or not to move their fleet to the Atlantic.

---

\* Casey Diaries, 25 June 1940.
† *DAFP*, Vol. III. p. xv.
‡ David Day, *Great Betrayal*, pp. 55–6.

Casey's campaign to interest the United States in the strategic value of Australia was based upon the concept of Australia and its neighbours as offering outstanding strategic assets for American strategy. In other words, the national interests of the United States would be served by coming to Australia's aid. Casey could well have declared the 'America Looks to Australia', playing on Curtin's future declaration. Casey's emphasis on the strategic considerations of the United States demonstrated not only his differences with the thinking embodied in Menzies' appeal but his keen understanding of Roosevelt's thinking. As for the message itself, it was acknowledgment that Britain was in desperate need of support. The other part of the message was that Australia was a valuable strategic asset for the United States.

In his cable to the Department on 28 June, Casey set down the arguments he was employing, 'publicly and privately' about Australia:

> Significance immensely greater than our population implies by reason of size, resources, location.
>
> Outpost of Western civilisation in Pacific Ocean.
>
> Purchases millions dollars worth of American goods last twelve years against 300,000 [pounds] exports to America.
>
> Australia is not a liability to its friends as witness last war and this war.
>
> Australia, with increasing population and strength will have increasing contribution to make towards economic development of the Pacific area.
>
> Glad to have other ideas in this connection.[*]

Four of the five points appealed to American self-interest. Casey's first point – Australia's size, resources and location – was the centrepiece of his gospel. Even the notion of Australia as an outpost of Western civilisation implied that Australia could serve the United States as an outpost in a military setting. Casey's message too, revolved around the connection of the oceans and

---

[*] Casey to External Affairs, 27 June 1940, cablegram, 140, AA A981, USA 79, I, NAA.

islands around Australia to the area of principal American strategic concern. As Casey put it to his diary in terms that he was using in his private diplomacy and public speeches:

> Australia is the bridge between the Pacific and Indian Oceans. Some columnists speak glibly of the possibility of letting the Netherlands East Indies go – without realising that it isn't the Netherlands East Indies alone but the whole western Pacific that will go if the NEI 'goes'.*

At this time, American thinking looked at the Philippines as its base for war against Japan, but Casey was providing his American listeners with a Plan B. Australia had many advantages – English speaking, several good port facilities, beyond the range of Japanese bombers, and the potential for dozens if not hundreds of air strips.

Casey's battle for Britain was then a challenge, but not a case of choosing between Britain and Australia. From Australia's perspective, everything depended upon the United States aiding Britain, while strengthening its commitment to the Pacific. The question was how to press this argument upon the Americans. Casey had quickly realised the ineffectiveness of the argument that Australia was worthy of assistance as a white, European outpost in Asia. He was only too aware that Roosevelt had remained quite unmoved when Churchill had appealed for assistance in mid-1940, citing the reason that if Britain, the last outpost of democracy in Europe, fell to the Nazi tyranny, the world would enter upon a dark period of oppression that would even threaten the very existence of the United States. Menzies' appeals of May and June 1940 were similarly predicated on the nobility of a European nation in a sea of Asian settlements. Roosevelt clearly took little notice of this reasoning. Instead, Casey pressed the case that the United States needed Britain to enforce the Monroe Doctrine and needed Australia if it were forced into a war against Japan.

It was in the interests of both the United States and Australia for the Americans to rearm, for the American fleet to base itself in the Pacific, and for the United States to look upon Australia as a potential base in the South West Pacific. Moreover, Casey's battle

---

\* Casey Diaries, 2 July 1940.

for Britain had planted him firmly within the circle of influential Americans discussing policy. Casey coped with his frustration by working ever harder at networking the Administration and other power brokers. He could not change the American position but he had made the necessary contacts and set down the basic message of his gospel about the importance of Australia for the next, and ultimately more important phase of his mission.

*Chapter Six*

# Autumn and Winter 1940–41: America Moves into the Pacific

Casey was desperate to influence events once the November election gave Roosevelt his third term. Indeed a change in Casey's strategy was evident from the late autumn of 1940 and reflected an appreciation of the growing threat from Japan. This change in focus led him to vary another segment of his strategy, that is, the targets, the people and institutions who might, in some way, influence the direction of American thinking. The focus of his activities would no longer be directed at convincing the Americans that the survival of Great Britain was essential to the security of the United States. Instead, Casey now faced the task of explaining the vital role that Australia must play in repulsing the common threat of a rampant Japan in the Pacific.

For Britain, the military situation improved in Europe in the autumn of 1940. Crucial for Britain was the dismantling of the so-called 'invasion fleet' on the French coast. Various intelligence reports from a wide range of sources signalling a build-up of German military strength on the eastern boundaries pointed to the possibility that Hitler was deferring, if not abandoning the cross-channel invasion and was contemplating if not planning an attack on the Soviet Union. Churchill's somewhat prolonged refusal to concede that the danger to Britain had passed by the late autumn of 1940 was still in evidence in 1941. Even in his broadcast of 23 June 1941, Churchill argued that the German invasion of the

Soviet Union was no more than a prelude to another attempt to invade Britain. Documents captured by the Allies at the end of the war fixed the date of Hitler's decision to postpone indefinitely the invasion of the British Isles at 17 September.* Publicly, in Britain, the conclusion that the invasion had been deferred if not abandoned was suppressed, the Cabinet believing that the war effort would be lessened if the threat of invasion no longer existed.

Churchill and Roosevelt met at Newfoundland on 9 August 1940, accompanied by advisors, Welles, Hopkins and Cadogan, chief of the Foreign Office, and some service chiefs. The 'Joint Declaration' or 'Atlantic Charter' that resulted on 14 August 1940 looked forward to a world freed from Nazi tyranny. On the other hand, this first meeting between Churchill and Roosevelt changed little on the ground. There is a conflict between what might be termed contemporary, private, and deep resentment of the inaction of the United States on the part of individuals like Churchill, Lothian, Cadogan and Casey and some of the historical commentary, which is far more sympathetic to Roosevelt and his administration. Norman Davies, for example, refers to Roosevelt 'shoring up Britain' in its moment of need. Moreover, while 'watching Britain's ordeal with sympathy, and aware of the fact that it was not in America's long-term interest for Britain to go under', American aid had to be 'surreptitious'.† Davies leaves us wondering exactly what this 'surreptitious' aid actually was. Frequently, the 'Destroyers for Bases' deal is quoted as the example of Roosevelt's courageous and generous assistance. In August 1940, the United States gradually settled on a plan that would give Britain some fifty old destroyers in return for 99-year use of certain British bases in the Atlantic and Caribbean. This was only token aid. Slow, obsolescent and clearly beyond their use-by date for the major purpose for which they were built but still useful for slow convoy duties, these ancient destroyers would have been of little practical value in the event of a German invasion. In any event, Roosevelt offered them to Britain on 2 September 1940 and they did not actually commence being

---

\* Kershaw, *Fateful Choices*, p. 84.
† Norman Davies, *No Simple Victory* (New York: Penguin Group, 2007), pp. 88–92.

handed over for some weeks, by which time, the threat of invasion had all but passed. Their chief effect was to establish which side the United States was on.

Other accounts refer to Roosevelt's authorising assistance to Britain, but the outcomes are questionable.* Burns, for example, cites Roosevelt's granting Churchill's request that a British battleship, HMS *Malaya*, badly damaged by a torpedo while escorting a convoy, be repaired in an American shipyard. Whether this comprised significant aid is open to debate. On the other hand, it must be acknowledged that even token aid created a great many political problems for Roosevelt. Within the United States, the destroyers deal led to a lively argument. Professor Herbert Briggs and Professor Edwin Borchard claimed that Roosevelt had acted unconstitutionally, the 'gift' being a violation of America's neutral status.†

Yet, as Reynolds has put it, there was 'from July to October 1940 ... a remarkable Anglo-American *rapprochement*' characterised by the growing belief in the United States that Britain would survive and 'the increasingly pro-British tone of American public statements on the war'.‡ Casey's optimism that the United States might 'come in' with Britain in the war against Nazi Germany had proved wide of the mark. However, his tireless efforts to promote the British war effort clearly contributed to this growing *rapprochement* and made the United States much more open to this new development.

Both Admiral Harold Stark, Chief of Naval Operations, and General George Marshall, the Army Chief were putting pressure on the President to begin planning for the inevitable entry of the United States into the European conflict. Marshall's arguments were based on first-hand reports on the military situation in Britain, submitted by Generals Emmons and Strong, who concluded that 'sooner or later, the United States will be drawn into this war'. This conclusion was given greater weight by reason of the same two officers finding that morale in Britain was high and that Britain may well have had

---

* John Eisenhower, *Allies. Pearl Harbor to D-Day* (Boston: Da Capo Press, 2010), p. xx; Ibid.; Reynolds, *From Munich to Pearl Harbor* (Chicago: Ivan R. Dee, 2001), p. 4.
† Tansill, *Back Door to War*, p. 599.
‡ Reynolds, *Creation of the Anglo-American Alliance*, p. 143.

the ability to withstand, if not repel invasion on its own.*

Marshall brought his report to the notice of the Standing Liaison Committee, the coordinating group of the Departments of War, Army and Navy on 23 September 1940.†

In the United States, earlier suspicions of Japan had hardened into an article of faith that Japan was contemplating aggression. Hoyt fixed the date of Japan's articulation of its ambitions as October 1921 when a group of young army officers made a secret agreement, effective when they reached senior staff level, to reorganize the Japanese army and to define the area which Japan needed to fulfil her needs and ambitions. These comprised Siberia, China, India, South east Asia, Indonesia, Australia and New Zealand.‡

From an Asian perspective, the American invasion of the Philippines with the defeat of Spain in 1898 added a new ingredient into the already potent mix. The rulers of Japan and China perceived the United States as a threat to their own emerging nationalist ambitions. Hunt and Levine define the beginnings of Japan's hostility as specifically directed to the United States and as early as the nineteenth century. The American occupation and subjugation of the Philippines, Hawaii, Midway and Pearl Harbor and the conflict with Germany over Samoa looked to China and especially Japan, to be naked American empire-building and constituting a threat to other Asian and Pacific nation states:

> As Japanese and Chinese observers clearly saw, the United States had become an imperial presence in eastern Asia. The very fact of conquest dramatically signalled the emergence of a powerful, confident country in the Pacific.§

Japan was in a far stronger position to flex its muscles against the new arrival than was China. Japan was conscious of its own lack of colonies, in contrast to the substantial colonial empires of the Western powers which constituted a basic foundation for

---

\* Ibid., p. 139.
† Lowenthal, 'Roosevelt and the Coming of the War', pp. 60–1.
‡ Edwin P. Hoyt, *Japan's War. The Great Pacific Conflict* (London: Hutchinson, London, 1986), p. 57.
§ Michael H. Hunt and Steven I. Levine, *Arc of Empire: America's Wars in Asia From the Philippines to Vietnam* (Chapel Hill: University of North Carolina Press, 2013), pp. 288–9.

international status and prestige. After World War One, Japan suffered indignities that fed the sense of resentment at the failure of Western Powers to recognise Japan's true standing or what Japan perceived as her true standing, internationally. The Versailles conference rejected Japan's request for a racial equality clause in the League of Nations Charter. Japan perceived the Washington Naval Agreement as unfair, despite the fact that it had the effect of strengthening Japan's relative standing in the Pacific. The Japanese Exclusion Act of 1924 severely restricted Japanese immigration to the United States and matched the Australian White Australia Policy in its anti-Japanese provisions. It was unsurprising therefore that these obstacles were perceived in Tokyo as deliberate attempts by Western Powers to keep Japan firmly in its place. During the years between the end of World War I and the beginning of World War II, the Versailles Treaties granted Japan trusteeship rights over strategic Pacific Islands. Small groups of Japanese Army and Navy officers were diverted to study international situations that could translate into armed intervention by the United States. The United States' disarmament and its withdrawal from its 'temporarily close association with the European colonial powers', after 1920, also contributed to the balance of power in the Pacific region swinging in favour of Japan.*

Yet the difficulty for Australia was that the Atlantic always appeared to take priority over the Pacific in the minds of American military planners. Casey continued to work on the State Department, especially Hull, Berle, and Hornbeck with a view to manoeuvring the United States into a greater commitment to the Pacific. Berle certainly sought out Casey for information. In September 1940 with the Japanese taking over French Indochina, Berle noted in his diary:

> The Australian Minister came in, at my request; I asked him whether they could supply any arms to Indo-China, if we replaced them. He said he would seek advice [from Canberra] but they were steering pretty clear of it. In a sense this is typical English; they want the Far East held down and they need that very badly. But they resolve somebody else shall do

---

\* Matloff and Snell, *Strategic Planning for Coalition Warfare*, pp. 1–3.

it and take the rap for it. This is permissible in the Australian case, I suppose, since they might not be able to resist.*

Following the 'Destroyers for Bases Deal', there were rumours in Washington that the United States might take over more British bases. Berle's diary entry of 20 September 1940 clearly indicates his recognition of Casey's growing influence at the highest level of the Washington Administration and simultaneously a fear of what that influence might mean:

> The various conversations which Secretary [of State], Hull is having with Lord Lothian [British Ambassador] and Mr Casey, the Australian Minister, are exciting a great deal of comment. Everybody suspects that another Anglo-American naval base deal may be in the making, which will give us joint occupation of the bases running all the way from Singapore around the Pacific.†

Berle argued that 'I think that there probably is danger that the British will try to do some such thing as that – since this would in substance imply that we were to defend the British Empire in the Far East – from some unnamed point in the Indian Ocean'. Yet Berle noted that if the matter of joint bases in the Far East were being discussed, he hoped that it would involve 'the southern Pacific route, not accessible to the Japanese fleet'.‡ At least there was recognition here that the desirability of bases and lines of communication safe from Japanese attack was paramount.

Casey attempted to enhance his influence by offering Berle opinions that differed from official British sources. In October 1940, Berle committed to his diary his surprise at Casey's criticism of the frequency with which Britain supplied misleading figures of the resources she held in the Far East. Casey claimed that the figures were understated by about half. Berle's long-held suspicion of Britain's motives and duplicity, no doubt, lay behind his observation that in relation to the misleading figures: 'This may be that they are merely giving the first line plane resources, which is not quite cricket, because the Japanese have only second rate stuff. Or it may

---
\* Adolf Berle Diary, 19 September 1940.
† Adolf Berle Diary, 20 September 1940.
‡ Ibid.

be that the British are piling on the agony hoping to get more out of us, which I think is probably the case'. Putting aside Berle's poor opinion of Japanese aircraft, an erroneous belief common to American, British, and Casey's thinking, it was significant that he found Casey's criticism of Britain, 'interesting' and Britain's subterfuge 'not quite cricket', a colloquialism, unusual for an American to use, but quite appropriate in that context.* It is apparent that by this stage people like Berle and Hornbeck were recognising Casey as an independent thinker, someone with worthwhile ideas to offer in their discussions and a clear understanding of the global aspects of the war.

Casey was privy to confidential sources. On the day before the United States Elections of 5 November 1940, Casey cabled Canberra that he had learnt, without revealing his source, that Japan believed that the United States might well engage in a Far East conflict but that they would do so, 'hesitatingly and too late'. Casey judged that intelligence to imply that if Japan acted with speed, both the United States and Australia would 'be faced with a fait accompli'.† The following week, Casey reported to Canberra that he had finally told Berle of this intelligence.‡ Given the frequency he met with Lothian, the closeness of the relationship and that each shared confidential matters with the other, it may be assumed that the intelligence had emanated from British sources. Less than three weeks after learning of that intelligence, on 22 November 1940, Casey had a night visit from Hornbeck.§ Casey had called upon both Hornbeck and Berle earlier that day and Hornbeck's unexpected return visit to Casey's home was to inform the Australian that he, Hornbeck, believed that Japanese forces were concentrating at Hainan and Southern Formosa so as to be ready to move by sea to an unknown destination, possibly Saigon or Camranh Bay. Hornbeck considered that Singapore should be reinforced by British and/or Australian aircraft. He was not in favour of American ships visiting Australia or Singapore,

---

\* Adolf Berle Diary, 21 October 1940.
† Casey to Canberra, 4 November 1940, cablegram, 358, A3300, 11, NAA.
‡ Casey to Canberra, 15 November 1940, cablegram, 379, A981, Far East 26A, NAA.
§ Casey Diaries, 22 November 1941.

which he believed would be too provocative. In reporting this new intelligence to Canberra, Casey emphasised Hornbeck's sensitivity about being quoted.*

Hornbeck's after-hours visit to Casey may be explained by his reluctance to be seen by his colleague, Berle, as supplying confidential information to Casey. In any case, important inferences may be drawn from these two incidents. Firstly, Casey's informing Berle of intelligence of which Berle was unaware, indicates the extent to which Casey had established valuable contacts and enjoyed sound relations with sources of such intelligence. Secondly, Hornbeck's night visit to Casey suggests that Casey clearly had positioned himself as an important broker of information and was perceived that way on all sides in Washington.

The passing of the Selective Training and Service Act in late October 1940 at least signalled American recognition of the fact that it might soon need more substantial armed forces. By November 1940, senior officers of British, American and Dutch forces had formed a committee to discuss what Casey termed, 'matters of high strategy'.† Hull wrote in his memoirs: 'I held several conversations with Lothian and Casey at the beginning of October to lay the basis for exchanges of information among the United States, Britain, Australia, New Zealand and the Dutch East Indies concerning the forces available in the Far East to resist a Japanese attack'.‡ There is no substantive proof that Casey was a key figure in these discussions, but in the light of Hull's reluctance to do anything provocative and given that Lothian was unwell and not proactive in expressing Britain's concern over developments in the Pacific, Hull's notations may be regarded as a further example of Casey's leadership and influence. The involvement of senior naval figures in the discussions clearly indicated that while the President might disown such claims, the Navy was considering and implicitly devising strategy for a future conflict. The presence of British and Dutch representatives, moreover, hinted that the Pacific was the region under discussion. Clearly, the chief interest surrounded the devising of a strategy for the expected conflict with Japan.

---
\* Casey to Canberra, cablegram, 389, A3300, II, NAA.
† Casey Diaries, 13 November 1941.
‡ Hull, *Memoirs*, Vol. I, p. 912.

Casey certainly had ample opportunity to develop his knowledge of political manoeuvring, military strategy and technology in the autumn of 1940. On 16 October 1940, Casey spoke with the President, Hull and Knox. Casey learned about new developments in air-engine manufacturing from Knox. From the President, Casey learned about American interest in a 'more southerly air route between USA and Australia' and establishing bases at various Pacific locations and Christmas Island.* This was the kind of thinking that Casey could only encourage given that a great deal of American thinking and resources was directed at shoring up the Philippines. Casey summed up his message in a note to his diary on 22 November 1940: 'Guam no fleet facilities. Little at Manila. Southern route to Australia and New Zealand all the more important'.†

It was in the aftermath of the November elections that Admiral Harold Stark in a celebrated Memorandum written on 12 November 1940, outlined what became known as the 'Beat Hitler First' strategy. Stark recommended that in a two-front war, the United States would give priority to defeating Germany over Japan. Stark, who had access to deciphered Japanese codes, took the view that Australia and New Zealand were not part of Japan's imperial ambition at that point. Much more likely was that Japan would attempt to conquer Hong Kong, Singapore and the resource-rich Malaya peninsula. Here too, his Memorandum was well informed.

Neither Stark nor Marshall opposed the granting of further aid to Britain. Stark went so far as to argue that an American goal should be the prevention of the 'disruption of the British Empire, with all that such a consummation implies'.‡ Stark was so confident of the strength of the arguments that he and Marshall had advanced that he told Admiral J.O. Richardson, Commander in chief, United States Fleet, that the President would 'give some definite pronouncement on it in order that I may send you something more authoritative than I otherwise could do'.§ Roosevelt did nothing of

---

\* Casey Diaries, 16 October 1940.
† Casey Diaries, 22 November 1940.
‡ Lowenthal, 'Roosevelt and the Coming of the War', p. 61.
§ Stark to Richardson, 12 November 1940, letter, quoted in Lowenthal, 'Roosevelt and the Coming of the War', p. 61.

the sort. Nonetheless, Stark had now made it clear that the Navy expected American involvement in a world war.

Casey's diary made no mention of the Memorandum, but his subsequent activity could be viewed as representing an attempt to water down the 'Beat Hitler First' strategy and to emphasise the threat from Japan in the Pacific. At one level, Casey was clearly in sympathy with a strategy that prioritised American and British cooperation in the Atlantic. 'Beat Hitler First' would become a cornerstone of the military alliance between Britain and the United States.* In a private letter to Menzies in November 1940, Casey confessed that he still saw the greatest menace to Australia as the possibility of Britain being beaten in Europe. Casey viewed Britain's commitment to the Pacific as the most that could be hoped for under the circumstances: '… I think the British government's statements regarding ensuring the safety of Australia and of Singapore are satisfactory …'† The hope at that time remained for Australia somehow to avoid war with Japan. Casey realised at the same time that in judging the German and Japanese threats, it was important to get the balance right

Casey certainly had ample opportunity to make his ideas known to American military planners. He was in frequent contact with officers of the War Plans Division of the Army and the War Plans Division of the Navy. When Commander Henry Burrell, the Royal Australian Navy's Director of Operations and Plans arrived clandestinely in Washington on 17 November 1940 to take part in high-level naval discussions, it was Casey who introduced Burrell to Berle, Hornbeck, Welles, Knox, and Stark.‡ It was not just high level policy-makers that Casey met in this period but those who a year later would be totally involved in the conflict with Japan. On 25 November 1940, Casey took Burrell to see Sherman Miles, Chief of Army Intelligence and later that day had Burrell dine with Admiral Walter Anderson, American Chief of Naval Intelligence, Commander Heard, also American Naval Intelligence, Stanley Goble who was the Australian liaison with the Air Training

* David Lowe, 'Australia in the World', in Joan Beaumont, *Australia's War 1939–1945* (Sydney: Allen and Unwin, 1996), p. 171.
† Casey to Menzies, 23 November 1940, letter, CP290/6/ bundle 2, NAA.
‡ Casey Diaries, 22, 25 and 26 November 1940.

Scheme, and Admiral Herbert Pott, formerly of the Royal Navy and now an attaché in the British Embassy in Washington. This last week in November 1940 was a busy time in terms of information gathering and cross fertilising the American, British and Australian information channels. Casey's diary entry for 24 November 1940 did not mention Burrell, but noted simply 'Lunched with General Marshall Chief of General Staff'. The same day as he lunched with Marshall, Casey had his first talks with Lothian after the latter's return from London.*

Because of his predilection for meeting as many senior political, media and government leaders as he could, Casey would have become aware of the shades of differences of views held in Washington. In his report to Canberra on 17 November 1940, he referred to the views of Knox in favour of 'preventive strategy' involving the deployment of American, British, Dutch and Australian warships to deter Japan from embarking on hostile actions. He also quoted Knox as favouring a substantial American naval force to visit Singapore, a tactic constantly opposed by the President and Hull as too provocative.†

Casey's interview with Hull on 12 November 1940 revolved around Hull's interest in the 'British naval and commercial shipping situation', which Casey put into the context of Hull's anxiety about the Far East. This was a few days after Roosevelt's re-election, a time when the Roosevelt Administration could have been expected to be more open and more enthusiastic about closer relations with Britain. Yet, American interest in the British Fleet clearly suggested a continuing fear that Britain might conduct negotiations with Germany in order to avoid the bloodshed and destruction of an invasion, but where the Fleet became one of Hitler's prizes. In this interview, Casey, not one to miss an opportunity, asked Hull if American warships would visit Australia and/or Singapore in the near future. Casey was being mischievously cute with this question. He had no reason to suppose that the Administration had changed its position. Avoiding a direct reply, the Secretary reasoned that placing American ships at Manila and sending British ships and

---
\* Casey Diaries, 24 November 1940.
† Casey to Canberra, 15 November 1940, cablegram, 358, A.3300.11, NAA.

Australian aircraft to Singapore would be a greater deterrent to Japan. Hull suggested that it might be possible for the United States to provide the aircraft, presumably involving payment.* Hull's avoidance of giving a direct reply to Casey's enquiry, in contrast to Knox's firm belief that US Navy ships should, in fact, visit Singapore, was another example of the differing views coming out of Washington. In his discussion with Hull, Casey argued that Britain's having to reinforce Singapore's defences, ipso facto, meant lesser resources being made available to 'other important areas' that were actual theatres of war.†

In a long session with Hull on 3 December 1940, it became evident to Casey that the Secretary of State had adopted a far more sympathetic stance concerning Britain's plight. Although the danger of invasion had passed and, with it, any possibility of negotiations between Germany and Britain, the loss of so many merchant ships in the Atlantic created a new and dangerous phase. That, anyway, was one of the explanations Hull offered for the new American attitude. Hull claimed to have spent much time impressing the gravity of the situation upon members of the Cabinet, the Defence Advisory Commission and leaders in the Congress. In reporting the conversation to Canberra, Casey said that he had emphasised to Hull the anxiety of the Australian government about Japan's next move. In the context of Australia placing a ban on the export of scrap iron, Hull did not offer any concrete support.

This lack of tangible aid continued to irritate the British and the Australians. The President delivered, on 27 December 1940, his 'Arsenal of Democracy' speech, which emphasised again that the United States was not about to fight in foreign wars, but rather to supply the 'implements of war'. Roosevelt claimed that the United States would provide 'real resistance' by strengthening those peoples attempting to resist the Axis invaders. Picking up a phrase uttered by Jean Monnet, the French resistance leader, Roosevelt ended his speech with a call to the American nation: 'We must be the great arsenal of democracy'. This phrase was meant to give heart

---

\* Casey to Minister for Foreign Affairs, 12 November 1940, cablegram, 373, 3300.40, NAA.
† Casey to Canberra, 4 December 1940, A981. War 45, NAA.

to Britain. The British leader saw it differently: as one historian has put it, 'In London, Churchill fumed and fretted'.* The Prime Minister was uncertain exactly what the President planned in the way of neighbourly assistance. As Churchill put it, 'Remember, Mr President, we do not know what you have in mind, exactly what the United States is going to do and we are fighting for our lives'.† By any measure, this expressed serious displeasure and concern on Churchill's part, an attitude that must have surprised Roosevelt. Churchill's mind was exercised by the American insistence that so much of this aid had to be paid for and that the costs were rapidly running down Britain's gold reserves. Casey, on a 'show the flag' visit to Florida, remained unmoved by the 'Arsenal of Democracy' speech. It may have represented an advance on Roosevelt's part towards a more helpful attitude towards Britain, but, realistically, it was a very small advance.‡

The scepticism is unsurprising because Roosevelt's intentions were difficult to read, even with the benefit of hindsight. Two factors lend themselves to a questioning of the timing of this harder American attitude. Firstly, the Presidential elections were out of the way, giving Roosevelt the opportunity to adopt a more belligerent attitude to the Axis powers at a lower political cost. Secondly, the postponement, if not the abandonment of a German invasion of Britain, certainly known by both London and Washington, enabled Washington to adopt a more pro-Allied attitude knowing that the United States would not have to deliver on its fine words.

Roosevelt's State of the Union message delivered in January 1941, spoke of the post-war world and of the need for 'four essential human freedoms'. The historiography of the message, its title fixed as 'The Four Freedoms Declaration' often depicted Roosevelt signalling a gradual but determined march to take the United States into what was expected to become another world war. Yet, a careful reading of the message does not necessarily lead to that conclusion. Roosevelt spoke of the four freedoms, speech,

---
* Lash, *Roosevelt and Churchill*, p. 271.
† Churchill's telegram of 30 December 1940 is cited in Warren Kimball, *The Most Unsordid Act: Lend-Lease, 1939–1941* (Baltimore: The Johns Hopkins University Press, 1969), p. 130.
‡ Casey Diaries, 29, 30 December 1940.

worship, freedom from want and from fear as attainable within his lifetime and not as some distant vision. It was the immediacy of this grand idea that led to the conclusion that the United States would have to take up arms in order to achieve the adoption, worldwide, of these freedoms. Inspiring as the sentiments may have been, they fell far short of providing any real expectation of a change in America's neutral position. The timing of the Four Freedoms Declaration, so soon after the crucial Presidential elections was a quintessential Roosevelt ploy, a lofty statement that would satisfy the Interventionists and hold them off for a further period and at the same time, reassure the Isolationists that military intervention was not on the Administration's agenda.

On the other hand, the promised material support for the Allies appeared more likely after the Lend Lease Bill was introduced into Congress on 10 January 1941. Lend Lease would become law despite an intense opposition campaign, mainly from Republicans, spurred on by a grass roots group known as America First, claiming a membership of over 800,000.[*] Casey, infuriated by what he regarded as empty gestures and posturing on the part of the United States, at least saw signs of hope of more useful assistance. Casey noted in his diary, 9 March 1941 that 'Lend Lease Bill passed Senate last night 60–31. Great sense of relief.'[†] Casey was quick to make apparent, Australia's readiness to participate in the scheme. The following day, he hosted a dinner at the Legation where the dinner guests comprised Secretary of the Treasury Henry Morgenthau, Head of US Steel and later of Lend Lease, Edward Stettinius, Berle and two naval officers, Admiral Pott and Admiral Turner.[‡] Clearly, Casey was intent on getting some key players together.

The task for the Americans now was to devise ways in which Lend Lease would fit into an ultimate victory programme and on 10 April 1941 the Secretary of War described the procedure to be followed under the Lend Lease Act.[§]

---

\* Edward Stettinius, Jnr, *Lend Lease. Weapon for Victory* (New York: Macmillan, 1944), pp. 71–89 and David Reynolds, *America, Empire of Liberty* (London: Allen Lane, 2009), p. 359.
† Casey Diaries, 9 March 1941.
‡ Casey Diaries, 10 March 1941.
§ Chief of Staff's notation of 14 February 1941 on General Moore's 3

Lend Lease was not the only important event from Casey's perspective. The Plan Dog memo written by Chief of Naval Operations, Harold Stark, in 1940, recognised the possibility of the United States being involved in war in both Europe and the Pacific. He formulated ideas on coping with the possibility, although recognising the need to 'Beat Germany First'. Stark's recommendation urged the President to approve US service chiefs holding talks with their British counter-parts, something the British had sought for months.

Roosevelt approved Stark's recommendation and the 'American British Conversation' or ABC1, ran from January to March 1941 and involved high level military delegations from both sides of the Atlantic. As Bridge has noted, Casey successfully had Burrell attached as an observer with the British military delegation.[*] This no doubt is part of the explanation of Casey being able to explain to Canberra accurately on the two main developments of relevance to Australia. Firstly, as the Stark Memorandum (Plan Dog) prefigured, the strategy was to 'Beat Hitler First' and to conduct a 'holding war' in the Pacific. Secondly, the Americans, against strong opposition from the British, had decided that Singapore was important but not vital in any conflict. This was the message conveyed by Casey to Canberra on 23 February 1941. While the United States was prepared, if necessary, to move ships from the Pacific to what it perceived to be the more important Atlantic theatre of the war, the expectation was that British capital ships would use this opportunity to reinforce the Far East.[†] The sweetener for Australia was, as Bridge put it, that for the first time there was recognition that holding Australia was crucial to any war against Japan.[‡]

Casey did his best to make the case for Singapore, which the British delegation at ABC1 considered vital for both India's and Australia's security. Casey was ill during the early days of the ABC1 talks. He was in hospital with influenza from 22 January to 1 February, followed by a week's convalescence. It is difficult at

---

February 1941 memo, AG381 92-17-41 MFM.
\* Bridge, 'R.G. Casey', pp. 183–4.
† Horner, *High Command*, p. 63.
‡ Bridge, 'R.G. Casey', p. 183.

this stage to conjecture if this affected Australia's arguments at the talks and whether his voice, added to that of the British, would have made a difference regarding Singapore. It must be remembered that Burrell was present during this period so Australia's opinions were represented. Casey met with Halifax on 4 February when he advised caution in issuing invitations to the Embassy at this time because of the atmosphere surrounding the Lend Lease Bill.\* It is obvious that he had the ability to 'bounce back' from ill health as he visited both Halifax and Hornbeck on 14 February and Cordell Hull the next day.† Among the many American contacts Casey made were two psychologists, Dr Hadley Cantril and Dr Lloyd Free, researching what Casey termed, 'the whole poll idea'. Clearly fascinated by the potential for political adaptation, Casey was interested to learn that, under the auspices of the Office of Public Opinion Research at Princeton University, the two were seeking to understand why vast numbers of Americans responded positively to simple prompts such as 'Constitution' and 'Panama'. Casey reported their interest in ascertaining the American reaction to prompts connected to the 'South West Pacific' such as 'Australia' and 'Singapore'.‡

Cantril's poll results gave heart to Casey and enabled him, on 17 February 1941 to report a 'most interesting public opinion poll… in respect of the Far East', copies of which he sent to Halifax, Hull, Hornbeck, and Frankfurter. The poll showed that Americans had 'a much greater appreciation of the value of Singapore than I had thought possible'.§ More than half those polled favoured American support for Singapore. For Casey, polling was an opportunity to exploit the public mood. He optimistically proposed that Wendell Willkie, the defeated presidential candidate, include Singapore on his itinerary for the latter's proposed trip to Australia. On 19 February 1941, he wrote the following in his diary:

> I have been spreading the Gospel far and wide lately – of the great importance of Singapore. There is a tendency in

---

\* Casey Diaries, 4 February 1941.
† Casey Diaries, 14 and 15 February 1941.
‡ Casey Diaries, 16 November 1940.
§ Casey Diaries, 17 February 1941.

some quarters here to regard the various theatres of war in watertight compartments and not from a global standing. The connection between Singapore and the main theatres in Europe and the Mediterranean has to be emphasised.*

To emphasise Singapore and the mistaken notion that Europe and Asia were utterly distinct theatres of war was to argue for moderation in the application of the 'Beat Hitler First' strategy favoured by the Americans at ABC1. For now, this was a battle that Casey could not win. The conclusions of ABC1 were the nucleus of the ultimate total strategy for the war. Yet, Singapore was for Casey, worth pursuing in the worrying context, as Horner has put it, that Australia's 'security was in the hands of American strategists who were more interested in the Atlantic than the Pacific'.†

There were other battles that Casey did win. He became an even more crucial intermediary during the northern winter because of the sudden death of Lothian on 12 December 1940. Like Casey, Lothian was quietly successful in winning friends in Washington. Churchill once described him thus: 'In all the years I had known him, he gave me the impression of high intellectual and aristocratic detachment from vulgar affairs. Airy, viewy, aloof, dignified, censorious, yet in a light and gay manner, he had always been good company'. Yet, by late 1940, Lothian, visiting Britain, had become, according to Churchill, a changed man, deeply conscious of the peril facing Britain.‡ Cadogan noted in his diaries that in Washington, Lothian had become subject to drowsiness. Clearly suffering from an undiagnosed illness, he refused medical attention because of his Christian Science beliefs and died shortly after.§ Lothian's death led to the American officials using Casey as a liaison with Britain.¶ Indeed, there was speculation in the American press that Casey would be Lothian's replacement as British ambassador.**

Instead, Casey played a dominant role in ensuring the

---

\* Casey Diaries, 19 February 1941.
† Horner, *High Command*, p. 64.
‡ Winston S. Churchill, *The Second World War* (London: Cassell, 1949), Vol. iii, p. 441.
§ Cadogan Diaries, p. 339.
¶ Hudson, *Casey*, p.11.
\*\* Bridge, 'The Other Blade of the Scissors', p. 142.

rejection of tentative soundings from London about David Lloyd George, the elderly, former Prime Minister, and an advocate of appeasement, being appointed British Ambassador to the United States. London enquired if he would be acceptable to Washington. In a Memorandum of Conversation, Berle described Casey's position on the proposed appointment as 'violently opposed'. Berle discerned that Casey believed his objections conveyed to London had had considerable influence in causing Lloyd George's name to be withdrawn; at the very least, Casey made it clear to Churchill that there was no support for Lloyd George among the Americans or Dominions.[*]

Lothian's eventual replacement was the taciturn Lord Halifax. A former Viceroy of India and with an imposing aristocratic background, he yet lacked the easy affability that Casey was able to call upon when the occasion demanded. His interests were said to be hunting and the Anglican Church, resulting in his nickname of the Holy Fox. Halifax reported to Churchill that he found the Americans and the American form of government difficult to deal with. In a personal letter to the Prime Minister dated 13 March 1941, Halifax complained about 'how terribly disjointed is the whole machinery of government. I don't think the President ties up awfully well; I am quite certain Harry Hopkins doesn't and as for government departments, they might almost as well be the administration of different countries ...'[†]

Nor did Halifax hit it off with Hull. Between February and May 1941, Hull was secretly meeting the Japanese Ambassador, Saburo Kurusu and the Special Envoy, Admiral Kichisaburo Nomura, for wide-ranging talks without even telling the British, a situation that infuriated Halifax when he found out.[‡] It was not within Halifax's capacity to engage in the kind of politicking or the new art of public relations employed by Casey. One of Casey's goals in spring 1941 was to bring Halifax into discussions with the Americans about practical issues such as the location of fleets and new deals over

---

[*] Berle, 3 December 1940, Memorandum of Conversation 40, Berle Papers, PSF, Box 94, Roosevelt Memorial Library, Bridge, 'The Other Blade of the Scissors', p. 142.
[†] Halifax to Churchill (Kew: Public Record Office, Prem. 4, 27/9.)
[‡] Reynolds, *The Creation of the Anglo-American Alliance*, p. 230.

bases. Hull was, it seems, referred to by his Assistant Secretary, Dean Acheson, as 'the old man from Tennessee'; he was extremely shy and felt quite intimidated by Halifax. Acheson described the situation thus: '[Hull] regarded Halifax as a combination of the holder of an ancient British peerage, Viceroy of India and a British Foreign Secretary, all rolled into one and he was scared to death of him'. Casey was asked if he could do anything about it. He initially raised it with Halifax, whose immediate reaction was: 'I hope he's not as scared of me as I am of him'. Casey arranged a small dinner party for Hull, Halifax and himself with an additional guest, Norman Davis, known to both. Food and drink were carefully chosen and Casey and Davis met beforehand 'and acted as honest brokers who made the running until the other two warmed up'. Apparently, the diffidence between the British Lord and the Tennessean Secretary of State evaporated thereafter.*

Few diplomats other than Casey would have the chutzpah to arrange such a dinner of opposites both of whom out-ranked Casey. Casey was pleased with his efforts, describing it as 'a most useful evening indeed'. This was the sort of diplomacy that Casey revelled in. According to Casey, Halifax 'tried my 'bases' proposal' and received a favourable response from Hull'. Casey was also pleased that he found himself on the same side as Hull in opposing any transfer of American naval vessels from the Pacific to the Atlantic.† The fact that the Australian Minister was routinely engaged in conversation with influential policy makers about military strategy helped to ensure that Australia remained part of the strategic conversation even after the Stark Memorandum. For a small nation that had had no previous diplomatic representation in the United States, Casey was clearly taken seriously by those responsible for the highest levels of American strategic planning.

When Casey arrived in the United States, it was made clear to him that Australia was not part of any American strategy. A year later, the situation had totally changed. The secret British and American Staff talks (ABC1) that took place in Washington in the first three months of 1941 made clear the American expectation of

---

\* Casey, *Personal Experience*, pp. 63–4.
† Casey Diaries, 5 May 1941.

entering the war on the Allied side. While both sides agreed that the first task would be to win the war in Europe, defending the British Commonwealth's interests in the Pacific became a priority, nonetheless. It was at this point, according to Burrell's report of 7 February 1941, that the Americans acknowledged that Australia and New Zealand had to be held by the allies. The implication was that if Britain could not 'save' Australia, then the United States might.[*] In any case, it is clear that, once the danger of an invasion of the British Isles had passed, Casey's priority was focusing American attention on the Pacific and the importance of Australia in defending American interests there. Again, a case of America needing to look to Australia, not the other way around, as expressed in the subsequent Curtin declaration.

---

[*] Bridge, 'R.G. Casey', p. 183.

*Chapter Seven*

# From the Menzies Visit to the Pearl Harbor

Throughout 1941, Japan's war-like intentions were obvious to more astute observers, but there was no agreement among the Allies about a response. After prolonged secret talks with three senior Japanese representatives, Hornbeck concluded that Japan wished to reduce her forces in China so as to have these forces available 'for possible activities in some other direction', which might be against British, Dutch, Soviet or even American interests.* Not too much weight should be given to this rather extraordinary claim by Hornbeck.

Japan's non-aggression treaty with the Soviet Union, signed in April 1941, clearly hinted that Japan was securing its northern frontier for the purposes of a southward invasion. On the other hand, the rapid progress of the Wehrmacht into the Soviet Union after the invasion in June 1941 invited the conclusion that Japan would use the opportunity to attack the Soviet Union on its eastern flank at a time when the latter was fighting on its western front for its very existence. The alternative view held that the treasures of oil and rubber, freely available and only lightly defended in the Southeast Asia region were vastly more vital to Japan's future.

This uncertainty over Japan was the shadow that hung over the visit of Menzies to Washington in May 1941. A measure of the greater sympathy for the Allied cause was reflected in confidential Briefing Notes prepared by the State Department for use by the President for the Menzies visit. These Briefing Notes, to my knowledge have never been cited in the literature, but are important

---

\* Lash, *Roosevelt and Churchill*, p. 333.

because they confirm that a change in American thinking about Australia had occurred. Significantly, the notes were prepared in the Department's Division of European Affairs, but were studied by Berle before they reached the President. In fact, the Briefing Notes' reflection of the frosty nature of American-Australian relations can be seen as Berle's contribution. The notes give insights into the relationship between the two nations, Australia and the United States, including frank judgments that relations had been highly unsatisfactory, at times, 'even acrimonious', that a 'trade war' existed between the two countries, and that the United States had 'black listed' Australia.

However, the State Department now saw other issues as relevant in the event of hostilities erupting in the Pacific region. Washington obviously believed that the long-standing issues that had inhibited closer relations between the United States and Australia for many years were no longer relevant. What was crucial was dealing with the growing aggressive nature of Japan.* From Washington's perspective, the two long-standing problems besetting the relationship were Australia's refusal both to allow American air services to land in Australia and to permit direct radio telegraph communications between the two countries. The notes described the long delays in telegraph services between the United States and Australia:

> Telegrams either go by radio via Canada or by cable via Canada or Great Britain ... the average delay on telegrams transmitted by radio originating in Australia and destined to [*sic*] the United States is five and one half hours. The American company, RCA had had a traffic agreement with Amalgamated Wireless [Australasia] Ltd. Since October 1931 for the establishment of a direct radio-telegraph circuit but the Australian government had not issued the necessary licence.†

Equally as inimical to the relationship were the poor trading arrangements, born of the excessive tariffs maintained by both

---

\* 'Briefing Notes', File 847.00 and File 1191-2, Reel 23, 711-99, Archives of the State Department.
† Ibid.

countries: 'It would be difficult to say which country has been more at fault in this regard'. The State Department notes clearly admit that the United States bore the major responsibility for the 'trade war' by its Tariff Acts of 1922 and 1930, which imposed excessive duties on Australia's principal exports to the United States, notably wool.

The Australian refusal to grant landing rights to Pan American Airlines arose solely from Australia's insistence that Britain be granted reciprocal rights to land in Hawaii. The American objection was based on the reality that the only suitable landing field in Hawaii was in the American Naval Station at Pearl Harbor, thus presenting grave security risks. The State Department noted that opening Hawaii to a British airline would enable that airline to operate a round-the-world service, a distinct commercial advantage and one that the United States would strenuously resist. A year earlier, Casey had complained to Berle that the British side had given away 'landing rights at Fiji and Auckland – and, had nothing in return'.* The Briefing Notes revealed that while the lack of a direct service between the two countries had been difficult from a 'purely commercial point of view, in the present emergency, a direct service becomes doubly important, not only for the United States and Australia but for the whole British Empire'.

This statement is important for two reasons. Firstly, the reference to the 'present emergency' at a time (8 May 1941) when the United States was neutral and the Pacific War was seven months away. Secondly, the notes referred to the British Empire in a manner that could be interpreted as showing concern, a departure from the conventional understanding that Roosevelt believed that the Empire should be broken up. It is only by a careful reading of the notes that the American position is fully understood. Clearly, the Roosevelt Administration was aware of the distinct possibility of Japanese-inspired conflict in the South Pacific and was attempting to create some sort of understanding with Australia that would facilitate American participation, if not intervention. Equally clearly, the United States was envisaging greater communication with and an improved relationship with Australia. Access by aircraft was an obvious means of establishing and maintaining that understanding.

---

\* Casey Diaries, 18 June 1940.

Important too was the need for rapid communication between the two nations. The identification of the need for direct radio telegraph facilities between the two nations signalled the growing American awareness of the approaching conflict in the Pacific.

The new importance of Australia is on display in the language of the notes: 'Should the United States become involved in war, particularly in the Far East, instantaneous telegraph communication with Australia would be of the utmost importance'. The same sentiment is expressed again: 'It is obviously desirable and helpful in cultivating closer ties between the United States and Australia, quite aside from mutual defence needs, to improve the communication facilities between the two countries'. The import and the motivation of the briefing notes thus becomes apparent. The United States was forecasting the role that Australia would be required to play in the events expected to unfold within the very near future.

The significance of the Briefing Notes lay in their confirming Burrell's belief that Australia had become part of the American strategy for the expected war in the Pacific. Equally significant was the fact that this document was written not by the American military or naval authorities but by the State Department. It is possible to speculate that the newly found American recognition of improving relations with Australia and the importance of Australia in Pacific defence strategy owed something to Casey's energetic wooing of the State Department and its senior officers. Berle and Acheson thus assume a more prominent place in the cast list of characters that Casey cultivated.

The Briefing Notes criticised what it perceived as Australia's attempt to 'establish its independent position vis-à-vis the United States and at the same time, expect us to accept her playing the Empire game in such a manner'. However, they concluded by emphasising that 'the current general situation offered an unusual, probable [sic] unique opportunity for attempting to solve, by moderate liberality, a deep-rooted conflict which puts a severe strain on United States-Australian relations in general – political as well as economic'.*

---

* Ibid.

Casey left nothing to chance in terms of cementing relationships upon the arrival of Menzies in Washington. His gathering of Washington's important people reveals the effectiveness of his networking. For example, in a letter to the Assistant Secretary of State that began 'My dear Adolf', he gave Berle a list of those who would be attending 'an informal men's dinner [black tie]' at the Australian Legation to meet the visiting Prime Minister, Menzies, on 9 May 1941, signing the letter, 'Dick Casey'. The list included Vice-President Henry Wallace, Secretary of War, Henry Stimson, Assistant Secretary of State, Dean Acheson and Special Adviser to the President, Harry Hopkins, along with other members of the Diplomatic Corps.*

The Menzies visit proceeded smoothly. Casey did his best to bring his intelligence up to date, noting in his diary the day before Menzies arrived: 'Lunched alone with Stimson [Secretary of War]. He wanted to explain his point of view regarding United States fleet proposals. We also discussed Philippines'.† No less an important meeting occurred on 12 May 1941 when General Marshall and Admiral Stark came to the Australian Legation to talk with Casey and Prime Minister Menzies. Casey would not have passed up this opportunity to spread his gospel that it was Australia that offered great benefits to American power in the Pacific. While Marshall and American strategy were still focused on the lost cause of somehow defending the Philippines and confining any Asian war to the ocean north of the equator, they would certainly not have been spared Casey's reminders about what a strategic asset Australia represented in the event of war with Japan. There were follow-up visits to Casey from American military leaders. On 9 June 1941, Admiral H.E. Kimmel, Commander-in-Chief of the US Pacific Fleet, and one of his planning officers Captain MacMorrow, called at the Legation to see Casey for a 'useful confidential discussion on Pacific'.‡

Impressing upon the Americans the importance of the Pacific,

---

\* Casey to Berle, *Berle Papers*, Car-Ce Box 30, Roosevelt Memorial Library.
† Casey Diaries, 8 May 1941.
‡ Casey Diaries, 9 June 1941.

despite the 'Beat Hitler First' strategy, was one of Casey's priorities. Another was seeking to encourage the Americans to look beyond the Philippines in the context of the looming Pacific War. Having made so many important contacts in Washington, Casey would have learnt of the existence of various colour-coded war plans created by a Joint Committee of the United States Army and the United States Navy. War Plan Orange was a strategy designed to deal with hostilities that were expected to break out in the Western Pacific involving a Japanese attack on the Philippines and Guam, both American protectorates. As early as 1905, Japan was perceived as the likely adversary in the Pacific, a belief that persisted, with varying degrees of conviction, until proven correct by the outbreak of the Pacific War in 1941. The Army and the Navy were required to develop their own tactical programs in accordance with the overall strategic concepts and objectives. Theoretically, the existence of clearly defined War Plans would have made it impossible for an outsider, such as Casey, to attempt to influence the political will of the United States in the specific areas of military and naval strategy. In reality, the colour plans never achieved what was hoped for and expected. Moreover, they were drawn up by serving and retired members of the Army and Navy, albeit of senior rank such as General Pershing and Admiral Dewey, but with insufficient political input. In retrospect, it is alarming to consider that two such elderly officers were involved in any sort of planning in the twentieth century, especially because of the rapid technological developments that changed the entire spectrum of weaponry and the actual conduct of twentieth century conflicts.

(Pershing fought in the Indian Wars, the Cuban War in 1898, he served in the Japanese army during the Russo-Japanese War, 1904–5, and in 1917, he was appointed commander-in-chief of the American Expeditionary Force in Europe during the Great War. He was chief of staff, US Army, 1921–24, while Dewey was commander of the US Asiatic Squadron that defeated the Spanish fleet in Manilla Bay in 1899.)

In fairness, there exist many different opinions on the value of the War Plans. Miller has claimed that 'War Plan Orange, the secret program of the United States to defeat Japan, was, in my opinion, history's most successful war plan'.* On the other hand, the Army's official history described these plans as far from realistic and hence little more than staff studies.† No War Plan was ever enacted by Congress or signed by a President. From the very beginning, American planning was based upon two major factors, firstly that the hostilities with Japan would be essentially a naval war and secondly, arising from that, a world class naval station and harbour was needed in the Western Pacific. Subic Bay or Manila Bay in the Philippines were invariably nominated for that role. Both propositions were problematic. The development of aircraft and aircraft carriers demolished the belief that hostilities with Japan would be entirely naval. Secondly, the declared need for a major naval base in the Western Pacific and the conclusion that the Philippines were the only possible place reflected poorly on the thinking that went into the creation of War Plan Orange. There was never a realistic chance that the Philippines were defensible. The agreements reached at the Washington Naval Conference in 1921–22 allowing Japan the smallest ratio of 5:5:3 in capital ships eventuated in Britain and the United States conceding Japan the right to strengthen her Pacific influence while denying the two Western countries the right to fortify their Pacific bases. In the words of a United States naval authority: 'Thus went all chance of defending the Philippines and providing a military sanction for American policy'.‡ At the first meeting of the Joint Board in 1919, after one of the many reviews, a Naval member, Captain Yarnell, questioned how could war plans be developed without a national policy being defined? What were America's interests in the Far East? If there were to be hostilities, would they be restricted to a limited war or was it the intention to decisively defeat the enemy? Could the Philippines be held and at what cost?

By 1922, Yarnell had concluded, 'it seems certain that in the course of time the Philippines and whatever else we may have there, will be captured', thus anticipating precisely the events of

---

\* Edward S. Miller, *War Plan Orange. The US Strategy to Defeat Japan, 1897–1945* (Annapolis: Naval Institute Press, 1991), p. xviii.
† Mark Skinner Watson, 'The War Department. Chief of Staff', p. 87.
‡ Louis Morton, 'War Plan Orange. Evolution of a Strategy', *World Politics*, Vol. 11, No. 2, January 1959, p. 224.

1941–42.* A senior Army officer, Brigadier (later General) Embrick argued that the Philippines 'had become a military liability of a constantly increasing gravity ... [that] the early dispatch of our fleet to Philippine waters would be literally an act of madness'.†

Between 1924 and 1938, Plan Orange was revised many times but the essential features remained unchanged. In April 1935, American strategic planners concluded that not only was Japan hell-bent on expansion of its empire, but that she could be defeated by the United States only in a long, costly war, in which the Philippines would early be lost. The American response would take the form of 'a progressive movement' through the mandated islands, beginning with the Marshalls and Carolines, to establish 'a secure line of communications to the Western Pacific'. Australia, despite its harbours and resources, was evidently too distant and too far south from where the Americans expected a Japanese attack, that is, the Philippines and the island of Guam. The vast expanses of the thinly-populated Pacific raised the question of whether the makers of American national policy were prepared to incur the obligation of engaging in such a war.‡

The revision of January 1938 recognised that the Royal Navy had responsibilities in the Pacific through Britain's access to the valuable resources in Australia, Malaya, Borneo and elsewhere. The 1938 Plan raised the possibility of greater co-operation between the navies of the United States and Britain in the event of war in the Pacific. Nonetheless, the Philippines always took priority over Singapore as the anti-Japan base in the Pacific, a situation that Casey was still complaining about bitterly in the weeks that followed Pearl Harbor.§

If the majority of the Naval hierarchy sought to prioritise holding the Philippines, the Army leadership was much more sceptical.¶ As the World's conflicts broke out, War Plan Orange was

---
\* Morton, 'War Plan Orange', p. 224.
† Quoted in Mark Skinner Watson, *US Army in WWII. Chief of Staff: Prewar Plans and Preparations* (Washington, D.C: History division of the Department of the Army, p. 415).
‡ Matloff and Snell, *Strategic Planning for Coalition Warfare*, p. 2.
§ Casey Diaries, 19 December 1941.
¶ Lowenthal, 'Roosevelt and the Coming of the War', p. 416.

succeeded by a series of Rainbow Plans, predicated on the belief that the next war would involve multiple countries and not just the United States and Japan. Rainbow Plan 1 aimed at preventing violation of the Monroe Doctrine, Rainbow Plan 2 the defeat of 'enemy forces' in the Pacific, while remaining 'in concert' with Great Britain and France. Rainbow Plan No. 3 provided for the 'protection of United States' vital interests in the Western Pacific by securing control in the Western Pacific as rapidly as possible'.* Whatever the plan, the belief that the Philippines could serve as the American base in the western Pacific in the event of war with Japan was held simultaneously with the fear that the Philippines could not be held in the face of a sustained Japanese attack. It doesn't take much imagination to conclude that planning for war with two such conflicting beliefs was a recipe for disaster.

In February and March 1941, as the ABC1 talks took place, Marshall and Stimson now expressed some confidence that the Philippines could be held once reinforced with the new B-17 Flying Fortress bombers. These long-range bombers could target Japan and help to deter an attack on Singapore. The effective takeover by Japanese forces of French Indochina in July 1941 was the background for Roosevelt strengthening American resolve to hold the Philippines.† On 31 July 1941 General Marshall announced that defending the Philippines was American policy.‡ The command of American forces in the Philippines was given to General Douglas Macarthur.

Ensuring that the United States did not restrict itself to prioritizing the Philippines therefore became the key element of Casey's mission in the months leading up to Pearl Harbor. It was a welcome development for Casey when, on 2 August 1941, he called on General Spaatz [Chief of US Army Air Corps] and General Scanlon [US Army Intelligence] regarding 'their desire for information re airfields in North Australia and the islands'.§ Casey was someone that the Americans clearly found necessary to bring into the discussion on this issue. Their interest must have delighted

* Matloff and Snell, *Strategic Planning for Coalition Warfare*, p. 8.
† Ibid., pp. 66–7.
‡ Reynolds, *Creation of the Anglo-American Alliance*, p. 235.
§ Casey Diaries, 2 August 1941.

him, suggesting, if not confirming that all his efforts were being heeded. Casey's diary for 11 October 1941 records, 'Called on President and had hour's talk, mainly on the part the Philippines may play in Far East and on economic aims in the future."* Casey advised Canberra that the President held out no hope of a permanent peace with Japan. Casey noted that the previous belief that the Philippines could not survive had been reviewed and it was now considered that the garrisons there could hold out for a longer period enabling Philippines-based aircraft to deter Japanese movement southward towards Singapore.† How Casey managed to blandly convey this message to Canberra indicates his skill at restraining what must have been a sense of incredulity. Casey's report of the meeting, sent to Canberra that night, indicated that the President spoke, at length, on 'the changeable attitude by the US Army and Navy' towards the Philippines.‡ The President, obviously aware of the doubts over whether the Philippines could be held, asked if Australia, in the event of war with Japan, might consider the practicability of Australian air squadrons operating from North Borneo, in order to co-operate with the United States air forces based in the Philippines. This was in itself a significant victory. It was recognition that the United States could not base its strategy solely on its holding the Philippines.

Menzies' hold on the Prime Ministership was always on a knife edge and he resigned on 27 August 1941. Arthur Fadden became Prime Minister for 40 days and when Wilson and Coles, two disaffected pro-Menzies backbenchers, crossed the floor, Labor came to power in a minority government. It would be wrong to see the removal of the United Australia Party from office as a decisive turning point in Australia's relationship with the United States. There were important elements of continuity, foremost among which was Casey himself who remained in Washington. In fact, Casey had initiated in a cable of 5 October 1941, the possibility of 'returning home for consultation', motivated in part, claims Bridge,

---

\* Casey Diaries, 11 October 1941.
† Casey to Dept. of External Affairs 11 October 1941, cablegram, 848, A981, Japan 178, NAA.
‡ Casey to Canberra 11 October 1941, cablegram, 848, A981 Japan 178, NAA.

by the prospect of assessing his chances of becoming UAP leader.* When this was denied Casey continued the diplomacy and the public relations campaign aimed at electing greater commitment from the United States to the security of the Pacific and Indian Oceans, and therefore to Australia.

The new Australian Prime Minister, John Curtin and his Minister of External Affairs, Doctor Herbert Vere Evatt, became involved in strategic discussions almost immediately. Long before he released 'Australia Looks to America' in the closing days of December 1941, Curtin was well aware of how far the Australia-United States military relationship had advanced under the previous government. On 13 October 1941, Curtin, as both Prime Minister and Minister for Defence Co-ordination, presented to the Australian Advisory War Cabinet a United States' request for Australia's assistance in various military matters. Curtin used the report to emphasise the increasing interest the United States was exhibiting in Pacific defence. Curtin was clearly aware of American plans. He cited various proposals: supplying equipment and technical assistance to make Rabaul a well-defended anchorage for possible use as a base for American fleet operations against the Caroline Islands and Japanese lines of communication passing eastward of the Philippines; American interest lay in establishing a chain of landing grounds suitable for heavy bombers between Honolulu and New Zealand, Australia, Malaya and the Philippines; advising the United States about conditions in New Caledonia, New Hebrides and the Solomons; and of increasing numbers of American planes arriving in Australia on their way to the Philippines.

The American requests were agreed to, some in principle subject to further investigation, but all were regarded favourably.† Although American service personnel were to staff the airfields for American aircraft, the request sought supplies and equipment including oil and gasoline, bombs, and ammunition. The motive for the American involvement was to facilitate the strengthening of the Philippines, but Australia's growing stature in American thinking was plain to see. In a message to Churchill in late October, Curtin

---

\* Casey to Curtin, A091/225, NAA. Cited in Bridge, *A Delicate Mission*, p. 189.
† War Cabinet Submission, Adendum, 13 October, A2671, 334/1941, NAA.

put the view that were the Commonwealth nations forced into a conflict with Japan, 'we will certainly have done all we can to deter her (Japan) and our defensive position in the Eastern Hemisphere will be all the stronger for the measures that have been taken'.*

Three days after this request, the Advisory War Cabinet received advice from Sir Robert Brooke-Popham, the British Commander-in-Chief, Far East when he attended their meeting on 16 October 1941. He told them that the whole region of Southeast Asia, comprising Burma, Malaya, the Netherlands East Indies, Australia, New Zealand and the Philippines comprised one strategic area. The defence of one affected the others. It was a perspective that reflected Casey's message to the Americans for much of the previous year. Yet, on other matters, Brooke-Popham proved to be wide of the mark. He assured the War Cabinet of the increasing strength of British forces in the Far East, with Malaya growing from strength to strength. The most welcome and the most inaccurate news of this message was that Japan probably was about to attack the Soviet Union rather than move south. As Brooke-Popham put it, 'Russia's preoccupation with the war with Germany presents an opportunity for Japan to rid itself of the Russian threat'.†

This optimistic view was abroad in Washington as well. Casey reported to Canberra that senior American service quarters believed that Japan was about to attack the Soviet Union and that the United States would remain neutral, so long as British and American interests were not also attacked.‡ As late as 25 October 1941, Casey was recording Welles as having 'a fairly hopeful attitude about the Far East, particularly about the probability [he thinks improbability] of their going south'.§ Yet, talks between Hull and the Japanese representatives, Admiral Kichisaburo Nomura and Special Envoy Saburo Kurusu, aimed at reducing the tensions between Japan and the United States, were achieving nothing.¶

\* Curtin to Churchill, 31 October 1941, cablegram, Johcu 2, A3196, 1941. O.17711, NAA.
† Advisory War Council Minutes, 16 October 1941, 533 A 2682, Vol. 3, NAA.
‡ Casey to Evatt, 17 October 1941, cablegram, 865, A981, Far East. 26A, NAA.
§ Casey Diaries, 25 October 1941.
¶ Casey to Curtin and Evatt, 18 November 1941, cablegram, 994, A981, Japan 178, NAA.

Contrary to the views held by some senior American service chiefs, Casey told Canberra in mid-November 1941 that Japanese-Anglo-American relations were 'heading fairly rapidly for a break'.* Casey's conscience was untroubled by his concentrating on conveying the worst possible scenario.

Japan's refusal to withdraw her troops from Indo-China and the American refusal to lift or reduce the restrictions and allow Japanese access to raw materials constituted major obstacles to a lessening of tensions. On 21 November, in a long message to Curtin, Casey trawled through the circumstances in which war in the Pacific might break out.† If Curtin and Evatt had entertained the hope that war with Japan would likely be avoided, Casey's latest message would have demolished that hope.

Simultaneously, Casey, was furiously pursuing all avenues to speed up Australia's rearmament. Australia was an important beneficiary of Lend-Lease and Casey was not afraid to voice his views about delays in the supply of equipment. He told Edward Stettinius, who was in charge of Lend-Lease, on 17 September 1941 that 'it was in his hands whether or not there was an Australian mechanised division in the field in mid-1942'.‡ In October 1941, he involved Welles, Hopkins and the President in a discussion of how well the Australians were using American-made machine tools.§ In November 1941 Casey congratulated himself on the fact that 'we have been getting our requisitions approved and orders placed at 2 to 3 times as great a rate, relatively, than any other beneficiaries, including the British'.¶

Casey hoped for an 'incident' that would bring the United States into the war but feared above all a situation where an embittered Japan struck out at British and Dutch interests with no guarantee of American assistance. Negotiations between Japan and the United States reached an impasse in November, and the United States knew from its MAGIC (US ability to collect and interpret

---
\* Casey to Evatt, 14 November 1941, cablegram, 969, A981, Japan 178, NAA.
† Casey to Curtin and Evatt, 21 November 1941, cablegram, 1014 A981, Japan 178, NAA.
‡ Casey Diaries, 17 September 1941.
§ Casey Diaries, 25 October 1941.
¶ Casey Diaries, 4 November 1941.

Japanese secret codes – hugely helpful in US devising strategy) intercepts that a date had been set in Tokyo for talks to come to an end. The United States had imposed ever tougher sanctions upon Japan. This was not a welcome development for the Australians who still hoped to buy time, avoid war with Japan altogether, or make sure that the United States, Australia and Britain entered a new war together.

Evatt, previously unimpressed by the Japanese threat, now as Minister and armed with Casey's intelligence, warned Parliament of the threat of war. Yet the Australians were still unclear as to how soon the collision with Japan might come. Casey on 29 November reported that a southward advance of a significant Japanese taskforce was expected.* At the same time, Evatt was greatly cheered in the last week in November 1941 by Casey's revelation that a draft proposal from Hull to the Japanese offered a *modus vivendi* that exchanged a retreat of Japan from its recent conquests in exchange for a resumption of trade.† The *modus vivendi* required that neither side would advance further in Asia or the Pacific. To Casey's chagrin, the *modus vivendi* was not ultimately part of the proposals that went to Tokyo. Casey blamed not only Japanese militarism but an intransigent Chinese nationalist movement for the removal of the *modus vivendi*, viewed in China as making too many concessions.‡ From that moment, it was simply a matter of where and when Japan would strike.

At the end of November, Casey reported on a long interview he had had with the Secretary of State. Casey told Curtin and Evatt that Hull now believed that relations with Japan had gone beyond the diplomatic stage and that so far as the United States was concerned, the matter was now up to the Army and Navy. Casey also noted that Hull had taken to using the word 'we' in the sense of the United States and British Commonwealth countries, a very encouraging signal.§

---

\* Horner, *High Command*, p. 135.
† Bob Wurth, *Saving Australia. Curtin's Secret Peace with Japan* (South Melbourne: Lothian, 2006), p. 118.
‡ Casey Diaries, 1 December 1941.
§ Casey to Curtin, Evatt, 29 November 1941, cablegram, 1053, A981, Japan 178, NAA.

Although he was careful to keep Canberra closely informed of his activities and, just as importantly, of what he learnt, it was obvious that Casey was on a fairly long leash. He sought Canberra's approval for various courses of action but the initiative was usually his own. An example was his private meeting with the Japanese Ambassador to the United States, Saburo Kurusu, and the Japanese Special Envoy, Admiral Kichisaburo Nomura, on 30 November 1941. In this case, Casey and Evatt had the same objective of miraculously postponing the looming war.* Bridge notes that Casey was the last diplomat to negotiate with Kurusu on the eve of Pearl Harbor. This was, as Bridge points out, not naivety on Casey's part, but a shrewd manoeuvre to remind the United States that Australia was in the front line of any Japanese attack and that the Americans had given no guarantee to Britain or Australia in relation to a Japanese attack on Malaya. Just such a guarantee did emerge on 1 December 1941.† If nothing else, this last-gasp conversation highlighted Casey's stature in Washington and his capacity to achieve results that worked in Australia's favour.

Casey's focus in 1941 was the looming Pacific War. He could not, by his own efforts, reverse the 'Beat Hitler First' strategy or American reliance upon the Philippines, let alone prevent a war with Japan. Yet the time spent by Casey and the energy employed – interviews, writing, dining, talking – propounding the interest of Australia and the role it could play in the war effort kept Australia's strategic value in plain sight of the military planners. The aftermath of Pearl Harbor would make all those Casey ideas suddenly relevant. Decision makers – both political and military – who had been hearing Casey's reasoned arguments and discussions in a wide range of meetings and gatherings found that ideas that were 'filed', but not actually dismissed, were now worth serious consideration, politically and strategically.

---

\* Casey to Curtin, 30 November 1941, cablegram, 1055, A981, Japan 178, NAA.
† Bridge, 'The Other Blade of the Scissors', pp. 142–3.

*Chapter Eight*

# Curtin and Casey

Bridge has made the point repeatedly that Casey was 'looking to America' long before Curtin put his name over these words in his statement of 27 December 1941. Yet, Curtin is the measuring stick by which most Australians still think about Australia's alliance with the United States. In traversing the path of the Australia-United States relationship in the crucial years of 1941 to 1945, Curtin looms large. If in fact, Casey did contribute to that formulation, the question arises, how do Casey's efforts compare with Curtin's? This might be seen as a fair question because Curtin has been afforded the accolades.

A key sentence in Curtin's 'Australia Looks to America' statement put Australia's international relationships in stark perspective: 'Without any inhibitions, I make it quite clear that Australia looks to America, free of any pangs as to our traditional links of kinship with the United Kingdom'. This sentence has become the symbol both of Curtin's foreign policy and indeed, of Curtin himself. The phrase is continually linked to Curtin and has entered the Australian political lexicon. The conventional wisdom is clearly based on the fact that within days of 'Australia Looks to America', thousands of American servicemen, growing to hundreds of thousands, plus ships, equipment and aircraft began arriving in Australia.

Thus, the phrase 'Australia Looks to America', which summed up neatly Australia's position in the crucial days following 7 December, constitutes one of the foundations upon which Curtin's status rests. The belief about Curtin ultimately led to his being perceived as the saviour of Australia.[*] Yet, the appellation is not justified. When

---
* Lee, *John Curtin. Saviour of Australia*.

Curtin issued that statement on 27 December (written incidentally by his Press Secretary, Don Rodgers), the Pacific War had been raging for almost three weeks. On this reasoning, nearly three weeks elapsed before Curtin publicly expressed these fears and referred to American assistance. This is clearly absurd. Moreover, the Curtin declaration is just that, a statement written for a newspaper. Many writers have described it and continue to describe it as an appeal. to the United States. It is no such thing. It is but a statement of Australian thinking, issued for the information of the Australian public and a call upon Australians to prepare for war.

The Japanese attacks on 7 December, plus the German declaration of war upon the United States four days later, virtually destroyed the isolationist cause and forced the hitherto neutral United States to become a combatant. As Casey put it on 8 December 1941: 'The Japanese attack has welded this country into one as nothing else could possibly have done'. In the days following Pearl Harbor, General George Marshall, Chief of Staff of the United States Army, took charge of the response to the Japanese attack. It was Marshall himself who decided that the major American base to counter the Japanese attack would be in Australia.* Upon reflection, it might seem obvious that it could hardly have been anyone else. While Roosevelt and Churchill may have been the political strategists for the United States and Britain, it was Marshall who was the chief military strategist for the Allied counter attack, certainly at that early stage of the war.

Immediately after Pearl Harbor, Marshall pensioned off his old guard in order to promote some of the bright young officers he had met during his career, George Smith Patton, Omar Bradley and Dwight Eisenhower. Eisenhower won much favourable comment over his brilliant conduct of war games in Louisiana in mid-1940, which led to his immediate promotion to brigadier general.† Marshall brought Eisenhower to Washington urgently. Arriving at Washington's Union Station on Sunday morning, 14 December, one week after Pearl Harbor, Eisenhower found the War Department surprisingly almost empty except for Marshall,

---

\* Lyon, *Eisenhower*, p. 94.
† Robert H. Ferrell (ed.), *The Eisenhower Diaries* (New York: W.W. Norton and Company, 1981), p. 39.

who told Eisenhower to put down on paper a plan for the strategic response to the surprise Japanese attack. Eisehower submitted a plan to Marshall the same day. Marshall gave it back to him, without actually rejecting it and told Eisenhower to make small but significant amendments. The new plan, completed by Eisenhower on 17 December, was submitted to Marshall who approved it for transmission to Roosevelt the same day.

While it is tempting to credit Eisenhower with the preparation of the American strategic response, it was Marshall who described in broad detail, the size, composition and time requirements of the American response and virtually instructed Eisenhower, to commit the proposals to paper, filling in some numerical blanks in the ordinance requirements, what might be termed 'the nuts and bolts'. He even included in his briefing to Eisenhower the proposal that was then being floated around Washington, to persuade the Soviet Union to take a belligerent stand against Japan and provide aid to those nations and areas under Japanese attack.* Eisenhower's recommendation was to 'use Australia as a base', which would entail making certain, the safety of Australia itself'.

Marshall's response to Eisenhower's recommendations about the Philippines – 'do your best to save them' – on the surface, at least, suggested no great urgency.† A more likely explanation was Marshall's recognition that in reality, the Philippines was a hopeless situation, but Eisenhower might come up with some tactic that would lessen the impact of total defeat. Yet the plan itself suggested an overwhelming reliance upon the Australian land mass. In his briefing, Marshall ignored the much-vaunted Rainbow Plan created for precisely this purpose. What he did include was a model of clear, concise directions that became the basis for the United States' conduct of the war in the Pacific and had the consequence of converting Australia into a vast arsenal that would, in effect, remove any possibility of Japanese forces invading the country. It is worthwhile to quote the Marshall/Eisenhower Plan, called 'Steps to Be Taken', in full:

---

\* Office of the Chief of Military History, 17 December 1941, Washington. OPD Exec, 8 Book A.
† Gelber, 'Turning Points', p. 78.

SECRET

Assistance to the Far East.

Steps to be taken.

Build up in Australia a base of operations from which critical supplies (planes and ammunition) and personnel can be moved into the Philippines – probably entirely by air. Speed is essential.

Influence Russia to enter the war, at least give us secret use of certain Siberian air fields.

Pursuit planes.

Move carrier with Army Pursuit planes, pilots, ammunition and bombs from San Diego to Brisbane, Australia.

Send fastest commercial vessel immediately available on West Coast, with pursuit planes, pilots, ammunition and bombs to Australia.

Ferry planes from Australia into Philippines.

Heavy Bombers

Move heavy bombers (B-24) – via Africa to Australia to set up a combined fighting-transport service from Darwin to Philippines. Also send B-17 heavy bombers in small groups across Pacific via the southern ferrying route from West Coast to Australia, if Christmas Island and Fiji fields can be used.

Transport Planes.

Establish in Australia, a transport plane ferrying service to move ammunition and supplies from Brisbane to Darwin, and possibly into Borneo or Manila.

Bombs and Ammunition.

Initially, utilize the bombs and ammunition now in Australia, others to be carried on carriers and fast merchant vessels with planes. Establish fast merchant ship supply service from US to Australia for maintenance. Ferry by plane from Australia to Philippines.

Clearly if there was a moment at which Australia was 'saved', this was it. Australia, not even on the radar as a base for the United States when Casey arrived in Washington in March 1940, was now central to American thinking. Of course, it was the 'incident' of Pearl Harbor that had brought about the transformation. Yet the situation had arrived at the point anticipated by Casey, whose achievement in disseminating his gospel of Australia being viewed as vital to American strategy in the looming war, had brought such a brilliant result. Although there is no direct evidence that Casey inspired Marshall's thinking, Marshall had met Casey before Pearl Harbor and was involved in many discussions with senior military figures who had also been in communication and negotiations with Casey. Casey's entreaties and suggestions about an American base in Australia were now relevant to detailed American planning at the highest level.

On the very day that he approved of the Marshall/Eisenhower plan, 17 December, Roosevelt called Casey to the Oval Office to tell him that he had read Curtin's offer to 'co-operate with the United States forces in the provision of a naval base at Rabaul and aerodrome facilities in territories under the control of the Commonwealth and at New Caledonia', which Casey had delivered to the President on 13 December.* Roosevelt explained that the United States regarded the whole South West Pacific as one area. As the President acknowledged, this notion that 'the South West Pacific is one unit' had been Casey's theme over a long period.† The war had to be regarded from 'a geographical rather than a national point of view ... and that the defence of Australia and its outlying islands were just as important as the defence of the Philippines', although Roosevelt believed that the Philippines were more immediately threatened. The President told Casey that they hoped to use Australia as the place to establish a bridgehead and a base.‡ Roosevelt asked Casey to 'please tell your government' that we have already started' on the matters raised in Curtin's message of 13 December.

As of 17 December 1941, there was presidential approval for Australia to become a major base for the American response

---

\* Curtin to Roosevelt, 13 December 1941, cablegram, 153 A981, War 53A, NAA.
† Casey Diaries, 17 December 1941.
‡ Casey to Curtin and Evatt, 17 December 1941, cablegram, 1162, A981, War 33,1 NAA.

to Japan. If Stimson is to be believed, the concept of Australia becoming a base had been locked into American thinking for some time.* It hardly needs to be said that the phrase, 'Australia Looks to America' is completely misleading. Rather, America looks to Australia. Australia was to be the basis of the American conduct of the Pacific War. This was the goal to which Casey had clearly been working, essentially since he arrived in Washington, in 1940 but which he had especially pushed in 1941. The Plan was more Marshall's than it was Eisenhower's. but more Casey's than it was anybody's. Casey had for the past two years, spoken to as many service people as he possibly could, always with the same message, the relevance of Australia in any plan for Pacific security. Given Casey's indefatigable energy, this message became well known to the various service people and became relevant when the full import of the Japanese attack began to sink in. Like Marshall, most of the important military leaders in the United States had heard first hand the Casey 'Gospel'.

If there is at the very least, a plausible case that Casey had influenced events positively from the perspective of the 'saving' of Australia, the same cannot be said of Curtin's 'Look to America'. That Don Rodgers, Curtin's Press Secretary, wrote this statement is now well established. Rodgers wrote it for Curtin, it was published over Curtin's name and, as Rodgers explained to this author, it represented Curtin's thinking at the time.† At that time, Curtin had enough to occupy his time without drafting press messages. He could never have anticipated that it would become, accidentally and wrongly, the historically significant document it has.

Historically significant it may be, but seriously flawed. 'Australia Looks to America' fulfils none of the criteria for being regarded as a definitive or significant document of national importance. Firstly, it was not drafted by any senior member of government, but by the Prime Minister's Press Secretary: the press release was merely scanned by the Prime Minister before being

---

\* Bridge, *A Delicate Mission*, p. 212.
† I conducted two interviews with Rodgers in 1977. Recordings of those interviews are held by the author and the Australian Museum of Democracy, Canberra.

sent to the newspaper.* Secondly, it was written by Rodgers simply in response to a request by the Editor of the *Melbourne Herald* for a New Year message and was published on 27 December 1941. Cyril Pearl, the editor of the new *Sunday Telegraph* (Sydney), saw what he considered was a new slant on the war effort, a switch in Australia's allegiances, and ran it prominently the next day. Pearl made a decision to concentrate on Australia seeking aid from the United States rather than the real message, that is, of Australia seeking aid from both the United States and the Soviet Union and encouraging an 'all in' effort on the home front.

Thirdly, it was never sent to the President, or indeed, anybody. It was essentially a Press release written for one newspaper. Fourthly, while it conveyed to the people of Australia a clear message that the war situation was rapidly deteriorating and that American and Soviet help was needed, Curtin knew at the time that it was issued that the United States was about to establish its major base in Australia. Essentially the American President had personally told both Casey and the Australian government of American strategy involving Australia. In the two weeks between Roosevelt's decision to approve the Marshall plan and the issuing of 'Australia Looks to America', Curtin was informed of the dimensions of the American aid in some detail. Initially, the information had come to him in a cablegram from Casey, within hours of Casey's being informed by the President himself, that he regarded Australia as a bridge-head and a base.†

There are at least two puzzling aspects of Curtin's statement. The first is what Curtin hoped to achieve with his American audience. Curtin may have intended 'Australia Looks to America' as an attempt to keep the United States focused upon the Pacific and Australia. Evatt would later claim that the Labor government was shocked when it learnt of Roosevelt's agreement to the 'Beat Hitler First' strategy. On the other hand, Bridge has shown that the Australian government did, in fact, know of the 'Beat Hitler First'

---

\* See also James Prior, 'How Curtin Became a War Casualty', *National Times*, 6–11 February 1978, p. 25.
† Casey to Department of External Affairs, 17 December 1941, cablegram, 1162, A981, War 33, 1, NAA.

policy within days of its formulation. While there has always been a degree of conjecture over the precise time of Australia's learning of the policy, Bridge notes that Casey notified the then acting Prime Minister, Arthur Fadden, in February 1941 that Roosevelt had made it quite clear that in the event of the United States becoming involved in a war with Japan, it would have to be 'a holding war'. To fight a war with Japan would be a dangerous diversion of forces and material from the main centre of operations, which in his [Roosevelt's] view was 'the Atlantic and Great Britain'.[*] It would be inconceivable for Curtin and the Labor members of the Advisory War Cabinet, although still in Opposition, to be ignorant of this.

In reality, the statement of 27 December was nothing more than a press release purporting to be a declaration of the Prime Minister informing the people of Australia where their future lay. The difficulty with that argument, however, is that, from the very beginning, the statement was regarded as an open appeal for the United States and the Soviet Union to come to the aid of Australia. Curtin made no attempt to place the statement in its correct context. In other words, the statement was misinterpreted and was, in fact, supposed to be something it was not. The blame for this lies both with the way it was written but also with the way it was treated by the press.

No matter how it is read, Curtin's 'Australia Looks to America' statement is misleading Nowhere does it acknowledge that Australia was about to become a huge American base. It remains a matter for conjecture why, in drafting the statement, Rodgers clearly constructed it that way. More importantly, it remains a matter for conjecture why Curtin, in approving its release, chose to not even hint that massive American help was already pouring into Australia. It is impossible to avoid the conclusion that in the matter of establishing a sound relationship with the American President, Curtin made a serious error of judgment in publicly calling for American aid when he already knew the details of the American strategy involving Australia. Indeed, as already stated, American forces started arriving in Australia on 22 December 1941.[†]

---

[*] Bridge, 'R.G. Casey', p. 184.
[†] The first American servicemen to arrive in Australia did so on 22

Roosevelt read it for the first time at the end of December, when it was reported in sections of the American press. The statement was published there on 28 December 1941.* The most frequently quoted sentence, 'Without any inhabitations of any kind, I make it quite clear that Australia looks to America, free of any pangs as to our traditional links or kinship with the United Kingdom' appeared in the second paragraph of both *New York Times* and *Washington Post* reports. Yet, Casey's diary for that week makes no reference to it perhaps because he soon learned that Roosevelt was extremely displeased.

Maie Casey recounted how President Roosevelt had called Casey to the White House and told him that if he thought that this statement would ingratiate Australia with the United States, he (Roosevelt) assured him that it would have the opposite effect. Maie Casey claims that the President insisted that his words were to be regarded as personal and not part of the official record.† Undoubtedly, this is the reason Casey neither made a note in his diary nor informed the Prime Minister. His silence on the matter for the rest of his life accorded with what he regarded as the honourable thing to do. The President had told him in confidence. Casey kept that confidence, despite the fact that Roosevelt's thoughts were of profound political and historical significance.

Hudson's biography of Casey deals only briefly with Casey's reaction to it. Casey committed to paper (but not his diary) his belief after talking to Roosevelt about it, and after the President put him under 'a seal of secrecy' that not only was the Curtin statement counter-productive, but was seen in Washington as almost treason against the major ally, Britain. Hudson found this (undated) 'scrap of paper' in a safe in Casey's house eight years after his death while researching the biography.‡

---

December 1941, dis-embarking from five troopships escorted by the USS *Pensacola*. The convoy was originally destined for the Philippines but was re-directed to Brisbane.

\* *New York Times*, 28 December 1941, p. 11 and *Washington Post*, 28 December 1941, p. 4.
† Maie Casey, *Tides and Eddies* (Harmondsworth: Penguin, 1969), p. 69. This statement appears in no official records.
‡ Hudson, *Casey*, p. 135.

Maie Casey recollected that 'Look to America' did not just offend Roosevelt, but also caused Casey anger and embarrassment.* It might be profitable to dwell on that sentence for a moment. Curtin's strongly worded plea for American assistance does not differ greatly from the message that Casey had been expressing from the time that he arrived in the United States. Curtin, however, used language that was far more assertive and demanding, far more aggressive even, reflecting the changed context. In Curtin's defence, Japan had commenced hostilities and the threat to Australian survival was real and growing daily.

It must be recognised that Casey too, often needed to be assertive and insistent. This invites the interpretation therefore, that if Casey was embarrassed and angered it may well have been at the reactions to Curtin's statement within the United States and Britain, and not to the statement itself. In other words, given Casey's passionate dedication to an American involvement in the conflict with the Axis powers, first Germany and subsequently Japan, the more probable grounds for his embarrassment or anger could have been the blunt, direct language used in the statement, language far removed from the felicitous periphrasis of his world of diplomacy.

The second puzzling aspect of 'Australia Looks to America' is that it was directed as much to Stalin as to Roosevelt. Curtin's 'Australia Looks to America' is in two parts. The first deals with Australia's foreign relations, the second part deals with the need for Australia, internally, to go on a war footing. The whole tenor of the statement reveals Curtin's belief that the war in the Pacific would be fought by a combination of the Soviet Union, the United States, the British Commonwealth, Dutch and Chinese forces. As Humphrey McQueen has pointed out, the strength of the appeal to the Soviet Union is no less than that of the appeal to the United States.† Of the thirty-two paragraphs of prose and the stanza of four lines that make up the Curtin statement, four deal with the justification of Australia seeking Soviet assistance, while three deal with the justification of Australia seeking American assistance.

\* Casey, *Tides and Eddies*, p. 83.
† Humphrey McQueen, *Japan to the Rescue. Australia's Security Around the Indonesian Archipelago during the American Century* (Melbourne: Heinemann, 1991), p. 1.

Two paragraphs refer to both nations. The summary within the statement reads: 'Summed up, Australian external policy will be shaped towards obtaining Russian aid and working out, with the United States as the major factor, a plan of Pacific strategy, along with British, Chinese and Dutch forces'.

Curtin's emphasis on the seeking of Soviet aid at a time when the Soviet Union was fighting for survival is, at first glance, mystifying. Curtin's statement explained it this way: 'As the Australian government enters 1942, it has behind it a record of realism in foreign affairs'. Specifically, Curtin pointed to what he called 'a forthright declaration in respect of Finland, Hungary and Romania' and which he said was followed by a declaration of war against those countries by the Democracies. Curtin was clearly raising the proposition that Australia could reasonably expect Soviet assistance because Australia had responded positively to the Soviet request for a declaration of war against Finland, Hungary and Romania. This is how Curtin put it: 'We felt that there should be no half-measures in our dealings with the Soviets when that nation was being assailed by the three countries mentioned'. Then came the argument for a negotiated pay-off: 'Similarly we put forward that a reciprocal agreement between Russia and Britain should be negotiated to meet an event of aggression by Japan. Our suggestion was then regarded, wrongly as time has proved, as premature. Now, with equal realism ... we should be able to look forward with reason to aid from Russia against Japan'.

The historian Peter Lyon described the urge to secure Soviet intervention in the war against Japan as 'a preposterous notion'.* It was, after all, only eight months since Stalin had signed a five-year neutrality pact with Japan. This was truly a pact that worked admirably for both countries. The Soviet Union, already suspicious of Germany and unsure of German intentions, specifically the possibility of a massive German invasion from the west, desperately wanted its eastern boundaries secure. Japan, for its part, needed just as desperately to keep her northern flank secure to facilitate a drive south. The pact therefore, was in the national interests of both the

---

\* Peter Lyon, *Eisenhower. Portrait of the Hero* (Boston: Little Brown and Company, 1974), p. 93.

Soviet Union and Japan. The subsequent German invasion of the Soviet Union did not violate the Soviet-Japan Neutrality Pact. Strained it no doubt but its preservation became even more vital to Soviet interests as the Wehrmacht stormed to the very gates of Moscow. Nothing could have been more inimical to Stalin's interests than a belligerent Japan on her eastern borders. Yet Curtin described as realistic an expectation of Soviet aid in the fight against Japan.

To be fair, Soviet intervention against Japan was a matter that was being discussed in Washington, London and Canberra throughout 1941. In a letter to Curtin in late October 1941, a day after he had called on Hornbeck and Loy Henderson of the Russian desk at the State Department, Casey reported to Canberra that there was information that Japan might shortly attack the Soviet Union.* Rather than extend southward, Japan would exploit the opportunity offered by Russia's precarious hold on its Eastern borders. From Australia's point of view, this could not be regarded as anything but favourable. A Japan engaged in fighting with the Soviet Union would be hardly likely to launch further aggressive moves involving Australia or indeed embark on any adventures in the Pacific region. In a submission to the Australian War Cabinet, Evatt proposed taking steps to seek the appointment of 'a Russian Consul-General', citing the following reasons:

> The necessity for giving the fullest material and moral support to Russia and continued Russian resistance [against the Wehrmacht], (b) Common political interests, in particular the consideration that Soviet policy in respect of Japan in the [Near] East is important to Australia, and (c) the potential importance of Australian-Russian trade.†

In Australia especially, the possibility of conflict between the Soviet Union and Japan was such an attractive one that a variation emerged. Rather than wait for Japan to strike the first blow, the Soviet Union might launch a massive attack on the islands of Japan, in other words, beat Japan to the first and possibly killer blow. Curtin

* Casey to Department of External Affairs, 17 October 1941, cablegram, 865, A981: Far East 26A, NAA.
† Dr H.V. Evatt, 4 November 1941 War Cabinet Submission, Agendum 367/1941, *DAFP*, Vol. V, Doc. 96, p. 160.

raised the matter of Soviet-Japan relations at a meeting of the Australian War Cabinet on 10 November. He proposed that Japan be warned that any attack by her on the Soviet Union would be resisted by the British Commonwealth, irrespective of the attitude of the United States. All members present were in agreement, although noting the New Zealand government's preference for caution and adopting a wait and see policy. Unable to speak for the whole of the Commonwealth or indeed to communicate directly with Japan, the War Cabinet simply conveyed to London the recommendation that such a warning be issued to Tokyo.* This would have been no surprise to London. Curtin had sent a similar message on 4 November.†

As the expectation of a Japanese attack on Australia heightened, Casey's interest in pressuring the Soviet Union to rattle the sabres at Japan also grew. Four days after the Pearl Harbor attack, when Britain, the United States and Australia were emerging from a state of shock, Curtin cabled London: 'We think time has now arrived to make earnest attempt to obtain Russia's intervention'.‡ Casey cabled Curtin three days later (14 December) that the 'great importance of active Russian co-operation against Japan' was fully realized in Washington but that an American approach had met with a negative reply by Stalin. Casey reported however, that in conveying Stalin's rejection, the Soviet Ambassador suggested to Hull that if the United States and Britain were able to make some kind of 'offers', Russian co-operation against Japan might be forthcoming.§ It seems that this faint offer by the Soviet leadership to join the Allies against Japan in return for some kind of 'offer' or deal was seized upon by the Curtin government with enthusiastic alacrity.

Whatever hopes that Casey had of the Soviet Union launching a preemptive strike against Japan received no support when he called upon the new Soviet ambassador, Maxim Litvinov, on 16 December 1941. Litvinov had served as foreign minister for a decade and knew the Japanese situation well. He told Casey that

---

\* Canberra to London, War Cabinet Submission, 2680, 134/1941, NAA.
† Curtin to London, 4 November 1941, A981, Japan 169 iii, NAA.
‡ Curtin to London, 11 December 1941, cablegram, 789, A981: War 33, Attachment B, NAA.
§ Casey to Curtin, 14 December 1941, cablegram, 1145, A981, War 54, NAA.

'a declaration of war on Japan would necessitate moving probably 20 divisions to Siberia'.* Litvinov noted that he could not see how attacking Siberia would be in Japan's interests either. Yet it must be acknowledged that hopes of Soviet military action against Japan remained very much alive in Allied thinking in 1942. After a meeting with Litvinov on 14 February, Casey noted that 'of set purpose I did not make any reference of Russia attacking Japan or Japan attacking Russia' for the State Department advised against provoking the Russians in this way'.† Yet clearly Casey's glacial avoidance of the subject must have been against his judgment. Russian intervention in the war was something that the Allies in general hoped to see as they scanned the international horizon. Equally clear is the fact that Curtin's appeal had as little effect on Stalin as it did on Roosevelt.

No man is without flaws and Curtin had his. His hidden personality is difficult to parse. His failure to anticipate Roosevelt's vexation at the issuing of 'Australia Looks to America' demonstrated either a level of insensitivity that jeopardised the relationship or a recklessness justified by the dire situation in which Australia found itself. Casey could have responded in a way that was less than complimentary to Curtin but it was not in his nature to go down that path. Of course it is often pointed out in Curtin's defence that 'Look to America' was designed to remind the United States of Australia's own challenges and simultaneously to challenge the 'Beat Hitler First' decision, taken by Churchill and Roosevelt earlier in the year. Curtin strongly believed that Australia must have the fullest say in Pacific strategy.‡ Even so, it is surely a myth that 'Australia Looks to America' was the catalyst that loosened Australia's ties with Great Britain and created, that is, gave birth to, the American Alliance. As a corollary, Curtin's identification with the creation of the American alliance is undeserved.

This conclusion needs to be acknowledged if Casey's contribution is to be fairly judged. In dealing with Curtin, much of the literature has been of an unquestioning character. Few writers have referred to Roosevelt's annoyance at the publication

---

\* Casey Diaries, 16 December 1941.
† Casey Diaries, 14 February 1942.
‡ Day, *The Politics of War*, p. 227.

of 'Australia Looks to America' at a time when Curtin was aware of the American decision to convert Australia into the jump-off base for the American offensive. Roosevelt could have concluded that Curtin, by issuing what seems like a virtual public appeal while knowing that the crucial decision had already been made and that, within a very short time, huge numbers of American servicemen and impressive quantities of American materiel would appear in Australia, was guilty of self-promotion and creating the belief that he exercised a powerful influence over the American President.

The kindest interpretation of Curtin's knowledge of the precise details of the American strategy at this time makes 'Australia Looks to America' seem less sincere and less convincing. A stricter interpretation would invite speculation about his attitude to and his relations with the Australian people. In wartime, it is not common for matters of strategy to be conveyed to the civilian populace. The Australian people at this time, late 1941, early 1942, however, were seriously concerned about the future of the nation and indeed, their own safety. The rapidity at which Japanese forces were moving southwards, approaching the Australian continent, created a state of anxiety. Colonel Gerald Wilkinson, who had been appointed British Liaison Officer with General MacArthur, in 1941, wrote in his diary that when he arrived in Australia from the Philippines, MacArthur had informed him that in 1942, Curtin had 'more or less offered him the country on a platter'. Wilkinson's own view was that Curtin was 'badly panicked and most un-statesman-like at the time'.* It might be reasonable to suppose that the nation's leader, who obviously appreciated the dire situation more than the civilian population, would assure the people that help was on its way, rather than keep them in the dark.

An interpretation of the sequence of events leads to the conclusion that Curtin had no significant role in the final American decision. This is not to deny the major role he took in the subsequent Pacific War. His battles with Churchill, his standing up to Roosevelt, the leadership he displayed as leader of the Australian people in their gravest hour have ensured his place

---

\* Papers of Gerald Wilkinson, April 1943, Churchill Archives Centre, Churchill College, Cambridge (Wilkinson Collection).

as an outstanding and courageous figure in the history of Australia. Yet it is difficult not to agree with the minority of commentators who look past Curtin when seeking an explanation of the alliance between Australia and the United States. Yet, as World War Two fades into history, Curtin's name and reputation continue to be invoked as much for the establishment of the alliance as they do for his wartime leadership role. As a consequence, the reputation of Casey and his role in establishing the alliance between the United States and Australia has been seriously underestimated. In effect, both Curtin and Casey were giving the same message. Yet, it is a matter of record that Curtin's message, in contrast to Casey's, failed to achieve anything in the United States.

*Chapter Nine*

# Pearl Harbor and Its Aftermath

It needs to be noted that some, mostly American, writers have chosen to overestimate Casey's influence with the President. The surprise Japanese attack on American warships and defence installations at Pearl Harbor on 7 December 1941 traumatised the United States and has generated a vast body of literature.* As well, there have been reports by the nine official investigations and enquiries into the attack, with the enquiry conducted by Senator Alben Barkely regarded as the most comprehensive and authoritative.† Central to the interest is the incredulity that a nation as powerful as the United States could be taken by surprise so easily. It could be expected, therefore, that much of the literature attempts to seek out a culprit or culprits upon whom the blame might be placed for this 'day that will live in infamy'.‡

Within eight weeks of the attack the local Army and Navy Commanders, General Short and Admiral Husband Kimmel, had been relieved, their careers and reputations permanently destroyed. Far from settling the issues raised, however, their removal only heightened the interest and stimulated the search for explanations.

---

* Louis Morton, *Pearl Harbor in Perspective*. A Bibliographical Survey of US Naval Institute Proceedings, LXXXI, April 1955, pp. 461–8.
† 'Investigation of the Pearl Harbor Attack Pursuant to S.Con. Resolution 27, 79th Congress'. Report and Hearings of the Joint Committee on the Investigation of the Pearl Harbor Attack. Congress of the United States (Washington: Government Printing Office, 1946). Hereafter referred to as PHA Report and PHA Hearings.
‡ President Franklin D. Roosevelt 'Address to Congress 8 December', *New York Times*, 9 December 1941, p. 1.

Senator Barkley, in introducing the resolution into the Senate for the final investigation, which began in November 1945, said that the first purpose of the Congressional investigation was that of 'fixing responsibility' for the Pearl Harbor disaster 'upon an individual, or a group of individuals, or upon a system under which they operated or co-operated, or failed to do either'.*

The final days of a neutral United States proved to be a period of infinite interest to American historians and writers. For Casey in Washington, it was a period of intense activity, a time in which he employed his diplomatic skills and his networking habits to the utmost and a period he seemed to enjoy. However, the historiography of that momentous period contains references to Casey that to this day have remained a mystery. The claim has often been made that on the afternoon of 6 December 1941, less than 24 hours before the Japanese attack, Casey called at the White House with British Ambassador, Lord Halifax, and conferred with President Roosevelt for an undisclosed period. What creates the mystery is that there is no record of such a meeting ever having taken place. It is unlikely that Casey would have conferred with the American President and not reported the meeting to Canberra. Yet, there is no mention of it in Casey's reports, diary, nor in the files held in the National Australian Archives. White House records contain no mention of it and the State Department searched twice through all relevant documents and found nothing.

An unrecorded visit to the American President by a relatively junior diplomat would not normally be of great interest to historians. Casey's supposed visit, however, became important for several reasons. Casey had access to the President and to the highest levels of the Roosevelt Administration to a degree greater than might be expected of a representative of a small nation member of the British Commonwealth. Australia's foreign policy sometimes echoed Britain's, yet Feis has noted that Americans were not as habituated to regard the aims of the Dominion of Australia with the same suspicion as those of Britain and that Casey, accordingly, sometimes 'found the path smoother that his British colleagues

---

\* Congressional Records, 6 September 1945, 8479–80.

[did]'.* Casey was a popular figure in Washington.

Moreover, just a few days previously, Casey had undertaken talks with the Japanese Ambassador, Kichisaburo Nomura and the Special Envoy, Saburo Kurusu, in an effort to break the deadlock that had arisen in the United States-Japan talks. Although Casey had the approval of the Australian Minister for External Affairs, Dr Evatt to undertake the talks, the initiative was entirely his own.†

From the viewpoint of many critics, Roosevelt was overly influenced by Churchill and privately, at least, anxious to lead the United States into war. From that position, several theories may be developed, ranging from the belief that despite ample knowledge that Pearl Harbor was about to be attacked, the Administration purposefully left it exposed and allowed the attack to happen, to another belief that the Administration manipulated and manoeuvred Japan into attacking by deliberately placing the bulk of the Pacific fleet at Pearl Harbor as an inviting and tempting target. This latter 'conspiracy theory' is described by Kenneth S. Davis.‡

A visit by an Australian diplomat who was close to the British Ambassador and who shared Britain's desire to see the United States enter the war became significant when no record of their conversation was kept and indeed, when all evidence of the visit was missing or simply, non-existent. The visit, moreover, was supposedly made less that twenty-four hours before the Japanese planes roared over the Hawaiian Islands. One American study, in bemoaning the absence of any record of the conversation, concludes: 'This phase of the pre-Pearl Harbor crisis is so poorly documented that it has invited very compromising interpretations'.§ The American historian, the appropriately-named Ladislas Farago, put it higher, calling the visit a 'mission': 'The Casey mission to FDR continues to remain one of the mysteries of the pre-Pearl Harbor diplomacy'.¶ The works referring to the Casey 'visit' multiplied over time and

---

\* Feis, *The Road to Pearl Harbor*, p. 135.
† Evatt to Casey, 29 November 1941, cablegram, 178, A0981, NAA.
‡ Kenneth S. Davis, *Experience in War* (MacMillan: New York, 1956).
§ W.L. Langer and S. E. Gleason, *The Undeclared War: 1940–1941*, New York, 1953, p. 920.
¶ Ladislas Farago, *The Broken Seal* (London: Arthur Barker Ltd, 1967).

featured prominently in at least nine substantial books.* The Australian historian, Roger Bell referred to it briefly in his 1977 work, 'Unequal Allies' quoting Esthus as his source.

The initial reference at the PHA Hearings to the Roosevelt-Casey meeting emerged when S. W. Richardson, the General Counsel assisting the Congressional Committee, learnt of a cablegram that Casey had dispatched to Curtin and Evatt on 6 December at 9.30 pm (Washington time). Richardson claimed that the cablegram discussed the procedures to be followed by Roosevelt in relation to a message he was proposing to send to Emperor Hirohito.† In May 1946, Richardson, acting through the State Department, asked the Australian Legation in Washington for information about Casey's cablegram of 6 December. He did not ask for an actual copy. The Legation's reply, dated 22 May and signed by L.R. McIntyre, stated, inter alia, 'the message was dispatched from Washington at 9.30 pm on 6 December 1941. The information contained therein regarding the procedure to be followed by the President had come orally from the President late in the afternoon of 6 December'.‡

The reply then went on to convey Roosevelt's concurrence to a joint warning that Britain and the Commonwealth nations proposed sending to Japan. It added that Roosevelt had decided to send a message to Emperor Hirohito and that if no reply was received from the Emperor by Monday evening, the President would issue a warning on Tuesday afternoon or evening. Roosevelt had asked that the British Commonwealth warning be held over

---

\* Esthus, *From Enmity to Alliance*, Charles A. Beard, *President Roosevelt and the Coming of the War, 1941* (New Haven: Yale University Press, 1948), Rear Admiral Robert A. Theobold, *The Final Secret of Pearl Harbor: the Washington contribution to the Japanese Attack* (New York, 1954), George Morgenstein, *Pearl Harbor* (New York, 1947), Joseph P. Lash, *Roosevelt and Churchill, 1939–1941. A Partnership that Saved the World* (London, 1977), David Bergamini, *Japan's Imperial Conspiracy. How Emperor Hirohito Led Japan into War Against the West* (London, 1971), Feis, *The Road to Pearl Harbor*, Farago, *The Broken Seal*, Langer and Gleason, *The Undeclared War*.
† PHA Hearings, Part 14, pp. 631–2.
‡ This quotation comes from the *Pearl Harbour Attack Hearings* and not from Australian sources. The Australian Embassy in Washington and the department files held by the NAA have been checked but no record can be found of McIntyre's letter of 22 May 1946.

until Wednesday morning, that is, after his own warning had been delivered to Tokyo.* What made the Australian message so interesting to the congressional Committee was that Roosevelt's reported proposals were contrary to the advice he was receiving from the State Department.

The wording of the reply from the Australian Legation in Washington seems to support the view that Casey had spoken to the President on that fateful afternoon. Furthermore, it is the Australian Legation report and nothing else, which was the basis for the speculation and conjecture in the above-mentioned histories of the period. It is now clear that the Casey visit did not take place. The advice contained in the letter of 22 May 1946 from the Australian Legation was correct but ambiguous and was seriously and consistently misinterpreted.

The key to establishing if Casey visited the White House on 6 December 1941, and, if he did, what was discussed, lies in his cables to Curtin and Evatt on the same date. Casey dispatched three cablegrams to Australia that day, 6 December, all addressed to Prime Minister Curtin and External Affairs Minister Evatt. The times of dispatch indicate that nothing more than the actual time each was logged out of Washington. The first was sent from Washington at 3.00 pm (incorrectly shown in *DAFP*, Vol. V, Doc. 167 as 3.00 am), the second at 3.37 pm and the last at 9.30 pm. This latter cablegram is the one paraphrased by the Australian Legation. The complete text of that cablegram, Casey to Curtin, is as follows:

> Washington, 6 December 1941. (9.30 pm)
>
> President sent for British ambassador late this afternoon to say that he was telegraphing Japanese Emperor (text follows in my immediate following telegram). President said that if he received no answer from Japanese Emperor by Monday evening he would give 'warning' to Japanese government on Tuesday afternoon or evening and suggests that in these circumstances British and others give their warnings on equivalent of Wednesday morning Washington time.
>
> The above time table is likely to be speeded up if the Japanese move more quickly. The President said that he was sending a confidential message to the Thai Prime Minister saying that

---

* PHA Report, pp. 428–9 and PHA Hearings, Part 14.

the United States Government would regard it as a 'hostile act' if Japan attacked Thailand, Netherlands East Indies, Malaya or Burma.

News is being published tonight here of two large heavily escorted convoys (totalling 35 ships escorted by 8 cruisers and numerous destroyers) having been seen this morning to S.E. of Point Camau (the southern point of Indo-China) steaming westward towards Gulf of Siam.

American estimates of numbers of Japanese troops in Southern Indo-China are also being given to press tonight, British Ambassador tells me that the President does not believe that the Japanese will make an aggressive move as soon as the Secretary of State does.*

That cablegram from Casey, with its clear indications in the first sentence of the first paragraph and in the last sentence of the final paragraph, that it was Halifax, the British Ambassador who had spoken to the President was subsequently paraphrased by the Australian Legation, inter alia, as follows: 'The information contained therein regarding the procedure to be followed came orally from the President late in the afternoon of December 6'.†

The information had certainly come orally from the President, but not to Casey. If the Australian Legation in 1946 had been precise, it would have told the Congressional Committee that the information reported by Casey had been told to him by the British Ambassador. It was this simple lack of precision in language paraphrasing that created the belief by the Pearl Harbor Attack Congressional Committee that Casey had visited the White House 'late in the afternoon of December 6.' and had received certain information 'orally from the President'.

It is well nigh unbelievable that for so many authors the history of the events leading up to the outbreak of the war in the Pacific could have been so distorted by a poorly written paraphrase. Equally as astounding is the widely held view (certainly by the nine writers) that Casey, a representative of a relatively small nation, could have played such a vital role at such a crucial time.

---

* *DAFP*, Vol. V, Doc. 169, p. 284.
† PHA Hearings, Vol. 14, p. 631.

Conspiracy theories aside, there is however ample evidence of Casey's influence in the winter of 1941–42. The attack on Pearl Harbor by no means heralded Casey's exit from the Washington scene. His major task, working towards an American participation in ensuring Pacific security had obviously been achieved beyond the best he could have possibly hoped for. It was to Casey that senior American service chiefs turned as they sought to bring order from the chaos and morale shattering events of 7 December. Casey came to fulfil the responsibilities of a major participant in the overall military planning as the American service chiefs battled to evolve a coherent and viable counterforce against the might of the Japanese Empire. It was Casey who knew intimately the resources and territorial characteristics of the Southwest Pacific. In the days and weeks following Pearl Harbor, Casey became involved in the implementation of the American counter attack, a recognition of the status he had achieved in Washington. The frenetic rounds of meetings between Casey and American military chiefs after Pearl Harbor were proof of his ever increasing importance. Although the Australian Legation, by this time, was staffed by military, air and naval attaches, their roles revolved around implementing decisions taken at a joint United States/Australia political level. It was Casey who had to pull the political strings as best as he could.

After Pearl Harbor, doors in Washington were opened to Casey to the degree that the Australian representative found himself in the regular company of the likes of Roosevelt, Churchill, and the senior military figures now running the war.[*] Casey already had a great deal of access and that many of those whom Casey spoke to after Pearl Harbor were the same individuals whom Casey had cultivated in the months leading up to this long anticipated 'incident'. However the welcoming doors now opened wider and with greater frequency.

Casey stayed in Washington until 1 April 1942. It must be said that this was the gloomiest period of the Pacific War for the Allied cause. The Philippines came under attack almost immediately after Pearl Harbor. Malaya was clearly vulnerable and its defenders badly panicked. The Americans and British at the Arcadia discussions

---
* Gelber, 'Turning Points', p. 79.

in Washington agreed that there would be an ABDA (America-British-Dutch-Australia) command stretching from Burma to the Philippines and, as a last-minute inclusion, south to the western part of northern Australia, including Darwin. The north east of Australia was included in the ANZAC area. The Japanese capture of Singapore on 15 February 1942 brought a premature end to ABDA and the ANZAC area, which would be transformed into the South West Pacific Area under General MacArthur who was to move from the Philippines to Australia. By mid-February, the Japanese had taken the Philippines and Singapore, a guerrilla war was under way in Timor, New Guinea was under threat and the Japanese had provided shattering evidence of their new found strategic reach and their capacity to harm Australia by capturing the 8$^{th}$ Division of the AIF at Singapore and bombing Darwin four days later. The turning of the tide in the Pacific would not arrive until the battles of the Coral Sea and Midway in May and June 1942.

Casey's private thoughts in the aftermath of Pearl Harbor suggest an abiding incomprehension and disdain of the superficiality of American preparedness and the almost sclerotic American response to Pearl Harbor, especially when compared with the manner in which Britain had reacted to being pitched into war in 1939. As Casey put it on 9 December 1941:

> The President spoke on the radio to the nation this evening. His speech did not carry the fire and conviction that the occasion demanded ... several minutes recounting of the individual countries that had been attacked without warning, which to me pointed the lesson that USA should have been more prepared, at Hawaii and elsewhere, to be attacked also without warning. *The lesson of a dozen countries seems to have been wasted on them.* [My emphasis.]
>
> Everyone I've met yesterday and today amongst senior American officials, Chief Justice Stone, Sumner Welles and several others have shown mortification and anger at the Hawaiian disaster. Not the least among them said that if the world can be saved, Britain would save it. Her bearing and steadfastness, without chatter, after the fall of France, 18 months ago, was a model for all people.

While Casey noted that the Japanese attack had galvanised the Americans into action, he seemed to doubt that the Americans had the necessary spirit to recover. As he told his diary:

> 11 December 1941. I called on Harry Hopkins at the White House. He looked very sick. I saw him in his combined bedroom-office ... my main object in seeing him was to seek to impress him with the idea that it would be wise to see that the President's mind was not bombarded with pessimism and depression by the US Army and Navy, who are mighty likely to be very down.*

Casey continued to wear his mask, however, balancing his obvious disgust at the failure of the United States to anticipate Japan's break-out in the Pacific with pep talks about the readiness of Australia and Britain to help. In his diary notation of 29 December 1941 Casey described how, since 7 December, his work had completely changed and that he was now nearly 100% engaged with Army, Navy and Air people and not diplomats or the State Department.†American resources were far from limitless. There were now manpower shortages, shipping shortages and all manner of equipment shortages. There were endless meetings with military people about all manner of military supplies that Australia desperately needed – shipping, aviation fuel, Kittyhawks and tank production-which occupied much of the discussion. After Pearl Harbor, Casey had to help supply Australia with much-needed materials of war while pursuing ever more vigorously his campaign to ensure that Americans did not lose sight of how much they needed Australia. His diary hints at the difficulties that he faced given that Australia was one priority among many and not the most immediately threatened.

In December 1941, the United States and Britain were concerned mainly about the Philippines and Singapore respectively. Both great powers were convinced, correctly as it eventuated, that Australia was not part of Japan's invasion plans at that stage. Japan's purpose was to prevent the Americans using Australia as their base and bridgehead by threatening ports, airfields and sea lanes. This

---

\* Casey Diaries, 9 and 11 December 1941.
† Casey Diaries, 29 December 1941

was not how matters were viewed in Australia or by Casey, for whom a Japanese invasion seemed a very real and growing threat. Often Casey had to work Australia into the conversation when his interlocutor had other priorities in mind. On 16 December 1941, for example, Casey had what he described as 'useful talks to McCloy (Under Secretary of War) about plans to reinforce the Philippines. Casey recorded that he 'renewed my suggestion to him about supply ships to Australia with relevant ammunition and spares for all American ships that might be using Australia as a base. He said he'd get on with it ..."* The next day, Casey records seeing 'General Arnold [Head of US Army Air Corps] about the United States aircraft that may be using or passing through Australia'. Typically Casey would deal with the person in charge, in this case Arnold, and then his subordinates; after seeing Arnold, Casey notes 'subsequently saw Col. John J. York ... and got full particulars'.†

At his meeting with the President on 17 December 1941, Casey was thanked for his tireless pressing of the message that 'the South West Pacific is one unit'. Less reassuringly, Roosevelt told Casey that 'Australia was just as important as the Philippines' but that 'the Philippines had a strategic position that might well save the whole SW Pacific'.‡ On 18 December, Casey saw Admiral Stark who was most keen for an 'agreed strategic plan for us all in the Pacific and Far East. Very well disposed ...'§ Casey was pleased with his meeting with Stimson on 19 December 1940, complaining afterwards that: 'it is noticeable that Singapore is always put a bad second in comparison with the Philippines.¶ Yet, Stimson's own diary suggests that a much more positive message emerged from this meeting. Stimson told Casey that should the Philippines and Singapore be lost, the United States would be 'making Australia our base, and fight it out there'.** Casey set himself the task of constantly reminding the Americans how important was Australia to their plans.

---

\* Casey Diaries, 16 December 1941.
† Casey Diaries, 17 December 1941.
‡ Ibid.
§ Casey Diaries, 18 December 1941.
¶ Casey Diaries, 19 December 1941.
\*\* Quoted in Bridge, *A Delicate Mission*, p. 212.

Events moved so swiftly in those post-Pearl Harbor days that it was impossible for him to record all his activities in his diaries.* Yet no day went past without Casey dealing with an influential service chief or functionary. He met with Marshall at least four times after Pearl Harbor: 29 December 1941, 6 January 1942, 25 January 1942 and 5 March 1942. These meetings appear to have proceeded smoothly. Marshall was not an easy man to impress. He was a cold, aloof person, 'remote and austere', according to Eisenhower, a 'man who forced everyone to keep his distance'. He did not have the charisma of his more glamourous colleague, Patton. President Roosevelt had tried at their first meeting to slap him on the back and call him 'George'. Marshall drew back and let the President know that the name was 'General Marshall' and 'General Marshall' it remained. He had few intimate friends. When he relaxed, he did it alone.† Casey experienced no such difficulties dealing with Marshall if his diary entry of 25 January 1942 can be believed:

> I saw General Marshall [Chief of US General Staff] on [the] same matters on which I saw the President yesterday – the situation in S.W. Pacific, and American reinforcements. I had nearly an hour with him on this and related subjects. He is very approachable and I should think, a balanced sane individual.‡

It was just as well that the relationship began well. After the fall of Singapore, Casey on 20 February had 'not an easy interview' with Marshall and Arnold in the light of Curtin's decision to recall the 6th and 7th Divisions of the AIF from the Middle East. Churchill's decision to ignore Curtin's entreaty and to send both Divisions to Burma, provoked a furious response from Curtin and which had the desired effect of Churchill reversing the decision. In a cable from Churchill, dated 23 February and sent by Deputy Prime Minister Clement Attlee, the Prime Minister wrote, 'My decision to move it northward during the few hours required to receive your final answer was necessary because otherwise your help, if given, might not have arrived in time.'§ This message infuriated Bruce, who considered it

---

\* Casey Diaries, 30 December 1941.
† Stephen Ambrose, *Eisenhower. Soldier General of the Army. President-Elect 1890–1952* (Boston: George Allen and Unwin, 1983), p. 135.
‡ Casey Diaries, 25 January 1942.
§ Attlee to Curtin, 23 February 1942, cablegram 241, *DAFP*, Vol. V, Doc. 362.

arrogant and appalling.* Casey handled this thorny issue as best he could and immediately went to Hopkins to help break the news to Roosevelt. Perhaps Casey's personal touch helped to ensure that the American reaction to the Australian decision to bring its troops home was much more muted than Churchill's.

The conversations with key military and political leaders became even more intense as the war progressed. Casey needed to be ready for discussions about the entirety of the war effort. On 26 January 1941, Casey talked to Admiral Ernest King about US naval forces designated to hold the 'Anzac area'. Then, on 27 January, he conferred with Arnold about 'air requirements of New Guinea area'. Arnold agreed that the ABDA area needed to be extended to New Guinea and as far as New Caledonia. According to Casey, it should also include the northern part of Australia. Casey's diary entry of 2 February tells how Hopkins had sought him out:

> Long talk to Harry Hopkins, at his request, late in the afternoon. He was obviously seeking to get a picture of the whole war against Japan, on which I aired the facts and my views on the facts for some time. He appeared to want to hear the ABDA area discussed – the Anzac area ... also what Australia is seeking in the way of fighter aircraft. He phoned General Arnold while I was there in an endeavour to help this along.†

This connection to Hopkins and the capacity to get Arnold on the phone immediately was unlikely to have been something that the average diplomat in Washington could achieve. Casey complained that not only were resources stretched to breaking point, but there was no centralised body to which Casey could petition about Australia's needs. Until the end of his appointment, Casey had to make his 'daily peregrinations round dozens of offices – seeing a series of highly placed individuals about our problems'.‡ These talks sometimes ended, as Casey would put it, 'unsatisfactorily'. It would be at that point that Casey's well-known hospitality techniques came into play. Hopkins' influence and networks were also a support that Casey could rely upon.

\* Bruce to Curtin, 23 February 1942, cablegram 33A, *DAFP*, Vol. V, Doc. 364.
† Casey Diaries, 2 February 1942.
‡ Casey Diaries, 3 March 1940.

There were many failures, although Casey was always quick to seize upon possible alternatives. Almost from the announcement of Lend Lease, Casey had hoped for the construction of tanks in Australia with a mechanised corps emerging some time in 1942. It became obvious that this would not happen, Casey on this occasion blaming decisions made in Australia rather than American priorities. On 6 March 1942, Casey urged the British Tank Mission representative 'to use any means of getting some medium tanks early. He made a useful suggestion that we offer to take some without 75 mm guns'.* While the Australian Army was anxious for a tank capable of matching the German models, Casey was desperate to have any tanks at all that were at least capable of matching it with the Japanese.† Casey needed to be pragmatic and facilitate solutions and compromises in conditions where resources were in short supply.

Casey, as ever, was deeply concerned about his position in the trading of information in Washington. He learned in February that information from Australian sources had found its way into Tokyo radio broadcasts. Casey was sufficiently worried to press Welles to 'speak to Marshall, King and Arnold in the sense that they could continue to talk to me with safety'.‡ Ultimately, Casey believed that the situation was retrieved. On 13 March 1942, he noted that he had 'a confidential talk with General Marshall. [He] Appears to have no reservations as to what he tells me'. On 26 March, Casey noted that he 'Saw General Marshall, talked about world problems'.§

Historians have recognised that Casey was often on the right side of these strategic debates. During the Arcadia talks post Pearl Harbor, involving both Roosevelt and Churchill, Casey successfully pressed the case for a unified command in the new South West Pacific theatre.¶ Reacting to plans for the new theatre, Evatt objected that Casey was off on a 'frolic of his own' only to find that the naval chiefs backed Casey.** On 2 February 1942 Casey expressed satisfaction that the Americans were now planning to

---

\* Casey Diaries, 6 March 1940.
† Bridge, *A Delicate Mission*, p. 236.
‡ Casey Diaries, 6 February 1942.
§ Casey Diaries, 13 and 26 March 1942.
¶ Bridge, 'R.G. Casey', p. 187.
\*\* Horner, *High Command*, p. 150.

use 'the Indian Ocean Route (Seychelles, Diego Garcia Cocos)', the route that Casey insisted that the Australian Air Department survey in 1939. According to Casey, he had painted a 'picture of the possibility of the Imperial Air Route being cut – at which, everyone laughed'.* On 16 February 1942 following the fall of Singapore, Casey described conferring with General Arnold about 'the Australian situation generally'. Casey summed up the position regarding Australia succinctly enough: 'Where else can the situation be retrieved?'† This had been Casey's message for a very long time and now in the desperate situation of the late winter of 1942, its importance was becoming increasingly obvious. Here Casey struck a tone of vindication, as well as desperation.

Australia still needed to make its voice heard, given the competing demands upon American decision makers. On 3 March 1942, Casey described his two principal troubles to Stimson, the lack of a body – as distinct from a series of individuals – where South West Pacific matters were discussed and the fact that Australia was in danger – yet the necessary war materials were not being shipped to Australia in sufficient quantities.‡ On 12 March 1942, he had talks with Roosevelt about 'the message for Curtin dealing with the co-ordination of all the air strength in Australia under one leader'.§ While his last weeks in Washington were fraught in terms of the storm surrounding his move to the Middle East, Casey continued to keep the key American strategists informed about Australia. Immediately before his departure, Casey described how he had military appraisals coming from Australia directly to the key American military decision makers:

> I saw Dill and Marshall and King – and handed each of them a copy of the Australian Chiefs of Staff appreciation of the situation in and near Australia – received from Australia by telegram this morning. I gave Marshall an extra copy for Arnold. It is a document of the highest importance and it is essential for all these four men to have it.¶

---

\* Casey Diaries, 2 February 1942.
† Casey Diaries, 16 February 1942.
‡ Casey Diaries, 3 March 1942.
§ Casey Diaries, 12 March 1942.
¶ Casey Diaries, 14 March 1942.

As he left Washington, Casey noted in his diary that: 'There is no more diplomacy to be done. The job here in future will be a military liaison job far below the top level ... Marshall and King are going to run the war'.*

Casey was perhaps offering a self-justification for leaving Washington before the war was won. On the other hand, his multiple gifts of strategic vision, superior networking skills, and mastery of technical military detail made him a crucial asset to Australia after 7 December. If his task were to save Australia, he could be well satisfied with his efforts. Casey came from and spoke of a country and a region that hitherto had not been in the American field of vision, in contemporary jargon, 'not on the radar'. He opened up a field of vision of great strategic potential. that would remain, even increase and enhance America's dominant pre-occupation with the Pacific region.

Significantly, of the discussions Casey had had with President Roosevelt, more than half occurred in the days and weeks immediately after America had entered the war. These talks indicate how important Australia had become in American strategic planning and that Casey was the individual to whom the Americans turned for advice and support.

It would be a mistake to argue that the obvious usefulness of Australia to the Americans after Pearl Harbor meant that Australia would be able to significantly influence the running of the war. Curtin and Evatt would find it brutally difficult to make an Australian voice heard in the crucial strategic debates.† Yet Casey's activity in the weeks that followed Pearl Harbor provided further evidence of his influence and capacities as a diplomatic all-rounder. His understanding of and contribution to Allied strategy, his mastery of military detail, and his successful networking enhanced Australia's visibility at a time when American strategists were scrambling to find a way to bounce back from the Pearl Harbor debacle and eventually, to bring about victory in the Pacific War.

---

\* Casey Diaries, 16 March 1942.
† Lowe, 'Australia in the World', p. 172.

# Conclusion

Trained as an engineer, Casey was a remarkable diplomatic all-rounder whose experiences were drawn from the military, business, academic and political worlds. There is clear evidence that he was capable of thinking strategically in both political and military terms. The two years he spent in Washington were years in which he not only sought to 'save' Australia but defined a future that placed Australia in a world-wide strategic axis with the United States. Just how difficult a task that this was, found expression in the message that Casey received upon arriving in Washington that Australia was not part of the American strategic picture. Perhaps sensing that Manila and Singapore would be lost in the first months of a Pacific War, Casey's message was that Australia was not distant from the conflict that might well break out in the Pacific.

Casey was engaging with politicians such as Roosevelt and non-elected officials such as Hull, Berle, Hornbeck and Acheson. He was arguing a case that was essentially strategic. His aim was to impose a strategic mind-set or vision on his American interlocutors who seemed beguiled by public opinion and dismissive of the existential danger to the United States. In 1941, Casey was beginning to move from this political Washington elite centred on the White House, the Congress and the State Department so as to work directly on the Service chiefs, Marshall, Arnold, Stark and King who would lead the fight in the air and on the seas and fields of battle that were crucial to Australia's survival. Casey understood better than most that the oceans around Australia and the large landmass of Australia itself might well be those fields of battle. Casey needed all the imagination, intelligence, and persistence he could muster. His endeavours on Australia's behalf, while heading the Legation in the United States required of him a careful reading and understanding of the American position in the fraught world situation, as well as qualities that could be summed up as sound judgment. Also necessary was the energy to implement all that he believed necessary.

Casey's activities at the top levels of the British government introduced him to the world of international relations, diplomacy and the personal attributes to effectively negotiate in the context of competing interests. All that experience was employed in full measure during his two years in the United States. Casey approached the United States with three different lines of attack. Firstly, through diplomacy, then almost simultaneously, through public opinion, that is moving the American people to see the need for greater American involvement in the conflict and finally, after diplomacy and public relations had achieved results, engaging the military. The data enumerating the interviews he conducted with the President, the Secretary of State and the Assistant Secretaries, other senior members of the Administration, newspaper publishers, radio network proprietors and perhaps most important of all, the heads of the military and the navy reveal the extraordinary range and scope of his activities, undertaken for one purpose, to influence events.

In the summer of 1940, Casey directed his efforts at appraising America of the mortal dangers confronting Britain and the dire effects such a loss would have on the rest of the word, especially the United States. Once the threat to Britain had passed, Casey sought to involve the United States in the affairs of the Asia-Pacific region with a view to ensuring American involvement in the long-expected conflict with the Empire of Japan. The evidence suggests that Casey was a rare example of a Dominion representative in the United States who stirred up the decision-makers of Washington, who attempted to make some impact upon American strategic thinking. Even before Pearl Harbor, Casey's endeavours brought him in contact with every influential figure and relevant organisation in the United States at that time. That he was accepted and recognised as a person of importance in the Oval Office, the State Department, the British Embassy, and senior American naval and military discussions; that his opinions were sought and listened to by the major American newspaper and radio executives; and that he spoke frequently to major and local organizations all point to the fact, that he fought way above his weight. His diplomatic skills and the fact that so many Americans, in a range of levels, listened to him, enhance his achievements.

The question needs to be asked as to whether all those he spoke to would have been prepared to include him in their reference groups if his views were of no relevance? There can be no doubt that Casey was hugely active in propagating greater American involvement in Pacific affairs. The results of those activities may be impossible to gauge. The essence of diplomacy is that things are done quietly, secretly, without public disclosure. Yet the evidence is overwhelming that the barn-storming did in fact, influence American thinking at the highest levels. It is a legitimate observation to wonder why the United States had shown less interest in the Pacific than what a keen student of international affairs might have.

The constant theme of Casey's public speeches and private urgings during 1940 and 1941 was the establishment of an American interest and presence in the Pacific. The conversion of Australia from an under-populated outpost of Empire into a vibrant American base virtually ensuring protection from Japanese invasion was undoubtedly Casey's underlying motive, but was not something that could be openly discussed in those terms. In all his discussions with American officials or at least those concerned with overall strategy, Casey was at pains to emphasise that the various theatres of war were vitally connected, a concatenation, that Roosevelt recognised as central to Casey's message. The American wartime reliance upon Australia as a base confirmed Casey's foresight.

Coinciding with Casey's years in the United States, there was a seismic shift in the thinking of the military and political powers of the United States in the two-year period leading up to Pearl Harbor. As Casey predicted, it was the pressure of events that drove the process and an 'incident' that catapulted the United States into the war. Yet it was Casey who patiently explained the strategic dimension of the Pacific War to his listeners in a way that prioritised Australia. The Marshall/Eisenhower plan might have been drawn up by Casey himself were he given the opportunity to do so.

The competing claims about the relative roles of Curtin

and Casey as instigators of the Australia-America Alliance may each be contested. Yet it has to be recognised that the decisions by the United States, after the shock of 7 December, owe a significant debt to the foresight and persistence of one man, Richard Gardiner Casey.

Casey's nimble and effective strategy and his well-developed networking skills enabled him to become a dynamic and effective force representing Australia in the corridors of American power at a time unique in Australian history when the future of the nation was uncertain. Casey would often be accused of lacking political acumen. Yet his approach to American politics was shrewd and exemplary. He eschewed the flowery language of civilisational bonds. Instead, he was tireless in his efforts to sell Australia as a base for American power in the Pacific. In his efforts to court public opinion and persuade American leaders, Casey was interventionist, he was assertive, too persistent to be ignored. He employed tactics and adopted an overall strategy that had clear and explicit aims. Significantly, he did all this without stirring up resentment, without earning a reputation as an interfering pest.

The aim of this book was to identify what Casey did to involve Australia in the American strategy for winning the Pacific War. The lack of recognition lies in Curtin's rather than Casey's name being attached to what really mattered in terms of the United States-Australia alliance, the transformation of Australia into an American base. The Australian historian, Caryn Coatney, in her book, *John Curtin. How He Won Over the Media* argues that Curtin manipulated the media to present himself as a strong wartime leader. This claim goes a long way towards explaining how Curtin receives plaudits for an achievement that in reality, owes nothing to him, the American alliance. As the good news from Hopkins recorded in Casey's diary on 22 December shows, Casey did in fact receive plaudits at the time even if his reports to Canberra failed to emphasise their significance. His reports frequently have the characteristics of British understatement. What is clear and beyond argument is that the final decisions of the Americans, the end result, even exceeded Casey's ambitions.

From an historical point of view, it is unfortunate that there is no official, weighty Proclamation conveying a Presidential or Congressional Declaration guaranteeing massive American support for Australia. Instead, we have Hopkins' verbal assurance, pledging virtually the same thing. It is clear that the American decision to make Australia the jumping-off base may have been formalised in the days immediately following Pearl Harbor but it was a decision that followed years of discussion, examination and persuasion, in which Casey played the crucial role. The corollary of all that is that Casey is due a recognition that hitherto accrued to Curtin.

In summation, Casey's endeavours and his influence were a real, tangible fact of life in pre-war America. It is impossible to measure quantitively the extent of that influence. All that can be said is that it existed, proof enough to conclude that Casey's reputation deserves greater recognition of the contribution he made to the joint Australia/America effort in the Pacific War, an effort which justifies revision of that reputation. Casey was not an insignificant player in the diplomatic game that led to the wartime alliance between the United States and Australia, but rather an influential participant, in fact, the key player whose contribution, albeit difficult to determine quantitively, was real. The position of Casey in the framework of Australian history therefore assumes a new relevance, one that recognises his vital role in determining that the United States looked to Australia in December 1941.

*Appendix*

# 'The Task Ahead' by John Curtin, *Herald*, 27 December 1941

> That reddish veil which o'er the face
> Of night-hag East is drawn ...
> Flames new disaster for the race?
> Or can it be the Dawn?

So wrote Bernard O'Dowd. I see 1942 as a year in which we shall know the answer.

I would, however, that we provide the answer. We can and we will. Therefore, I see 1942 as a year of immense change in Australian life.

The Australian Government's policy has been grounded on two facts. One is that the war with Japan is not a phase of the struggle with the Axis powers, but is a new war.

The second is that Australia must go on in a war footing.

Those two facts involve two lines of action – one in the direction of external policy as to our dealings with Britain, the United States, Russia, the Netherlands, East Indies and China in the higher direction of the war in the Pacific.

The second is the reshaping, in fact, the revolutionising, of the Australian way of life until a war footing is attained quickly, efficiently and without question.

As the Australian Government enters 1942, it has behind it a record of realism in respect of foreign affairs. I point to the forthright declaration in respect of Finland, Hungary and Rumania, which was followed with little delay by a declaration of war against those countries by the Democracies.

We felt that there could be no half-measures in our dealings with the Soviet when that nation was being assailed by the three countries mentioned

Similarly, as we put forward that a reciprocal agreement should be negotiated to meet an event of aggression by Japan. Our suggestion was then regarded, wrongly as time as proved, as premature.

Now, with equal realism, we take the view that while the determination of military policy is the Soviet's business, we should be able to look forward with reason to aid from Russia against Japan.

We look for a solid and impregnable barrier of the democracies against the three Axis powers, and we refuse to accept the dictum that the Pacific struggle must be treated as a subordinate segment of the general conflict.

By that it is not meant that any one of the other theatres of war is of less importance than the Pacific, but that Australia asks for a concerted plan evoking the greatest strength at the Democracies' disposal, determined upon hurling Japan back.

\*\*\*

The Australian Government therefore regards the Pacific struggle as primarily one in which the United States and Australia must have the fullest say in the direction of the Democracies' fighting plan.

Without any inhibitions of any kind I make it quite clear that Australia looks to America, free of any pangs as to our traditional links or kinship with the United Kingdom.

We know the problems that the United Kingdom faces. We know the constant threat of invasion. We know the dangers of dispersal of strength. But we know too that Australia can go, and Britain can still hold on.

We are therefore determined that Australia shall not go, and we shall exert all our energies toward the shaping of a plan, with the

United States as it s keystone, which will give to our country some confidence of being able to hold out until the tide of battle swings against the enemy.

Summed up, Australia external policy will be shaped toward obtaining Russian aid, and working out, with the United States as the major factor, a plan of Pacific strategy, along with British, Chinese and Dutch forces.

\*\*\*

Australian internal policy has undergone striking changes in the past few weeks. These, and those that will inevitably come before 1942 is far advanced, have been prompted by several reasons.

In the first place, the Commonwealth Government found it exceedingly difficult to bring the Australian people to a realization of what, after two years of war, our position had become. Even the entry of Japan, bringing a direct threat in our own waters, was met with a subconscious view that the Americans would deal with the short-sighted, under-fed and fanatical Japanese.

The announcement that no further appeals would be made to the Australian people, and the decisions that followed, were motivated by psychological factors. They had an arresting effect. They awakened in the somewhat lackadaisical Australian mind the attitude that was imperative if we were to save ourselves, to enter an all-in effort in the only possible manner.

That experiment in psychology was eminently successful, and we commenced 1942 with a better realization, by a greater number of Australians, of what the war means than in the whole preceding two years.

The decisions were prompted by other reasons, all related to the necessity of getting on to a war footing, and the results so far achieved have been most heartening, especially in respect of production and conservation of stocks.

I make it clear the experiment undertaken was never intended as one to awaken Australian patriotism or sense of duty. Those qualities have been ever-present; but the response to leadership and direction had; never been requested of the people, and desirable talents and untapped resources had lain dormant.

Our task for 1942 is stern. The Government is under no illusions as to 'something cropping up' in the future.

The nadir of our fortunes in this struggle, as compared with 1914–1918, has yet to be reached.

Let there be no mistake about that. The position Australia faces internally far exceeds in potential and sweeping dangers anything that confronted us in 1914–1918.

The year 1942 will impose supreme tests. These range from resistance to invasion to deprivation or more and more amenities, not only the amenities of peacetime but those enjoyed in time of war.

\*\*\*

Australians must realise that to place the nation on a war footing every citizen must place himself, his private and business affairs, his entire mode of living, on a war footing. The civilian way of life cannot be any less rigorous, can contribute no less than that which the fighting men have to follow.

I demand that Australians everywhere realise that Australia is now inside the fighting lines.

Australian governmental policy will be directed strictly on those lines. We have to regard our country and its 7,000,000 people as though we were a nation and a people with the enemy hammering at our frontier.

Australians must be perpetually on guard; on guard against the possibility, at any hour without warning, of raid or invasion; on guard against spending money, or doing anything that cannot be justified; on guard against hampering by disputation or idle, irresponsible chatter, the decisions of the Government taken for the welfare of all.

All Australian is the stake in this war. All Australia must stand together to hold that stake. We face a powerful, ably led and unbelievable courageous foe.

We must watch the enemy accordingly. We shall watch him accordingly.

# Bibliography

## Primary Sources

Archives of United States State Department, Washington.

Berle Papers, Box 212, Roosevelt Library, Washington.

Cadogan Diaries, *The Diaries of Sir Alexander Cadogan, O.M. 1938–1945*, David Dilks (ed.) (New York: G.P. Putnam, 1972).

Casey Papers, MS 6150, Vol. 1, Box 24, National Library of Australia, Canberra.

Moffat, J.P. *Moffatt Diaries*, Moffatt Collection, Vol. 37, N.H. Hooker (ed.) (Cambridge, Mass: Harvard University, 1959).

National Archives of Australia, Canberra.

National Archives, Kew.

Wilkinson Papers. Diaries of Gerald Wilkinson, Wilkinson Collection, Churchill Archive Centre, Cambridge.

## Secondary Sources

Alexander, Fred, *Australia Since Federation* (Melbourne: Thomas Nelson, 1967).

Alexander, Fred, *From Curtin to Menzies and After* (Melbourne: Thomas Nelson, 1973).

Alomes, Stephen, *A Nation at Last. The Changing Character of Australian Nationalism 1880–1988* (Sydney: Angus and Robertson, 1988).

Ambrose, Stephen E., *Eisenhower. Soldier, General of the Army, President-Elect, 1890–1952* (Boston: George Allen and Unwin, 1983).

*Australian Dictionary of Biography*, Vol. 13. Bede Nairn and Geoffrey Serle (eds.) (Carlton: Melbourne University Press, 1983).

Ball, Christopher, 'The 'Singapore Strategy' and the Deterrance of Japan:

Winston Churchill, the Admiralty and the Despatch of Force Z', in *The English Historical Review,* Vol. 116, No. 467, June 2001, pp. 604–34.

Ballantine, Joseph W., 'Mukden to Pearl Harbor. The Foreign Policies of Japan', *Foreign Affairs,* Vol. 27. October 1948.

Baxter, Christopher and Andrew Stewart (eds.), *Diplomats at War. British and Commonwealth Diplomacy in Wartime* (Leiden: Martinus Nijhoff, 2008).

Beard, Charles A., *American Foreign Policy in the Making, 1932–1940* (New Haven: Yale University Press, 1946).

Beard, Charles A., *President Roosevelt and the Coming War. 1941* (New Haven: Yale University Press, 1948).

Beaumont, Joan, Waters, Christopher, Lowe, David, and Woodward, Garry, *Ministers, Mandarins and Diplomats. Australian Foreign Policy Making 1941–1969* (Carlton: Melbourne University Press, 2003).

Beeson, Mark, 'Australia, the United States and the Unassailable Alliance' in John Dumbrell and Alex Schafer (eds.) *America's Special Relationships* (London: Routledge, 2006).

Bell, Roger, *Unequal Allies* (Carlton: Melbourne University Press, 1977).

Bergamini, David, *Japan's Imperial Conspiracy. How Emperor Hirohito Led Japan into War Against the West* (London: Heinemann, 1971).

Birgan, Michael, 'Lord Casey: Britain's Secret Service Agent', *The Bulletin,* 20 November 1984.

Booker, Malcolm, *The Last Domino. Aspects of Australia's Foreign Relations* (Sydney: Collins, 1976).

Bridge, Carl, *'Special Relationships'. Australia, Britain and the United States since 1941* (London: Sir Robert Menzies Centre for Australian Studies, 1991).

Bridge, Carl, *A Delicate Mission. The Washington Diaries of R.G. Casey, 1940–1942* (Canberra: National Library of Australia, 2008).

Bridge, Carl, 'R.G. Casey, Australia's First Washington Legation and the Origins of the Pacific War, 1940–1942', *Australian Journal of Politics and History,* 1982, Vol. 28, No. 2, pp. 181–9.

Bridge, Carl, 'R.G. Casey's Contribution to Australian War Policy, 1939 to 1942: Some Myths', *Journal of the Historical Society of South Australia,* 1981, No. 9.

Bridge, Carl (ed.), *Munich to Vietnam. Australia's Relations with Britain and the United States Since the 1930s* (Melbourne: Melbourne University Press, 1991).

Bridge, Carl, 'The Other Blade of the Scissors', in Baxter, Christopher and Andrew Stewart, *Diplomats at War, British and Commonwealth Diplomacy in Wartime* (Leiden: Martinus Nijhoff, 2008).

Bridge, Carl, *William Hughes. Australia* (London: Haus Publishers, 2011).

Buckley, Ken, Dale, Barbara, Reynolds, Wayne, *Doc Evatt. Patriot, Internationalist, Fighter and Scholar* (Melbourne: Longman Cheshire, 1994).

Burke, Anthony, *Fear of Security. Australia's Invasion Anxiety* (Cambridge: Cambridge University Press, 2008).

Burns, James McGregor, *Roosevelt, the Soldier of Freedom, 1940–1945* (New York: Harcourt, Brown, Jovanovich, 1970).

Burns, James McGregor, *Roosevelt. The Lion and the Fox. 1882–1940* (New York: Harcourt Brace, 1956).

Casey, Maie, *Tides and Eddies* (Hammondsworth: Penguin, 1969).

Casey, Richard G., *Friends and Neighbours. Australia and the World* (Melbourne: F.W. Cheshire, 1954).

Casey, Richard G., 'Australia's Voice in Imperial Affairs' in Duncan, W.G.K. (ed.), *Australia's Foreign Policy* (Sydney: Angus and Roberton in conjunction with the Australian Institute of Political Science, 1938).

Casey, Richard G., *Personal Experience 1939–1946* (London: Constable, 1962).

Casey, Richard G., *My Dear PM R.G. Casey Letters to Bruce 1924–1929,* Hudson, W.J. and North, Jane (eds.) (Canberra: Australian Government Publishing Service, 1980).

Charmley, John, *Churchill's Grand Alliance. The Anglo-American Special Relationship 1940–57* (New York: Harcourt Brace and Company, 1998).

Churchill, Sir Winston, *The Second World War,* Vols. II and III (London: Cassell, 1950).

Clark, C.M.H., *A History of Australia*. Vol. VI (Carlton: Melbourne University Press, 1987).

Coatney, Caryn, *John Curtin. How He Won Over the Media* (Melbourne. Australian Scholarly Publishing, 2016).

Cole, Wayne S., *Roosevelt and the Isolationists, 1932–1945* (Lincoln: University of Nebraska Press, 1983).

Conway, Ronald, *Land of the Long Weekend* (Melbourne: Sun Books, 1978).

Cumpson, I.M, *History of Australian Foreign Policy. 1901–1991* (Canberra: I.M. Cumpson, 1995).

Cuneen, Chris, 'A Question of Colour' in Stannage, Tom, Saunders, Kay, Nile, Richard (eds.), *Paul Hasluck in Australian History. Civic Personality and Public Life* (St Lucia: University of Queensland Press, 1999).

Curran, James, *Curtin's Empire* (Melbourne: Cambridge University Press, 2011).

Dallin, David J., *The Big Three. The United States, Britain, Russia* (New Haven: Yale University Press, 1945).

Daly, Fred, *From Curtin to Hawke* (Melbourne: Sun Books, The Macmillan Company, 1985).

Davies, Norman, *No Simple Victory* (New York: Penguin Group, 2007).

Davis, Kenneth S., *Invincible Summer. An Intimate Portrait of the Roosevelts Based on the Recollections of Marion Dickerman* (New York: Atheneum, 1974).

Davis, Kenneth, *Experience in War* (New York: MacMillan, 1956).

Day, David, *The Great Betrayal. Britain, Australia and the Onset of the Pacific War. 1939–32* (Sydney: Angus and Robertson, 1988).

Day, David, *The Politics of War. Australia at War 1939–45* (Sydney: Harper Collins, 2003).

Day, David, *Menzies and Churchill at War* (North Ryde: Angus and Robertson, 1986).

Divine, Robert, *Roosevelt and World War II* (Baltimore: The Johns Hopkins University Press, 1969).

Duncan, W.G.K. (ed.), *Australia's Foreign Policy* (Sydney: Angus and Robertson, 1938)

Edwards, Cecil, *Bruce of Melbourne. Man of Two Worlds* (London: Heineman, 1954).

Edwards, Peter G., 'Dr Walter Henderson – A South Australian in Charge of an Australian Foreign Office, 1924–1930' *Journal of Historical Society of South Australia*, 1982, pp. 3–14.

Edwards, Peter G., *Prime Ministers and Diplomats. The Making of Australian Foreign Policy* (Melbourne: Oxford University Press, 1983).

Edwards, Peter, *Arthur Tange, the Last of the Mandarins* (Sydney: Allen and Unwin, 2006).

Edwards, Peter (ed.), *Australia Through American Eyes, 1935–1945. Observations by American Diplomats* (St Lucia: University of Queensland Press, 1979).

Edwards, Peter, *Crises and Commitments. The Politics and Diplomacy of Australia's Involvement in Southeast Asian Conflicts 1948–1965* (North Sydney: Allen and Unwin, 1992).

Edwards, Peter, 'R.G. Menzies Appeals to the United States. May–June 1940', *Australian Outlook*, XXVII, 1974, pp. 64–70.

Ellery, David, 'Furphies a'plenty in Long ANZUS Alliance', *Canberra Times*, 18 November 2011.

Esthus, Raymond A., *From Enmity to Alliance. US-Australian Relations, 1931–1941* (Seattle, Washington: University of Washington Press, 1964).

Farago, Ladislas, *The Broken Seal. The Dramatic Story of Operation Magic and the Pearl Harbor Disaster* (New York: A Mayflower Paperback, 1969).

Feis, Herbert, *The Road to Pearl Harbor. The Coming of the War Between the United States and Japan* (Princeton: Princeton University Press, 1950).

Ferrell, Robert H. (ed.), *The Eisenhower Diaries* (New York: W.W. Norton and Company, 1981).

Fewster, Alan, *Trusty and Well Beloved. A Life of Keith Officer, Australia's First Diplomat* (Melbourne: Miegunyah Press, 2009).

Fitzhardinge, L.F., *William Morris Hughes*, Vol. 1 (Sydney: Angus and Ronertson, 1964).

Flynn, John T., *The Roosevelt Myth* (New York: Putmans, 1956).

Frame, Tom, *Pacific Partners* (Sydney: Stoughton and Houghton, 1992).

Fredman, L.E., *The United States Enters the Pacific* (Sydney: Angus and Robertson, 1969).

Gates, Eleanor, *End of the Affair. The Collapse of the Anglo-French Alliance, 1939–1940* (London: George Allen and Unwin, 1981).

Gelber, Harry, 'Turning Points. Richard Casey and the Development of an Australian Foreign Service', *Quadrant*, April 2009.

Gelber, Harry, *The Australian American Alliance. Costs and Benefits* (Middlesex: Penguin, 1968).

Goralski, Robert, *World War II Almanac, 1931–1945* (London: Hamish Hamilton, 1981).

Green, Frank, *Servant of the House* (Melbourne: Heinemann, 1969).

Greenwood, Gordon, *Approaches to Asia. Australian Postwar Policies and Attitudes* (Sydney: McGraw Hill Book Company, 1974).

Griffen-Foley, 'The Kangaroo is Coming into its Own: R.G. Casey, Earl Newsom and Public Relations in the 1940's', *Australian Journal of American Studies*, Vol. 23, No. 2, December 2004.

Gunther, John, *Roosevelt in Retrospect* (London: Hamish Hamilton, 1950).

Hawke, R.J. 'Foreword' in Norman E. Lee, *John Curtin, Saviour of Australia* (Melbourne: Longman Cheshire, 1983).

Hasluck, Paul, *The Chance of Politics* (Western Australia: Freshwater Bay Press, 1997).

Hasluck, Paul, *The Government and the People. 1939–1941. Australia in the War of 1939–1945*. Series 4 (Civil) Vol. I (Canberra: The Australian War Memorial, 1962).

Heinrichs, Waldo, *Threshold of War. Franklin D. Roosevelt and American Entry into World War II* (New York: Oxford University Press, 1988).

Henderson, Anne, *Enid Lyons. Leading Lady to a Nation* (Australia: Pluto Press, 2008).

Henderson, Anne, *Menzies At War* (Sydney: New South Publishers, 2014).

Henderson, Gerard, *Menzies' Child. The Liberal Party of Australia* (Sydney: Harper Collins, 1994).

Hoyt, Edwin P., *Japan's War. The Great Pacific Conflict. 1853–1952* (London: Hutchinson, 1987).

Horner, David, *High Command. Australia and Allied Strategy 1939–1940* (Sydney: Allen and Unwin, 1982).

Hudson, W. and Way, Wendy, *Letters from a Secret Service Agent* (Canberra: Australian Government Printing Service, 1986).

Hudson, W.J., *Australian Diplomacy* (Australia: Macmillan, 1970).

Hudson, W.J. and Jane North (eds.), *My Dear PM R.G. Casey's Letters to S.M. Bruce, 1924–1929* (Canberra: Melbourne University Press, 1981).

Hudson, W.J., *Casey* (Sydney: Oxford University Press, 1986).

Hughes, Colin A., *Australian Prime Ministers 1901–1972* (Melbourne: Oxford University Press, 1976).

Hull, Cordell, *The Memoirs of Cordell Hull* (New York: Macmillan Company, 1948).

Hunt, Michael, and Steven I. Levine, *Arc of Empire: America's Wars in Asia From the Philippines to Vietnam* (Chapel Hill: University of North Carolina Press, 2012).

Inglis, K.S., *This is the ABC* (Carlton: Melbourne University Press, 1983).

Joske, Percy, *Sir Robert Menzies, 1894–1978. A New Informal Memoir* (Sydney: Angus and Robertson, 1978).

Kennan, George F., *American Diplomacy 1900–1950* (New York: The New American Library, 1951).

Kershaw, Ian, *Fateful Choices. Ten Decisions that Changed the World. 1940–1941* (London: Penguin Books, 2007).

Kieser, Egbert, *Hitler on the Doorstep – Operation Sealion. The German Plan to Invade Britain, 1940* (London: Arms and Armour Press, 1997).

Killen, James, *Inside Australian Politics* (North Ryde: Methuen Haynes, 1985).

Kimball, Warren F., *The Most Unsordid Act: Lend Lease, 1939–1941* (Baltimore: The Johns Hopkins University Press, 1969).

Knapp, Wilfrid, *A History of War and Peace. 1939–1965* (London: Oxford University Press, 1967).

Kobler, John, *Luce. His Time, Life and Fortune* (London: Macdonald Publishing, 1968).

LaNauze, J.A., *Alfred Deakin* (Carlton: Melbourne University Press, 1965).

Langer W.L. and Gleason, S.E., *The Undisclosed War 1940–41. The World Crisis and American Foreign Policy* (New York: Harper, 1953).

Laquer, Walter (ed.), *The Second World War. Essays in Military and Political History* (London: Sage Publications, 1982).

Lash, Joseph (ed.), *From the Diaries of Felix Frankfurter* (New York: Oxford University Press, 1975).

Lash, Joseph P., *Roosevelt and Churchill 1939–1941. The Partnership That Saved the West* (London: Andre Deutsch, 1977).

Lebra, Joyce C., *Japan's Greater East Asia Co-Prosperity Sphere in World War II* (Tokyo: Oxford University Press, 1975).

Lee, David, 'Stanley Bruce at the Wartime High Commission' in Christopher Baxter and Andrew Stewart (eds.), *Diplomats at War* (Leiden: Martinus Nijhoff, 2008).

Lee, Norman E., *John Curtin. Saviour of Australia* (Melbourne: Longman Cheshire, 1983).

Liang, Chin-tung, *The Sinister Face of the Mukden Incident* (New York: St John's University Press, 1969).

Lowe, David, *Australian Between Empires. The Life of Percy Spender* (London: Chatto and Pickering, 2010).

Lowe, David, 'Brave New Liberal: Percy Spender', *Australian Journal of Politics and History*, Vol. 51, No. 3, 2005, pp. 389–99.

Lowe, David, 'Australia in the World' in Joan Beaumont (ed.), *Australia's War, 1939–45* (Sydney: Allen and Unwin, 1996).

Lowe, David and Gary Smith, 'Howard, Downer and the Liberals' Realist tradition', *Australian Journal of Politics and History*, Vol. 51, No. 3, 2005, pp. 459–72.

Lowenheim, Langley and Jones, *Roosevelt and Churchill. Their Secret Wartime Correspondence* (New York: Saturday Review Press, 1975).

Lowenthal, Mark M., Roosevelt and the Coming of the War. The Search for United States Policy, 1937–41, *Journal of Contemporary History*, Vol. 16, No. 3, July 1981, pp. 413–40.

Lowenthal, Mark, 'Roosevelt and the Coming of the War' in Walter Laqueur (ed.), *The Second World War. Essays in Military and Political History* (London: Sage Publications Ltd, 1982).

Lukacs, John, *Five Days in London, May, 1940* (New Haven: Yale University Press, 1999).

Lyon, Peter, *Portrait of a Hero* (Boston: Little, Brown and Co., 1974).

Lyons, Dame Enid, *Among the Carrion Crows* (Adelaide: Rigby, 1972).

McCarthy, J.M., *Australia and Imperial Defence. 1918–1939* (St Lucia: University of Queensland Press, 1976).

McCoy, Donald, *Coming of Age* (New York: Penguin Books, 1973).

McCullough, David, *Truman* (New York: Simon and Schuster, 1992).

McLean, Craig, *R.G. Casey and Australian Foreign Policy: Engaging with China and Southeast Asia, 1951–1960*, Phd. Dissertation. Victoria University, 2008.

McNicoll, David, *Luck's a Fortune* (Sydney: Wildcat Press, 1979).

McQueen, Humphrey, *Japan to the Rescue. Australia's Security Around the Indonesian Archipeligo During the American Century* (Melbourne: Heinemann, 1991).

Magnusson, Magnus (ed.), *Chambers Biographical Dictionary* (Edinburgh: Chambers, 1992).

Maisky, Ivan, *Memoirs of a Soviet Ambassador* (New Haven: Yale University Press, 1950).

Manchester, William, *American Caesar. Douglas MacArthur 1880–1964* (Australia: Hutchinson, 1978).

Manchester, William, *The Caged Lion. Winston Spencer Churchill, 1932–1940* (London: Sphere Books, 1989).

Manchester, William. *The Glory and the Dream* (London: Michael Joseph Ltd, 1974).

Martin, A.W. and Hardy, Patsy (eds.), 'Menzies' 1941 Diary', in *Dark and Hurrying Days* (Canberra: National Library of Australia, 1993).

Martin, M.W., *The Whig View of Australian History* (Carlton: Melbourne University Press, 2007).

Matloff, Maurice and Snell, Edwin M., *Strategic Planning for Coalition Warfare, 1941–1942. United States Army in World War II* (Washington, D.C: Office of the Chief of Military History, Department of the Army, 1953).

McKernan, Michael, 'Independence Day' in Gare, Deborah and Ritter, David, *Making Australian History. Perspectives on the Past since 1788* (South Melbourne: Thomson, 2008).

Megaw, Ruth, 'Undiplomatic Channels: Australian Representation in the United States, 1918–1939', *Historical Studies*, Vol. 15, No. 60, 1973, pp. 110–30.

Megaw, Ruth, 'Australia and the Great White Fleet 1908', *Journal of Royal Australian Historical Society*, No. 56, June 1970, pp, 121–33.

Menzies, Sir Robert, *Afternoon Light* (Australia: Cassell, 1967).

Menzies, Sir Robert, *The Measure of the Years* (London: Cornet Books, 1970).

Millar, T.B., *Australia in Peace and War. External Relations 1788–1977* (Canberra: Australian National University, 1978).

Miller, Edward S., *War Plan Orange. The US Strategy to Defeat Japan 1897–1945* (Washington: Naval Institute Press, 1991).

Morrison, Samuel Eliot, Commager, Henry Steele and Leuchtenburg, William E., *The Growth of the American Republic*. Vol. II (London: Oxford University Press, 1969).

Morton, Louis, 'War Plan Orange. Evolution of a Strategy', *World Politics*, Vol. 11, No. 2, January 1959, pp. 221–50.

Morton, Louis, *Pearl Harbor in Perspective*, A Bibliographical Survey of United States Institute proceedings LXXXI.

Mosley, Leonard, *Marshall. Organiser of Victory* (New York: Methuen, 1982).

Overy, Richard and Wheatcroft, Andrew, *The Road to War* (London: Macmillan, 1989).

Parker, R.A.C., *Chamberlain and Appeasement. British Policy and the Coming of the Second World War* (London: Penguin, 1993).

Parrish, Thomas, *To Keep the British Isles Afloat* (New York: Harper Collins, 2009).

Phillips, P.D., 'Australia in a Changing World', in Duncan, W.G.K. (ed.), *Australia's Foreign Policy* (Sydney: Angus and Robertson, 1938).

Poynter, J.R., 'The Yo-Yo Variations: Initiative and Dependence in Australia's External Relations, 1918–1923', *Australian Historical Studies*, Vol. 14, No. 54, 1970.

Pratt, John L., *A History of United States Foreign Policy* (Princeton: Princeton University Press, 1955).

Prange, Gordon W., *December 7, 1941. The Day the Japanese Attacked Pearl Harbor* (London: Harrap Ltd, 1988).

Prior, James, 'How Curtin Became a War Casualty', *National Times*, Sydney, February 1978.

Reckner, J.R., *Teddy Roosevelt's Great White Fleet* (Annapolis: Naval Institute Press, 1988).

Reese, Trevor R., *Australia, New Zealand and the United States. A Survey of International Relations* (London: Oxford University Press, 1969).

Reid, Alan, *The Gorton Experiment* (Sydney: Shakespeare Head Press: 1971).

Renouf, Alan, *Let Justice Be Done. The Foreign Policy of Dr H.V. Evatt* (St Lucia: University of Queensland Press, 1983).

Reynolds, David, *America. Empire of Liberty* (London: Allen Lane, 2009).

Reynolds, David, *From Munich to Pearl Harbor* (Chicago: Ivan R. Dee, 2001).

Reynolds, David, *The Command of History. Churchill Fighting and Writing the Second World War* (London: Allen Lane, 2004).

Reynolds, David, *The Creation of the Anglo-American Alliance 1937–1941. A Study in Competitive Co-operation* (London: Europe Publications, 1981).

Rivett, Rohan, *Australian Citizen. Herbert Brookes, 1867–1963* (Carlton: Melbourne University Press, 1965).

Rock, William R, *Chamberlain and Roosevelt. British Foreign Policy and the United States. 1937–1940* (Columbus, Ohio: Ohio State University, 1988).

Roosevelt, Elliott and Brough, James, *The Roosevelts of the White House. A Rendezvous with Destiny* (New York: Putnams, 1952).

Rosenman, Samuel L. (ed.), *The Public Papers and Addresses of Franklin D. Roosevelt*. Vol. 9 (New York: Harper Brothers, 1940).

Ross, Andrew, T., *Armed and Ready: The Industrial Development and Defence of Australia, 1900–1945* (Sydney: Turton and Armstrong, 1995).

Saunders, Kay, *Notorious Australian Women* (Australia: Harper Collins, 2011).

Schedvin, C.B., *Australia and the Great Depression* (Sydney: Sydney University Press, 1988).

Schlesinger, Arthur, Jr, *The Age of Roosevelt. The Politics of Upheaval* (Boston: Houghton Mifflin Company, 1960).

Shirer, William L., *The Rise and Fall of the Third Reich* (London: Secker and Warburg, 1960).

Smith, Gary, Cox, Dave, Burchill, Scott, *Australia in the World* (Sydney: Oxford University Press, 1996).

Souter, Gavin, *Acts of Parliament. A narrative History of the Senate and House of Representatives*, Commonwealth of Australia (Carlton: Melbourne University Press, 1988).

Souter, Gavin, *Lion and Kangaroo. The Initiation of Australia 1901–1919* (Sydney: William Collins, 1976).

Spector, Ronald H., *Eagle Against the Sun* (New York: Viking Penguin, 1985).

Spender, Percy, *Politics and a Man* (Oxford: Blackwell, 1972).

Stanley, Peter, *Invading Australia. Japan and the Battle for Australia, 1942* (Camberwell: Penguin, 2008).

Stannage, Tom, Saunders, Kay and Nile, Richard (eds.), *Paul Hasluck in Australian History, Civic Personality and Public Life* (St Lucia: University of Queensland Press, 1999).

Stargardt, A.W., *Australia's Asian Policies: The History of Debate: 1839–1972* (Hamburg: Institute of Asian Affairs, 1977).

Stettinius, Edward Jnr, *Lend Lease. Weapon for Victory* (New York: Macmillan, 1944).

Stokes, H.J.W. and Edwards, P.G. (eds.), *Documents on Australian Foreign Policy* (Canberra: Australian Government Publishing Service, 1979).

Stoler, Mark, *Allies in War. Britain and America Against the Axis Powers. 1940–1945* (London: Hodder Arnold, 2005).

Tansill, Charles Callan, *Back Door to War. The Roosevelt Foreign Policy 1933–1941* (Chicago: Henry Rigney Company, 1954).

Tennant, Kylie, *Evatt. Politics and Justice* (Sydney: Angus and Robertson, 1970).

Thorne, Christopher, *Allies of a Kind* (London: Hamish Hamilton, 1978).

Thorne, Christopher, *The Far Eastern War. States and Societies. 1941–1945* (Boston: Unwin Paperbacks, 1980).

Tiver, P.G., *The Liberal Party. Principles and Performance* (Queensland: Jacaranda Press, 1978).

Tugwell, Rexford G., *The Democratic Roosevelt* (Baltimore: Penguin Books, 1957).

Vita, I.D., *The Making of British Foreign Policy* (London: Unwin Paperbacks, 1968).

Von Vorys, Karl, *American National Interest. Virtue and Power in Foreign Policy* (New York: Praeger, 1990).

Waller, Sir Keith, 'A Day in the Life of an Ambassador' in W.J. Hudson (ed.), *Australia in World Affairs* (Sydney: George Allen and Unwin, 1980).

Waters, Christopher, 'Cold War Liberals: Richard Casey and the Department of External Affairs, 1951–60' in Beaumont, Waters, Lowe and Woodard (eds.), *Ministers, Mandarins and Diplomats* (Melbourne University Press: Carlton, 2003).

Waters, Christopher, *Australia and Appeasement. Imperial Foreign Policy and the Origins of World War II* (London: I.B. Tauris and Company, 2012).

Waters, Christopher, 'Casey. Four Decades in the Making of Australian Foreign Policy', *Australian Journal of Politics and History*, Vol. 51, No. 3, 2005, pp. 380–8.

Watson, Mark Skinner, *United States Army in World War II. Chief of Staff: Prewar Plans and Preparations* (Washington, D.C: Historical Division, Department of the Army, 1950).

Watt, Alan, *The Evolution of Australian Foreign Policy 1938–1965* (London: Cambridge University Press, 1967).

Wesley, Michael, 'The Rich Tradition of Australian Realism', *Australian Journal of Politics and History*. Vol. 55, No. 3, 2009, pp. 324–34.

Wolfsohn, Hugo, 'The Evolution of Australia in World Affairs', *Australian Outlook*, March 1953.

Woolcott, Richard, *The Hot Seat. Reflections on Diplomacy from Stalin's Death to the Bali Bombings* (Sydney: Harper Collins, 2003).

Wurth, Bob, *Saving Australia. Curtin's Secret Peace with Japan* (South Melbourne: Lothian, 2006).

## Newspaper Articles

*The Age*, 17 March 1908.

*Boston American*, 16 June 1941.

*Journal* (Lewiston, Maine), 16 June 1941.

*Lewiston Evening Journal*, 16 June 1941.

*New York Enquirer*, 26 June 1941.

*New York Sun*, 16 June 1941.

*New York Times*, 21 February 1940.

*New York Times*, 25 December 1939.

*New York Times*, 28 December 1941.

*New York Times*, 9 December 1941.

*Portland*, Maine Express, 16 June 1941.

*Republican* (Springfield, Mass), 16 June 1941.

*Sunday Times* (London), 23 August 1908.

*Washington Post*, 28 December 1941.

*Washington Post*, 9 January 1940.

# Index

Acheson, Dean 76–7, 140, 145–6, 188
Arnold, Harold H. 19, 182–6, 188

Barkley, Alben W. 174
Bell, Roger J. 19, 176
Berle, Adolf 14, 53, 57, 66–78, 88, 93, 108, 112, 126–9, 131, 135, 139, 143–6, 188
Brains Trust 66–7
Bridge, Carl 9, 11, 16, 20, 24, 136, 151, 156–7, 163–4
Brooke-Popham, Robert 153
Bruce, Stanley Melbourne 3–4, 9–10, 12–13, 20, 25, 39–43, 46, 51–6, 79, 89–90, 97–8, 100, 109, 183
Burrell, Henry Mackay 131–2, 136–7, 141, 145

Cadogan, Alexander 95, 123, 138
Cairo 21–2, 77
Canberra 13, 56, 64, 66, 87, 89, 92, 97, 102, 114, 117, 126, 128–9, 132–3, 136, 151, 153–4, 156, 168, 174, 191
Casey, Maie 4, 14–15, 89, 165–6
Casey, Richard Gardiner *passim*
Chamberlain, Neville 8, 10, 44, 63, 74, 95–7
Churchill, Winston Spencer 8, 15, 20–3, 30, 58, 74, 95–101, 113, 120, 122, 123–4, 134, 138–9, 152, 158, 170–1, 175, 179, 183–5
Curran, James 20

Curtin, John 20–2, 25, 28, 100, 119, 141, 152, 154–5, 157–8, 161–72, 176–7, 183, 186–7, 190–3

Eisenhower, Dwight D. 158–9, 161–2, 183, 190
Evatt, Herbert Vere 6, 15, 20–2, 24–6, 28–9, 40, 152, 154–6, 163, 168, 175–7, 185, 187

Farago, Ladislas 175
Feis, Herbert 174

Germany 10, 32, 39, 41, 44, 51–2, 61–2, 69–70, 72, 80, 91, 94–5, 103–4, 108–9, 112, 114–15, 124–5, 130, 132–3, 136, 153, 166–7
Great Britain 8, 31, 49, 51, 100, 105, 109, 122, 143, 150, 164, 170
Gullett, Henry 9, 45, 49–50

Halifax, Edward Frederick Lindley Wood 17–18, 45, 51, 73–4, 96–7, 101, 137, 139–40, 174, 178
Hasluck, Paul 16, 24–5
Hawaii 125, 144, 175, 180
Hitler, Adolf 20, 44, 60, 62, 95–6, 98, 101–2, 112–13, 122–3, 130–2, 136, 138, 147, 156, 163, 170
Hopkins, Harry 14–15, 19, 67, 85, 123, 139, 146, 154, 181, 184, 191–2

Hornbeck, Stanley 53, 57, 73, 76, 78, 116–18, 126, 128–9, 131, 137, 142, 168, 188
Hudson, William 1–2, 4, 7–8, 16, 18, 22–3, 25, 29, 33, 40, 65–6, 86, 89, 165
Hull, Cordell 11, 14, 19, 21, 49, 53, 59, 66, 68, 78, 83, 102, 109–10, 112–13, 115, 126–7, 129–30, 132–3, 137, 139–40, 153, 155, 169, 188

Japan 9–10, 17, 21, 32, 34–9, 41–6, 48, 51–3, 55–6, 58, 61, 71, 74–7, 88, 91–2, 99, 112–18, 120, 122, 125–33, 136, 139, 142–4, 146–56, 158–9, 162, 164, 166–71, 173–82, 184–5, 189–90, 193–5

Kershaw, Ian 58, 96
Kimmel, Husband E. 146, 173
King, Ernest J. 19, 184–8
Knox, Frank 21, 78, 130–3
Kurusu, Saburo 139, 153, 156, 175

London 3–5, 7, 9–15, 20, 23, 26, 33–5, 40–2, 45–6, 51–4, 65, 89–91, 95, 98, 100, 102–3, 132, 134, 139, 168–9
Lowe, David 9
Lyons, Joseph 4–6, 8–9, 24, 41–3, 45

McEwen, John 50, 57, 61, 76, 81, 89–90, 93, 107, 110, 114, 117
Marshall, George 19, 112, 124–5, 130, 132, 146, 149–50, 158–9, 161–3, 183, 185–8, 190
Melbourne 2–3, 22, 34–5
Menzies, Robert Gordon 4, 7–13, 18, 22, 25, 29, 32, 44–7, 52–5, 59, 83–4, 95, 97–8, 100–1, 105, 119–20, 131, 142, 146, 151

Nomura, Kichisaburo 139, 153, 156, 175

Officer, Keith 14
Oval Office 15, 65, 69, 73, 75, 161, 189

Pacific region 10–11, 13, 18, 20, 32–8, 40–3, 46–7, 53, 55–6, 63, 71, 74–5, 77, 83, 87, 91–2, 99–101, 105, 107–8, 112, 115–20, 122, 125–7, 129–31, 136–8, 140–1, 143–50, 152, 154–6, 158–63, 166–8, 170–1, 175, 178–83, 185–95
Page, Earle 20
Pearl Harbor 16–17, 20, 30, 63, 77, 90, 92, 112, 125, 142, 144, 149–50, 156, 158, 161, 163, 169, 173–5, 178–81, 183, 185, 187, 189–90, 192

Reynolds, David 66, 68, 97, 124
Roosevelt, Eleanor 14–15
Roosevelt, Franklin Delano 13–15, 17–20, 43, 47, 49, 52, 54–63, 66–72, 74–6, 78, 83–4, 93, 98–110, 112–13, 117, 119–20, 122–4, 130, 132–6, 144, 150, 158–9, 161, 163–6, 170–1, 174–7, 179, 182–8, 190

Short, Walter C. 173
Southeast Asia 38, 47, 112, 116, 125, 142, 153
Spaatz, Carl 150
Spender, Percy 16–17, 29, 45, 86
Stark, Harold R. 14, 112, 124, 130–1, 136, 140, 146, 182, 188
Stettinius, Edward 135, 154
Stimson, Henry L. 21, 41, 146, 150, 162, 182, 186
Sydney 28, 35, 163

United States 3, 8, 11–15, 17,
   20–1, 24–6, 30, 33–6, 38, 42–9,
   51–9, 61–6, 69–80, 82–9, 91–2,
   97, 99–104, 106–9, 111–20,
   122–31, 133–6, 139–41, 143–67,
   169–70, 172–5, 178–9, 181–2,
   188–95

Wallace, Henry 78, 146
Washington 1, 3, 7, 9, 11–22, 24–9,
   35, 38, 41–2, 45, 47, 51–5, 57,
   64–7, 70, 74, 77–82, 85–6, 91–4,
   97–102, 104, 114–15, 126–7,
   129, 131–4, 138–40, 142–3,
   146–8, 151, 153, 156, 158–60,
   162, 165, 168–9, 174–7, 179–80,
   184–9
Watt, Alan 14–16, 26
Welles, Sumner 66, 73, 78, 109,
   113, 116, 123, 131, 153–4, 180,
   185
White House 14–15, 18, 55, 65–9,
   71, 74, 77, 165, 174, 177–8, 181,
   188

www.ingramcontent.com/pod-product-compliance
Lightning Source LLC
Chambersburg PA
CBHW030853170426
43193CB00009BA/591